RECONSIDERING
THE LIFE OF POWER

SUNY series in Chinese Philosophy and Culture
───────────
Roger T. Ames, editor

RECONSIDERING THE LIFE OF POWER

Ritual, Body, and Art in Critical Theory
and Chinese Philosophy

James Garrison

Cover image courtesy of the author. Reprinted with permission.

Published by State University of New York Press, Albany

© 2021 State University of New York

All rights reserved

Printed in the United States of America

No part of this book may be used or reproduced in any manner whatsoever without written permission. No part of this book may be stored in a retrieval system or transmitted in any form or by any means including electronic, electrostatic, magnetic tape, mechanical, photocopying, recording, or otherwise without the prior permission in writing of the publisher.

For information, contact State University of New York Press, Albany, NY
www.sunypress.edu

Library of Congress Cataloging-in-Publication Data

Name: Garrison, James, 1982-author.
Title: Reconsidering the life of power : ritual, body, and art in critical theory and Chinese philosophy / James Garrison.
Description: Albany : State University of New York Press, 2021. | Series: SUNY series in Chinese philosophy and culture | Includes bibliographical references and index.
Identifiers: LCCN 2020024802 | ISBN 9781438482118 (hardcover : alk. paper) | ISBN 9781438482101 (pbk. : alk. paper) | ISBN 9781438482125 (ebook)
Subjects: LCSH: Philosophy, Chinese. | Aesthetics, Chinese. | Critical theory—China.
Classification: LCC B5231 .G37 2021 | DDC 181/.11—dc23
LC record available at https://lccn.loc.gov/2020024802

10 9 8 7 6 5 4 3 2 1

Contents

Acknowledgments	vii
Introduction	1
Intercultural and Interdisciplinary Work: A Statement on Method	21
1 Subjectivation/Subjection	47
2 Autonomy and Appearance in Artful Ritual Practice	81
3 Confucianism and *Lǐ* 禮/礼: Ritual Propriety, Music, and the Arts	97
4 Subjectality	119
5 Technique in Appearance	135
6 Somaesthetics	157
Final Thoughts	185
Notes	201
Index	223

Acknowledgments

This work uses text that the author has republished with permission, including the following:

Garrison, James. "The Aesthetic Life of Power: Theories in Subjectivation and Subjectality (An Overview)." *Annals of the University of Craiova, Philosophy Series*, no. 34 (2014): 30–47. "Introduction" is a newer version of this work.

———. "Intercultural and Interdisciplinary Work: A Statement on Method." In *Orte des Denkens / Places of Thinking*, edited by Murat Ates et al., 80–98. Freiburg: Verlag Karl Alber, 2016. "Intercultural and Interdisciplinary Work: A Statement on Method" is a newer version of this work.

———. "Reconsidering Richard Shusterman's Somaesthetics: The Confucian Debate between Mèng Zǐ and Xún Zǐ." *Contemporary Pragmatism* 12, no. 1 (2015): 135–55. Chapter 6, "Somaesthetics," is a newer version of this work.

———. "Revolution in Kant's Relation of Aesthetics to Morality: Regarding Negatively Free Beauty and Respecting Positively Free Will." In *Kant und die Philosophie in weltbürgerlicher Absicht: Akten des XI. Kant-Kongresses 2010*, edited by Stefano Bacin et al., vol. 4, 47–57. Berlin: Walter de Gruyter, 2013. Chapter 1, "Subjectivation/Subjection," uses material from this earlier version.

———. "The Social Value of Ritual and Music in Classical Chinese Thought." *Teorema: Revista internacional de filosofía* 31, no. 3 (2012): 209–22. Chapter 3, "Confucianism and *Lǐ* 禮/礼: Ritual Propriety, Music, and the Arts," uses material from this earlier version.

———. "What Should the World Look Like? Li Zehou, Confucius, Kant, and the World Observer." In *Li Zehou and Confucian Philosophy*, edited by Roger T. Ames and Jinhua Jia, 118–34. Honolulu: University of

Hawai'i Press, 2018. Chapter 4, "Subjectality," is a newer version of this work.

If there is anything worthwhile here, it owes first and foremost to the writing, teaching, mentorship, and authoritative conduct of Professor Roger Ames, whose great work I hope here with this effort to *appreciate* in turn.

Additionally, this work was undertaken with substantial support from the University of Vienna's Department of Philosophy, with Prof. Dr. Georg Stenger and Ms. Andrea Schönbauer meriting particular thanks. Prof. Richard Shusterman, Dr. Sophie Loidolt, Dr. Anthony Everett, Dr. Megan Blomfeld, Dr. Anke Graneß, Prof. Henry Rosemont (RIP), Prof. Tao-chung "Ted" Yao 姚道中 (RIP), Prof. Eliot Deutsch (RIP), Prof. Graham Parkes, Prof. Douglas Berger, Murat Ates, William White, and Robert Willem Diem also deserve substantial appreciation for the help that each provided along the way. Scripps College, particularly Professors Sheila Walker and Yuval Avnur deserve appreciation, as does the Consortium for Faculty Diversity, which made my time there possible. Likewise, thanks goes out to the University of Puget Sound, particularly Justin Tiehen, Ariela Tubert, Sam Liao, Sara Protasi, and Bill Beardsley in the Philosophy Department and Kris Imbrigotta and Kent Hooper in the German Department. Thanks are also due to Ruhr Universität-Bochum's Theatre Studies Department and Meike Hinnenberg. Further thanks go to my new institution, Baldwin Wallace University, and my colleagues in the Philosophy Department, Amy Lebo, and Kelly Coble. Professors Ron Bontekoe, Arindam Chakrabarti, Thomas Jackson, and David McCraw at my first graduate institution, the University of Hawai'i at Mānoa, deserve recognition as well. Thanks also go to my undergraduate home, Whitman College, and particularly to Professors Patrick Frierson, Julia Ireland, James Soden (RIP) and Tom Davis, the latter of whom introduced me to philosophy and posed the question that prompted this very book, along with Trustee Emeritus John Stanton for first bringing me as an IT intern to Vienna, where I would later compose much of this book.

My mother, Judy Leonard, and my brothers, Joseph and Jesse Garrison, of course deserve thanks for their kindness and love, along with my aunts, Carol Leonard and Alicia Rinehart. My deep and abiding gratitude also goes to Matt McMurrer, David Beckley, Kevin Phillips, Bryan Haynes, Alyssa Hays, and Vana Sarkisian each for being profoundly great friends. Anneliese Rieger of *PenArt Zeitschrift* deserves heartfelt thanks for her crucial support, feedback, care, and love during the time that this was written.

Introduction

> It must cease forever describing the effects of power in negative terms: it "excludes," it "represses," it "suppresses," it "censors," it "abstracts," it "masks," it "conceals." In fact power produces; it produces reality; it produces domains of objects and rituals of truth.[1]
>
> —Michel Foucault

The task of accounting for how persons, how subjects, are made brings a convergence between what Euro-American traditions tend to deem to be the separate domains of ethics and aesthetics. It is in this regard that alternative voices, particularly those from East Asia, and even more particularly from the Confucian tradition, possess a distinct advantage. Having had such a long history in which to develop its own terms, Confucianism can address the conjunctions of ethics, aesthetics, and politics that occur in person-making in ways that the best, though still ultimately tradition-bound and reactive efforts from Euro-American critical theory cannot.

Here the path is sixfold, going through the critical post-structuralist notion of (1) becoming subject—subjectivation—and the accompanying idea of (2) autonomy alongside (3) the classical Confucian idea of ritual—*lǐ* 礼—as well as contemporary notions of (4) subjectality, a Confucian/Marxian-materialist approach to collective unconsciousness in social ritual, (5) technique in appearance, and (6) somaesthetic (bodily) practice. This results in an intercultural and interdisciplinary account of how a set of traditions, some newer and reacting to dominant traditions and others relatively older and with longer histories of internal conceptual development, still nonetheless converge on an important issue for philosophy generally—understanding and broadening the radically (a) relational, (b) discursive, (c) bodily, (d) ritually impelled self.

Subjectivation

The first key word here is subjectivation. Judith Butler follows Michel Foucault in using a variant of this term—subjection—to describe how melancholy defines the emergence of subjects as the question of survival induces them to perform a kind of ritually driven life in order to gain recognition from broader social forces. Butler specifically breaks down her account in terms of five key paradigms—Hegel's unhappy consciousness, Nietzsche's bad conscience, Freud's ego, Althusser's interpellation, and Foucault's power-resistance dynamic (with bits from Lacan and other writers). All of these sources form her narrative of the body being turned on itself and trapped in a skin-tight prison, sentenced to go through a rigmarole of ritual motions in order to get through the day, with the repetition itself bringing a meager measure of freedom in the form of rage and the reappropriation of the terms of the ritual/symbolic field. However, this view of rage *as* resistance *as* reappropriation offers little more than the temporary relief that a prisoner might likewise obtain through using "the routine" of prison life against itself. The argument here starts from the finding that this subversive reclaiming of slurs like "n-----" or "f-----" and of more extended ritual behavioral norms cannot be the endgame, and that, even as an intermediate strategy, it should be but one approach. Even with its somewhat unsatisfying conclusions, Butler's paradigm remains compelling as a framework for considering subject life and the challenge of possibly improving this psychic dimension of life amidst the machinations of power.

As a base premise, Butler holds that a subject's identity arises from external normativity, which initiates and continually takes up residence within an inner sphere of self-consciousness.[2] In her view, what Hegel sees as the split between recognized master and recognizing slave internalized in unhappy consciousness, Nietzsche rearticulates in his notion of the bad conscience as a socially driven split of the self into tormenter and tormented, creditor and debtor.[3] Working from this convergence, Butler develops the insight in psychoanalytic terms, reasoning that melancholy occurs as social forces form the psyche, with the social regulating the psychic sphere so that the subject's conduct occurs within social norms.[4] In her readings of Hegel, Nietzsche, and Freud, social forces establish the layout of the mind, regulating it and foreclosing socially unacceptable behavior. Therefore, for Butler, the social regulates the psychic, leading to an internalizing of society's values. All of this enables the will to be tame enough to get by in society. The self, being so constituted, does not really possess its own will, but is formed in relation to others. Hence, in explaining the relational self, Butler writes, "The 'will' is not . . . the will of a subject, nor is it an effect fully cultivated by and through social norms."[5] She suggests instead that the will is "the site at which the social implicates the psychic in its very formation—or, to be more precise, as its very formation and formativity."[6] Moreover, her more recent work sees Butler further repudiate the "interesting posture" taken by "many people [who] act *as if* they were not formed."[7] With her emphasis on relationality, she couches her critique in terms of Kierkegaard's notion of despair. She thus examines the anguish resulting from "denying the place of God as the true author of human existence," to use similar, more secular language to flesh out her decidedly less theological project in terms of a common understanding of the misery that results from the chauvinistic insistence that one is one's own sovereign person simpliciter.[8] This all signals that, as understood in terms of subjectivation, the subject is (a) deeply relational.

Butler goes on to distill her notion of a will that formatively turns on itself with the help of Louis Althusser. Imagine Althusser's hypothetical scene where a police officer yells, "Hey, you there!"[9]

"You" turn around, recognizing yourself in this hail with a literal turning of the self back upon self. The self, so recognized, guiltily submits before the law without reason. This plays out thousands of times in the subject's life, where outright pejoratives, lesser slights, and indirect cultural messages hail the subject into being, into acting out a certain role—a kind of ominous unsettling speech act of vocation. A physician declaring "It's [hereby] a girl" is a speech act calling the infant to be, to look, and to act in certain ways. Calls to be this or that (or both in certain circumstances) enact the psychic constitution of particular subjects and enable the performance of roles, highlighting (b) the discursive character of subjectivation.

This scene of Althusser's, like Hegel's master-slave antagonism and the imposition of bad conscience in Nietzsche's creditor-debtor model, greatly influences the subjectivation model put forth by Butler, but the scene is seldom reducible to two parties. Indeed, for Foucault, those granting recognition are themselves subjects, watching and surveilling each other in society's grand, self-regulating, panoptical prison. In any case, similarly pernicious effects result. The subject body unthinkingly turns on itself, disciplined and preternaturally ready to submit, be it to Althusser's singular authority or that of innumerable, invisible, displaced, and paradoxically ubiquitous "Others." This body, ready to turn on itself, is initially inchoate, undefined, and unintelligible in a way that Butler likens to Aristotelian prime matter.[10]

Calls to be this and/or to be that stamp raw bodily matter into a recognizable form. Thus these impressions form a subject, where the subject *is* a body that matters and, in order to matter, betrays itself for continued subject life. This calls attention to (c) the bodily nature of subjectivation.

Before long, the subject ego is continually comporting the body in order to achieve a dubious form of social recognition. Taking up Foucault's language, repetition becomes the basis for discipline, whether it be within physical prison walls or those figuratively built by society as a means of control. Within this repetition, behavior thus becomes patterned, while conduct becomes a type of ritual performance driven by a need to maintain a level of recognition and legitimacy. This shows subjectivation to have (d) a profoundly ritualistic character.

This turning of the self back upon the self occurs in such a way that there is no inside or outside prior to the formative turn, because that barrier is precisely what is being formed.[11] There is no core, no eternal soul that comes prior to the social implication of the psyche. Peeling back the onion only yields more onion and sifting through the sediment of past social relationships only unearths more sediment. There is no redemption, in the sense of recovery of original essence or original soul, precisely because the soul qua psyche, so considered, is not a pregiven quantity, being instead always in the making. This marks a break with conventional notions of the soul, and in this regard Butler's project is less about redemption and more about rehabilitation. Though Butler does not put it this way in her reading of Nietzsche and the imposition of *slave* morality, the implication is there—the challenge here is gaining, or perhaps regaining, a sense of *nobility* for this (a) relational, (b) discursive, (c) bodily, and (d) ritually impelled subject.

Tabling the issue of subject nobility for the moment, Butler looks to Nietzsche's bad conscience and Freud's id-ego-superego dynamic for inspiration here, particularly as concerns the former's remark "that bad conscience *fabricates* the soul."[12] For both Nietzsche and Butler, this fabrication is "artistic" in nature. This means that the subject, the coarticulation of psychic form and somatic matter, is itself a work of art created by our moral life. In appropriating Nietzsche, Butler describes the subject "as a kind of necessary fiction, [being] also one of the first artistic accomplishments presupposed by morality."[13] Following Nietzsche, Butler describes bad conscience as "the instinct for freedom made latent."[14] She continues and, reminiscent of Nietzsche, claims that this form of self-consciousness is "a peculiar deformation of artistry" and that "the soul is precisely what a certain violent artistry produces when it takes itself as its own object."[15]

However, Butler does not adequately follow up on the link between art and freedom, neither within the context of her analysis of Nietzsche nor within the broader scope of her general project. Regarding Nietzsche, it is almost as if her appropriation stops precisely at the second stage of what his Zarathustra calls the metamorphoses of spirit, that of the lion, of the beast who snarls "no" and violently refuses the dragon that embodies a thousand years of old values with its golden scales each emblazoned with a gleaming "Thou Shalt!"[16]

Considered in these terms, Butler follows much of Nietzsche's template regarding the assumption of society's burdensome norms in the first "camel" stage and the subsequent contrarian denial of those values in the second "lion" stage, but she by and large disregards the third stage—the child stage.[17] Understood in terms of Nietzsche's Zarathustra, this means that after saying "yes" to conventional norms and then saying "no" to imposed, internalized morality, as the lion does, there is little room in Butler's view for psychic life beyond everyday good and evil. In her account there is no joy of saying "yes" to oneself, to artistry, to constructive artistry, a new type of *moral* artistry, to spontaneity, and to the creation of novel values for the self. Now, it may well be the case that Zarathustra's particular deus ex machina resolution would ill serve the more sober work of Foucault and Butler on subjectivation/subjection. But putting the eccentricities of Nietzsche's project aside, there still remains the challenge set forth by him of *affirming* (a) relational, (b) discursive, (c) bodily, and (d) ritually impelled subject life in a way that links artistry and autonomy.

Autonomy

For Butler, though, the subject has no real resources except those problematically granted by power structures and thus no way out. This leaves only metonymy in the form of enraged resistance to twist already given terms of discourse. Just like the game in which one repeats a word to the point where it strangely ceases to sound like a "real word," this kind of strategic repetition of terms is meant to expose the more obvious absurdity of social constructions like pink being for girls and blue being for boys or of race being presented as an objective fact, as well as of the illogic at play in more subtle ritualized normative performances in the everyday.

Therefore, in order to supplement, and not undermine, subjectivation theory, I propose looking at another possibility, first by examining alternate notions of autonomy beyond the problematic version precariously obtained in the process of subjectivation, namely, the type of autonomy exhibited by works of art, and then secondly using intercultural approaches to apply this artistic sensibility to the locus of subjectivation—the body that matters because of social ritual.

What is needed here is a reconsideration of autonomy, particularly of how the subject attains this dubious state in and though the "Other." Butler's paradigm explores how the need to survive and be recognized as a valid subject by society at large marks the subject as mediated self-conciousness. This means that rather than immediately expressing will in the manner of artistic creativity praised by Nietzsche, the will instead doubles back on itself and uses its now deformed artistry to devise new ways to torment itself with this implement called conscience so as to try, however haltingly, to pay back the debt owed to "Other" as part of the subject's continued, supposedly autonomous existence.[18]

However, this constellation of autonomy, artistry, and the "Other" need not be the end of the story, and indeed the first phase of this argument involves reconfiguring these notions in terms of artworks. Simply put, people are not the only kind of "Other." The world presents objects, natural and artificial, that variously make claims on us, demanding that attention be given to what is variously sublime or beautiful (the latter being the focus of this account), and thereby form a sense of self for subjects, i.e., self-consciousness.

Honing attention to what is made, contingent, and nonetheless powerful in art's claim on our attention and its ability to speak to the subject can show the ability of artworks to serve as a different kind of "Other" through which the subject might enter into a mode of self-recognition, which, despite being fleeting, would not be so bound up with demands that the subject take up a self-monitoring, self-berating posture in wielding the force of conscience to determine itself as this and/or that type of subject in order to survive. Because it does not arise from the Faustian bargain for survival that characterizes subject life, the less deterministic brand of autonomy manifest in art and artifice makes it possible to begin to recognize the contingency at the heart of the human world and all of its power structures, thereby loosening the stifling strictures of subjectivation.

Turning to art is only a start; the second phase is making one's own bodily life an artwork and indeed a different kind of "Other." And so, the argument presented here applies this notion of self-recognition through art to the ritualized subject body formed in the course of subjectivation. This makes sense, as subjectivation is all about a body turning on itself in order to gain recognition and status through embodying social norms and roles ritually performed in everyday life. The question then turns to developing an account of artful, ritual cultivation of the body.

Ritual Propriety—Lǐ 礼

Butler and the thinkers crucial to her account are already somewhat at odds with the dominant orientation of the Euro-American tradition, which itself does not provide many resources for talking about ritual and body that do not at some point lapse into the kind of mind/body hierarchical dualisms that are problematic both to her account and more generally speaking. The vocabulary and the root premises need to change.

Why not then step outside of this tradition and these geographic bounds, especially when there are so many intriguing insights into ritual and body? Why not then look at a body of philosophical thought that excels in its sensitivity to (a) the relational self, to (b) discursively formed roles, to (c) the body, and to (d) ritual performance *and* that has the added benefit of being more attuned to the artful side of subject life than post-structuralism? Why not look to other sources like this? Why not, at least as a starting point for the time being, look at what may be the most influential philosophical tradition in East Asia, namely, Confucianism?

Stemming from what Karl Jaspers calls the "axial age," the defining period for Athenian philosophy and for Buddhism around 500–400 BCE, the still-living tradition of Confucianism set the stage for ensuing East Asian philosophical schools. It continues to furnish a great deal of the basic vocabulary of both academic discourse and everyday life in the region, with Confucian perspectives on role-based ethics, ritual, and family proving particularly influential up into the present day.[19]

The benefit of Confucianism, spanning the classic and the contemporary, is that here it can do what the largely reactive enterprises of critical theorists often cannot—that is, Confucianism can speak in its own voice about person-making. Confucianism can supply its *own* vocabulary of body and ritual without having to reckon with a mind/body hierarchy entrenched in thinking spanning millennia. If fruitful points of connection can be found with the subjectivation paradigm, which itself is at odds with major frameworks in the Euro-American tradition, this would allow for looking at the relational self in terms beyond endless struggle in ways that point to real autonomy.

Therefore, a historical reading of the key Confucian terminology relating to society and self will drive the first part of the investigation here, allowing for evaluation of the major debates within the Chinese tradition. Confucians have dealt with the issues at play here in fights with Mohists and Daoists as well as in quarrels within the tradition, for example, in the clash between Mencius (Mèng Zǐ 孟子) and Xun Zǐ 荀子 on human nature. Parsing these arguments with respect to the historical development of Confucianism can help anticipate major topics only recently emerging for critical theorists and point to novel senses of autonomy.

And so, perhaps unexpectedly, the third key word is *lǐ* 礼. Unlike post-structuralism, which, as a new field, seeks to redefine terms like "body," "power," "subject," and so on, Confucian philosophy has developed on its own terms and has its own vocabulary for dealing with many of these issues, with *lǐ* being perhaps the most important here because of its (a) relational, (b) discursive, (c) bodily, *and* (d) ritualistic senses.

Lǐ means ritual propriety, broadly connoting everything from the subtly ritual-habitual to grandiose formalities.[20] *Lǐ*, though rendered here in terms of a singular concept for the sake of smooth translation, is a bit more ambiguous, *also* connoting the plural form of ritual acts in a way that points to deep pluralism in the transactions of the everyday. Simply put, *lǐ* is social grammar.[21]

Lǐ, as Confucius (Kǒng Zǐ 孔子) puns, provides knowledge of where to stand.[22] *Lǐ* coordinates the where and when of social comings and goings. *Lǐ* attends to gesture and comportment. *Lǐ* describes how the players and the audience each take their various places, and act just so at just the right time.[23] *Lǐ* forms a pair with *yuè* 乐, music, or, more precisely, musical theater, with connections to all arts.[24] *Lǐ* brings a convergence of bodily movement and moral excellence.[25] *Lǐ* is both a social grammar *and* a social choreography. *Lǐ* encompasses what the classifications of academic philosophy might label the ethical and the aesthetic nature of (a) the relational self.

Lǐ speaks to how language stands in society. *Lǐ* connects the regulation of cultural expression and of society. *Lǐ* sets up codes of difference and deferral in the basic historical movement of discourse. *Lǐ* addresses much of what Derrida does with *différance*.[26] *Lǐ* expresses how (b) the discursive climate defines how people live up (or down) to social role archetypes.[27]

Lǐ describes the body that stands. *Lǐ* relates linguistically to *tǐ* 体, the corpus, with a sense surpassing simple physical matter, pointing to the dynamic, ongoing arrangement of bodies.[28] *Lǐ* grounds self-cultivation, *xiūshēn* 修身 in Chinese, literally habilitating the person, the body. *Lǐ* addresses the role of ritual in physical growth, coordination, and habituation. *Lǐ* works in relational processes. *Lǐ*, which, depending on context, could be rendered in English in the singular or in the plural, thus deals with both (c) "individual" human bodies and common bodies politic.

Lǐ provides knowledge of when to make a stand. *Lǐ* conditions social relations. *Lǐ* establishes bounds and bidirectional demands between ruler and advisor, parent and child. *Lǐ* refers to (d) a ritual-based sense of appropriateness, including knowing when and how to call out inappropriate failure to fulfill a name or role.[29]

In sum, *lǐ* points to the thread running through human development, and through the work of Butler and Foucault as well—the artful process of cultural sedimentation and normative subjectivation.

This similar, though distinct, vocabulary opens up a new avenue for dealing with the (a) relational, (b) discursive, (c) bodily, and (d) ritually impelled self of subjectivation, and this can show how society's grand apparatus of normative rites, what Foucault might call power, might enable as well as constrain. Though Foucault and Butler do indeed make this point themselves, their political and theoretical commitments lead them to focus on the latter as expressed in notions like bodily subject life being a prison and discourse occurring through the proliferation of sign chains that might be refashioned in the course of repetitive use. Could there be perhaps another side to things here? Could rites, could *lǐ*, taken with a bodily and artistic sense, serve not just as a tool of power against the subject, but perhaps a tool *for* the subject's self-cultivation? Might *lǐ* help not only to empower the subject, but also aid in the project of subjecting power to reappraisal, especially as regards the basic dynamic of contingency, necessity, and autonomy underlying subjectivation?

Subjectality

Subjectality is the fourth term here, and this neologism speaks to the historical roots of subject life and the use of collective cultural psychology as a tool to define human society. Subjectality is the term that contemporary philosopher Lǐ Zéhòu 李泽厚 crafts to translate the phrase *zhǔtǐxìng* 主体性, literally "subject-body nature," in describing ritual's formative role in human social life and its artful use as a tool for human survival. Post-structural subjectivation does well in talking about technologies of the self, but subjectality gets at the root *tekhnē*, with its blend of premises from Marx, Confucius, and Kant.

Briefly, Lǐ uses Marx's statements on the "humanization of nature" and the "naturalization of humanity" to explain how shamanistic art, music, and rituals operated as tools for social cohesion in the early material economy of human survival.[30] Moving forward historically, Lǐ Zéhòu sees Confucianism as being particularly apt (but not exclusively so) at describing and formalizing the cultural/psychological edifice that sediments over time in subject rationality.[31] Finally, Lǐ turns to Kant and Marx in reconsidering the Confucian framework of "being inspired by poetry, taking a stand with *lǐ* [rites], and finding perfection in music"[32] to describe how tools like ritual artifice form humankind's suprabiological body, thus allowing for labor on an object, on a "noumenal humanity" akin to "Jung's collective unconsciousness," that can provide an aesthetically structured source of internal freedom.[33]

For Lǐ Zéhòu, the ground of this freedom lies in how humans naturally excel at artifice,[34] at the art and craft of building society and culture in the deployment of labor and material. This approach gives hope that, if the species is naturally capable of the sometimes dark artistry behind the social formation of ritual normativity, individuals might then rehabilitate this prior, though often concealed, form of creativity and put it to work in daily life.

Subjectivation, while being useful in talking about the machinery of person-making, can lose view of what can be termed the *tekhnē* behind the machine. Lǐ Zéhòu attends to this oversight with his notion of subjectality and the formation of collective ritual normative structures.[35] Subjectality extends subjectivation by showing the constitutive role of artistic creativity in the unconscious rhythm of the everyday. This rhythm, this background hum of ritual practice, can become a symphony when properly attuned. This is what it means to refine *lǐ* in practices like t'ai chi ch'uan (tàijíquán 太极拳) and the martial arts, where the body takes on *a life of its own*, as a more artful kind of other.

These practices thus transform rigid, regular, and sometimes punishing discipline into a type of learned and practiced spontaneity. This phrasing might seem counterintuitive if not outright contradictory, but such disciplined spontaneity accords well common phenomena. Take, for example, the way in which in the arts, in music in particular, training is necessary for genuine, skillful improvisation. Confucianism, starting from well before Lǐ Zéhòu, has understood this and addressed the nature of practiced spontaneity in subject life more generally, to wit:

The Master said: "At fifteen, I was determined to learn; at thirty I took my stand; at forty there was no longer any doubt; at fifty I realized the propensities of the heavens; at sixty my ear was attuned; at seventy I could follow my heart-and-mind freely without going too far."³⁶

In short, discipline, properly attuned, gives way to mastery, gives way to autonomy and spontaneity. The twist here lies in bringing improvisation and a measure of unanticipated and unregulated autonomy to the discipline meted out in the course of the subject's psychic life. It is in this way that self-disciplined self-cultivation can open up novel modes of self-recognition that outstrip any founding disciplinary powers, thereby changing the basic stakes for subject autonomy.

Lǐ Zéhòu's work on subjectality shows the need for subjectivation theorists to better address the aesthetic side of subject life in the ongoing creation of the social field. Though he is not directly addressing subjectivation theorists, Lǐ perhaps nonetheless surpasses the post-structuralists in responding to the following gauntlet thrown by Foucault:

> It must cease forever describing the effects of power in negative terms: it "excludes," it "represses," it "suppresses," it "censors," it "abstracts," it "masks," it "conceals." In fact power produces; it produces reality; it produces domains of objects and rituals of truth.³⁷

Lǐ Zéhòu does precisely this in describing the historical material roots of subjectality. What is the upshot of this, then?

To some extent Nietzsche anticipates the benefit of an approach like that of Lǐ Zéhòu's. Though the bolder statements of Zarathustra on creativity occurring in terms of an ineffable, child-like, yes-saying spontaneity pose difficulties, elsewhere Nietzsche points to how understanding the formation of social custom can bring a realistic, plausible possibility of self-growth. On the confinement of thought by language and social habit, Nietzsche writes:

> Only by forgetting this primitive metaphor-world . . . only through the undefeatable belief that this sun, window, and table might have a truth in itself, in short, that one forgets oneself as a subject, and indeed an artistically creating subject, does one live with any calm, security, and consistency: if one could get out of the prison walls of this belief for a moment, then "self-consciousness" would immediately be gone.³⁸

And here, the language of subjectivation, particularly the voice of Judith Butler comes back into the conversation. What Nietzsche is pointing to, much like Lǐ Zéhòu, is a dynamic of foreclosure. Here the idea is that a type of constitutive forgetfulness occurs as habits sediment in the most basic use of religious-cultural-aesthetic-normative technologies, forming something akin to what is described by Jung where he speaks of collective unconsciousness. A kind of practiced forgetting of the everyday that instead remembers and recovers unconscious cultural resources to loosen the strictures of subject self-consciousness is thus needed to get past the lion stage that characterizes Butler's approach and into the stage of the child marked by "a forgetting, a new beginning."[39]

It may be that Nietzsche's somewhat untenable description of attaining the third stage concerns reckoning with time and the possibility of the interwoven moments and deeds of one's life recurring eternally, but time per se will not be the key to this attempt to square Butler's second-stage, no-saying lion with Nietzsche's third-stage, self-affirming child (though time will factor into this account). Instead, given that the task laid out in this project concerns a practiced forgetting the ritual performance of normative subject life in the everyday, the contention here is that this must take place in and through the body and the ritualized bind of having to appear as a body that matters in order to get by.

Technique in Appearance

And so, the fifth key term here is "technique in appearance," and, as the connotation suggests, phenomenology enters the conversation at this juncture, bringing memory (and thus time) to bear on the technology of ritual. It is in this regard that Bernard Stiegler's exploration of the Promethean myth's insights into technique and memory has a great number of intriguing connections to the discussion here. Of particular interest is his description of how the proliferation of "technization" leads humanity to a profound forgetfulness, where access to origins is lost and remembering original, authentic temporality occurs through attention not to organic or inorganic matter, but to how we organize matter, that is, the conjunction of technique and time.[40] Though Stiegler's work represents a somewhat anthropological approach to Dasein that might upset chapter-and-verse Heideggerians, it excels in showing how the development of humanity and future-oriented care for being, born of anticipation and ultimately being-toward-death, occurs neither through the subject (who?) nor the object (what?) of primeval techniques, but with "*différance* . . . below and beyond the who and the what."[41]

And so, humans invent techniques *and* techniques invent humanity, both on a macro level of the ongoing, continual development of the human species and on the micro level of the human individual and "the accents of his speech, the style of his gait, the force of his gesture, the unity of his world."[42] Putting his own gloss on Heidegger's reading of *tekhnē* (τέχνη), Stiegler defines techniques in terms of savoir faire or skill, pointing to "politeness, elegance, and cuisine" as techniques, and he observes that only with the latter, cuisine, does one find the kind of overtly material "*productive*" technique that dominates conventional understanding whereby an artisan serves as the efficient cause of bringing forth, or *poiēsis* (ποίησις).[43]

For Stiegler, following Marx and detouring through evolutionary anthropology, such technique is best understood in terms of the humanization of nature and the naturalization of humanity, which, in this reading, is where the question emerges concerning the meaning of being. Stiegler, addressing what he sees as shortcomings in Heidegger's account vis-à-vis the "dynamic of *organization*," maintains that this occurs through techniques that themselves are the constitutive organon of the interior and exterior, of the who and the what, of the subject and the object, of the technician and the material.[44] With historical, cultural, and economical forces sedimenting and concealing the temporality of techniques, the interior/who/subject/technician/Aristotelian efficient cause becomes the star of a narrative where human subjects stand over objects and master more and more banal technology at the expense of authentic technique.[45]

Now, in terms of his greater phenomenological project, Stiegler is calling for a reconsideration of *tekhnē* with regard to the meaning of being. Taking a cue from Judith Butler and Hannah Arendt, what is at issue here is the technology that draws together being and appearance in public political society and the way in which this dynamic runs prior to and suffuses the process of subjectivation and the experience of subject life with a deep ritual history.[46] And so, within the space of *this* book's project and *its* theme of normative subject life, that call echoes with a similar appeal to return attention to the finer technologies of ritual, of *lǐ*. And so, despite the complexity of their works and their varying theoretical commitments, there is a convergence in how Bernard Stiegler and Lǐ Zéhòu frame the issue of how finer techniques with a ritual basis lie at the root of human life (with whatever scope or definition) and how such techniques become covered over and lost with the passage of time. Though the idioms differ and perfect translation remains elusive, the conversation ultimately has great bearing on the main topic here—that of something being lost and foreclosed in becoming a normative subject and the possibility of recovery through artful ritual technique.

The point to which Lǐ, Nietzsche, and Stiegler all variously draw attention is that the cultural, traditional, political, human animal has always had an aesthetic bearing rooted in the ritualized organization of labor and material and that there are structural reasons why human subjects work ceaselessly to forget this. But is this forgetfulness a total foreclosure? An *ur*-foreclosure? What would an ur-foreclosure be? How can this forgetfulness be understood not just as a mere memory lapse, but as having the specific structure of "never, never" and ungrieved grief so crucial to Butler's account? How can Stiegler's language of forgetfulness of authentic temporality and Lǐ's of the sedimentation of collective unconsciousness connect to the terminology of foreclosure set out by Butler? And most importantly, how does any of this help with the question of the subject's plight?

Recall that, for Butler, subjectivation on an individual level occurs through the foreclosure of certain possibilities for attachment. Foreclosure here has the specific meaning of "never loved, never lost" such that subject life occurs as a type of melancholy, a preempted mourning, a grief that can never be grieved because what is lost, even in the subtle losses of what Freud terms "setbacks and disappointments," is an "object-loss [is] withdrawn from consciousness" for subjects intent on and *dependent* on self-monitoring and self-punishment.[47] The subject stays intact as a subject through disciplinary power, as internalized in the watching, surveilling superego in a way that closes off the possibility of even thinking about certain forms of attachment (e.g., queer and interracial, to give a few specific examples from Butler's work on contemporary power structures).[48]

The ur-foreclosure is such that, to use Nietzsche's words, "one forgets oneself as a subject, and indeed an artistically creating subject." The "never, never" structure occurs in the subject never being attached to something other than the necessity-contingency dynamic of subjectivation, such that the very idea of indeed being an artistically creating subject becomes lost. The etymology of the word "subject" itself, that is, the confining notion of being "thrown under," indicates the extent of not only what has been lost, but of what has been foreclosed *as* lost. The artful side of subject life is what is lost and never properly grieved in an ur-foreclosure stretching back to the very formation of early human ritual life in what Nietzsche calls "this primitive metaphor-world."[49] Though not directly responding to

Nietzsche, the point that both Stiegler and Lǐ end up making in varying ways to his dilemma is that attunement to this ur-foreclosure, occurring through real *bodily, material* work, can help to recover what has been lost. Putting it all together and responding to the issues highlighted by Foucault and Butler, this means making the bodily ritual material of subject life in some way artful.

And so, thinking in terms of subjectality opens up the possibility of attuning oneself to the artistic fashioning of the long-sedimented and often unconsciously neglected world of signs, gestures, rituals, and cultural productions in and through which subjects emerge. If the sign chains of discourse and the skin-tight prison of the subject's body are themselves understood as having been built, as a sort of artistic achievement of social technology, then society appears contingent, much like the self. The basis of power is recognition; and recognition requires repetition; and repetition requires a ritual performance so that the power structure of recognition might be embodied and internalized over time. If all of that is a human invention, what Foucault might call a technology of self, why then be limited to the unconscious, sometimes slavish performance of everyday normative rituals that paradoxically mark self-consciousness? Why not then explore the possibility of empowering subjects, especially in the bodily dimension, through ritual and bringing conscious attention to what slumbers unconscious in culture?

These questions prompt reconsideration of Butler's *The Psychic Life of Power*. And so, the particular approach taken up here is aesthetic because of its attunement to body, sense, and feeling—the proper domain of aesthetics as αἴσθησῐς. It is artful insofar as it reveals and thrusts the contingent technology of subjectivation into unconcealment and opens up the possibility of bodily purposiveness without the determinate trappings of conventional purpose. The response lies in ritual attention to the body, or, to borrow a somewhat recently coined word, it lies in "somaesthetics."

Somaesthetics

Somaesthetics is the sixth and final key word here, and it refers to a pragmatic, intercultural approach to conscious bodily/somatic cultivation with the aim of broadening subject life. Somaesthetics is the signature paradigm of Richard Shusterman, a leading philosopher with a distinct American pragmatist and intercultural bent. Shusterman resists using the term "body" because of its connection to oppositional mind/body dualism, and he instead opts to use the term "soma" to refer to what he calls "a living, feeling, sentient body rather than a mere physical body that could be devoid of life and sensation."[50] Though he does not base his project on Chinese thinking per se, he quite aptly points out the way in which core Confucian vocabulary takes the crucial role of bodily life as a basic premise, leading him to describe his own usage of "soma" in terms of the Chinese word for body, *shēntǐ* 身体, where he writes:

> If the *ti* body in classical thought is closely associated with generative powers of physical life and growth and the multiplicity of parts (such as the [bodies'] four limbs), the *shen* body is closely identified with the person's ethical, perceptive, purposive body that one cultivates and so it even serves as a term for self. The concept of *shenti* thus suggests the soma's double status as living thing and perceiving subjectivity.[51]

Likewise in his use of the term "aesthetics," Shusterman simultaneously emphasizes soma as both perceiving and self-fashioning, as observer and artist, as it were. "I thus both am body and have a body," as Shusterman says.[52]

When it comes to artistically cultivating the soma, Shusterman is interested in many practices, including "various diets, forms of grooming and decoration (including body painting, piercing, and scarification as well as more familiar modes of cosmetics, jewelry, and clothing fashions), dance, yoga, massage, aerobics, bodybuilding, calisthenics, martial and erotic arts, and modern psychosomatic disciplines like Alexander Technique and Feldenkrais Method."[53] The connections here to *lǐ* are obvious, since all of these approaches bring together ritual and self-cultivation, as are the connections to Foucault's work on care for the self, both of which Shusterman references. The practices of interest to Shusterman all can provoke somatic awareness, albeit in different ways, but for him a similar effect obtains in a kind of family resemblance, namely, a new sense of self in everyday relations. The thinking here is that, as one becomes more attuned to the soma, unconscious habit likewise becomes conscious practice.

When ritual bodily practice takes on a life of its own, genuine autonomy becomes possible with self-recognition not being wholly determined by the Master, the creditor, the power structures of the day, or the pejorative "Other." And so, much like subjectivation, somaesthetic practice takes repetition and turns it into autonomy, though the mode of self-recognition here brings a measure of freedom from outside norms unlike the quasi-autonomy promised by the recognition of others and of the "Other" in subjectivation. Looking at somaesthetic practice with subjectivation in mind, it is thus possible to see how the basic stakes of contingency, necessity, and autonomy can undergo a definite shift *and* how this can change subject life for the better. While superficially similar as regards repetition, this is unlike Zarathustra finding grand spontaneity in embracing the eternal return of the same, as this program of repetitive, disciplined somaesthetic self-cultivation points to perhaps a more realistic notion of free growth modeled on the social, affective, and cognitive play that *recurring* experiences of art, artistry, and artfulness generally bring.

Reconsidering the life of power in terms of subjectality and somaesthetics in this way is not meant to counter, but rather to enrich, the observations made by Foucault on subjectivation and Butler's extension of that work in her work *The Psychic Life of Power*. In that book, Butler sets out a strategy for resistance against harmful, life-threatening power structures using the weakness inherit in what Nietzsche calls "sign chains." As Butler explains, the passage of time and the accrual of historical accidents make it such that "a sign is bound to signify in ways that estrange the sign from the originating intentions by which it is mobilized."[54] Since it is impossible for a single person acting alone simply to "invent" discourse without using material at hand, since it is impossible to invent out of nothing the terms whereby society recognizes self and self recognizes self, the strategy of Butler's work is instead to exploit, through resignification, the weakness of terms given by power for the initial purposes of subjectivation, subjugation, and subjection.

A common, if somewhat prosaic, example can be found in the subcultural reappropriation of words like "n-----" and "q----."[55] As Butler describes, such slurs can in fact be reclaimed because of how they "live and thrive in and as the flesh of the addressee . . . [because of] how these slurs accumulate over time, dissimulating their history, taking on the semblance of the natural, configuring and restricting the *doxa* that counts as 'reality.'"[56] It is through already having become a material part of social reality inhering in the body that such reappropriated discourse and associated behavior norms can have real effect over and above any doomed attempt to "invent" or "introduce" novel discourse out of nothing.

Perhaps a better illustration, and Butler's own preferred example, is the hyperbolic reappropriation of conventional gender norms in drag performance, which allegorizes heterosexual melancholy and the way in which those norms are formed through the loss of a loss, through the foreclosure of certain socially dangerous possibilities.[57] Put roughly, the approach set forth by Butler does not promise freedom from the sign chains of subjectivation, but it suggests that some small freedom of movement might be possible as those chains inevitably rust.

The assertion being made here in this project is somewhat different. The claim is that it is possible to use the sign chains of power to chain power, that it is possible to tie power up in its own knots. With subjectality theory and somaesthetic practice drawing attention to the contingency of entrenched power structures, there exists the possibility of new forms of self-recognition not fixed by the terribly sublime necessity of the powers that be. This is to say that, by feeding the basic premises of a system back upon itself, paradoxes unanticipated by that system may result. Here, somaesthetic practice informed by subjectality takes one of the major "rules" for subject life, that it be ritually regulated, and it uses ritual self-regulation to expose the contingency of those originally given rules. And so, in keeping with Butler's approach to resistance, this approach does not posit the use of anything beyond the sign chains already there, nor does it depend on miraculous redemption à la Nietzsche. But going beyond Butler's approach and the negativity and rage to which it necessarily and with good right leads, the claim of this book is that reconsidering the aesthetic dimensions of the life of power can open up some *minor* possibility for affirmation and hope.

To take what might be a more familiar and pleasantly accessible example, consider the character of the Wizard of Oz. Seeing past the imposing simulacrum of the Wizard of Oz to the doddering figure at the machine does not change the circumstances for Dorothy and the rest, but knowing that his "power" is similarly contingent allows the heroes to realize that they have been able to face those circumstances with this less grandiose type of power all along.[58] Now, nothing so dramatic as an all-revealing pull of a curtain is possible in the case of the subject, for subjectivation takes place through a multitude of encounters where countless different rituals are enacted with a variety of other subjects. But just as subjectivation occurs from a thousand different points, so too can a thousand tiny curtains be pulled back in a thousand particular contexts, all aggregating into burgeoning recognition of the ultimate contingency of subjectivation's rites and rituals. The material, bodily, and somaesthetic work of realizing this contingency takes place across a manifold of settings and it does not erase the subject's basic needs, meaning that there is no easy answer like that of Dorothy tapping her heels together three times and chanting, "There's no place like home." Home does not even make sense for this kind of relational subject, this kind of soul in the making, if only because the fragmented discipline of subject life proves so far from home, so uncanny, so *unheimlich*, that it precludes any simple A-to-B-and-back-again narrative. Indeed, the deeply public nature of appearance and the social character of ritual indicate that whatever limited improvement may be possible might not rest in an *atomically individual* subject per se, as indeed Butler herself raises the question, "What difference does it make when bodies act in concert, together[?]"[59] Nonetheless, even if nothing like Zarathustra's redemption of the will or a ruby-slipper return trip to Kansas is in the offing, exposing the contingency of subjectivation through conscious ritual work on the body and bodily norms can bring genuine improvement to the plight of subjects generally.

Conclusion

To sum up, this approach does not completely solve the problems of (1) subjectivation, but, by providing a new sense of (2) autonomy through attention to how (3) *lǐ*, in the process of (4) subjectality, leads to a sedimentation of (5) techniques of appearance in collective unconsciousness, (6) somaesthetic practices can ameliorate the dilemma bit by bit. This approach is meant to supplement rather than supplant resistance strategies exploiting sign chain rust by also creating tension with sign-chain knots.

The claim being advanced in this project is that, by confronting the effects of (1) subjectivation and obtaining (2) newfound autonomy with conscious attention to (3) *lǐ*, (4) subjectality, (5) technique in appearance, and (6) somaesthetic feeling, subjects can go past what Slavoj Žižek terms Butler's "mere 'performative reconfiguration' . . . within the hegemonic field"[60] in appropriating the technologies *of* the self for use *on* the self, resulting in a restructuring of the playing field, as Žižek wishes, and perhaps setting a new direction for critical theory (one hopes).

Moreover, a framework so built on the notions of (1) subjectivation, (2) autonomy, (3) *lǐ*, (4) subjectality, (5) technique in appearance, and (6) somaesthetics furthers the enterprise of intercultural philosophy. This approach advances intercultural thinking by pointing to a fruitful convergence being possible amid supposedly disparate bodies of thought, and it does so not out of intellectual vanity, but in its response to the genuine philosophical call to think through how the (a) relational, (b) discursive, (c) bodily, (d) ritualistic subject might encounter itself anew as a work of art hewn with other subjects in the medium of everyday practice.

Intercultural and Interdisciplinary Work
A Statement on Method

> The Confucian position of "embodying our experience" (*ti* 體) and "pursuing a ritual propriety in our roles and relations" (*li* 禮) differs . . . only in that it is more radical, going beyond the twentieth-century philosophical preoccupation with "language" and "mind" to claim that our entire psychophysical persons are involved in the process of assimilating and transforming the world as it is experienced. [The] further argument would be that cultural differences in thinking and living are fundamental to this transformative process.[1]
>
> —Roger T. Ames

Rhizomes, Embryos, and Growth in Between

With a project like this, questions of method are bound to emerge. This project is marked by its occurrence in the spaces in between, in between cultures and in between disciplines. This is so because the aim is better understanding the conditions and the conditioning of cultural norms and normativity, of discipline and disciplinarity, in bodily subject life. There may be other ways, but with the co-formation of cultural norms and of disciplinary schemes being the matter under discussion, it makes sense to avoid any kind of blinding allegiance to, affection for, or affiliation with any one particular cultural field or disciplinary system. Hence the approach here is both interdisciplinary and intercultural, and very self-consciously pursuing its own doctrine of the mean, of trying to become more at home and stake out some kind of center amid the complex and multivalent dynamics of subject life.

At the outset, this project may seem somewhat unwieldy, crossing disciplines and philosophical traditions as it does; however, all of this does have a point. Foucault's question, his charge and challenge, presents a genuine philosophical quandary. Again, to reiterate, Foucault puts the issue thusly:

> It must cease forever describing the effects of power in negative terms: it "excludes," it "represses," it "suppresses," it "censors," it "abstracts," it "masks," it "conceals." In fact power produces; it produces reality; it produces domains of objects and rituals of truth.[2]

Even if one does not subscribe to Foucault's notion of power per se, there is still something here. There is the demand to find a way of accounting for and dealing with society as both confining *and* enabling. With this background in place, what is posed here is ultimately a philosophical problem that stands on its own apart from any particular idiom of Foucault, Butler, or any other critical theorist. There still remains the issue of finding a way to deal with the necessary and productive ills of society.

Why then turn to Foucault, Butler, and this language of subjectivation at all? What precisely is the upshot?

While they in no way exhaust what is possible here, Foucault and Butler provide a well-developed, rigorous, worst-case way of thinking through the issue of the socially formed subject who is bereft of resources and without any deus ex machina to come to the rescue. This has value in and of itself, since the lack of presumption does not shy away from the dilemma of actions, decisions, behaviors, gestures, bodily life, and normativity as such all being in some way programmed into self-regulating subjects. This makes freedom and spontaneity genuine theoretical challenges.

Moreover, the approach of Foucault and Butler provides the additional benefit of highlighting a line of thought emphasizing the self as (a) relational, (b) discursive, (c) bodily, and (d) ritually impelled. However, these notions have only just recently begun to be explored in earnest in the Euro-American sphere. Luckily though, these ideas have much greater historical purchase elsewhere in the world. As such, this branch of subjectivation theory can serve as a point of departure for intercultural philosophical engagement with schools of thought that have longer, richer traditions of dealing with dynamics of self and society on consonant (but far from identical) terms. This is what happens here in this project and its engagement with classical and contemporary Confucianism, where the aim is to build upon possible convergences and meaningful differences in approaching the larger philosophical issue of accounting for the social field and its necessary constraints in person-making.

Now, by no means do either the idea of subjectivation as developed by Foucault and Butler or the varying perspectives from classical and contemporary Confucianism address everything possible with this topic; it would be rather surprising if they could. But these approaches *do* lend themselves to each other, to fruitful connections. Moreover, there are further links with contemporary approaches to tools and technologies of ritual on a species level, as happens with Hannah Arendt's political phenomenology and the specifically Marxist phenomenology of Bernard Steigler, and on an individual level, and as happens with the somaesthetics of Richard Shusterman.

This might seem a bit confusing though. True, there is no A-leads-to-B-leads-to-C narrative of how these schools of thought develop along a clear vector, a clear line of thought, but this is hardly a failing. This interdisciplinary approach spanning traditions separated by time and space and including domains like philosophy, psychology, political theory, anthropology, and kinesiology is not taken up as a matter of caprice. Rather, the nature of this project demands not only an interdisciplinary approach, but also one that proceeds and grows from multiple points. This would mean growing like a potato or ginger root, like a rhizome. Gilles Deleuze and Félix Guattari advocate such a rhizomatic approach in their own considerations of philosophical method, writing:

> 1st and 2nd principles of connection and heterogeneity: any point of a rhizome can be connected to anything other, and should be. This is very different from the tree or root, which fixes a point, an order. The linguistic tree in the manner of Chomsky still begins at a point S and proceeds by way of dichotomy. On the contrary, not every trait in a rhizome is necessarily linked to a linguistic feature: semiotic chains of every nature are connected to very diverse modes of coding—biological, political, economic chains, and so forth—bringing not only different regimes of signs into play but also states of things of differing status.[3]

Setting aside for the moment Deleuze and Guattari's own theoretical commitments (which are numerous and byzantine), the basic point being taken up by this inquiry is that the interplay of the various sign chains (biological, political, economic, etc.) constitutive of society and self tends toward tangles and knots, such that any account of these strands will be likewise tangled and knotted. As they go on to explain:

> A rhizome never ceases in establishing connections between semiotic chains, organizations of power, and occurrences relative to the arts, sciences, and social conflict. A semiotic chain is like a tuber agglomerating very diverse acts, linguistic, but also perceptive, mimetic, gestural, and cognitive: there is no language in itself, nor is there any universality of language, only a concurrence of dialects, patois, slangs, and specialized languages.[4]

When a bit of thought is given, this rhizomatic approach makes sense if one does in fact commit to the notion of subjectivation. What is at issue here is not language as such, but a kind of theory of everything as pertains to normativity, signs, and social life. Hence it is not at all strange to expect a sprawling account, and though Deleuze and Guattari seem to incautiously overstate it in their own work, the general point remains, "any point of a rhizome can be connected to anything other, and *must be*."[5]

In any case, bringing in Deleuze and Guattari makes sense here, for the idea of discourse at play in subjectivation theory encompasses what they themselves call the "perceptive, mimetic, gestural, and cognitive."[6] With these domains interconnected in this way, there is no central standpoint, no objective middle from which an account of discourse and its development can proceed without obscuring one particular aspect. Continuing their tree/rhizome contrast, Deleuze and Guattari write:

> It is always possible to decompose language down into internal structures, it is not fundamentally different from a search for roots. There is always something of genealogy about a tree; it is not a method for the people. On the contrary, a method of the rhizome type can analyze language by decentering it onto other dimensions and other registers.[7]

So understood, the development of discourse for the human species and for individuals is not just perceptual; it is not just ritually mimetic; it is not just gestural; it is not just about the terms of our cognition; it is not just a matter of inscription and the written word; it is not just the spoken word. It is all of these at the same time. It is discipline as such, connecting the facets of the social disciplining, regulating, and assignment both of individuals into particular roles and of human knowledge itself into particular disciplines.

Discipline, understood on such terms, cannot be dealt with from inside of a single discipline without replicating in some way that particular local configuration of disciplinary power. If there is to be any hope of grappling with disciplinary power in its wholeness, as something both repressive and necessarily productive, then it will have to be through an interdisciplinary, rhizomatic approach without any one particular center. This approach to discipline will have centers *plural*; it will proceed out of interconnected and intertwined issues falling across what only now happen to be different disciplines.

Furthermore, beyond the proliferation of disciplines calling for interdisciplinarity, what is being talked about here, in a certain sense, is inchoate; it is human development as such, with discipline and disciplines serving to intertwine the levels of society and individual. With society and individual there is already a chicken and egg problem, already a difficulty of assigning a primary locus for situating the inquiry. Sure, mapping correspondences between society and individual, individual and society is not a new idea, just look at Plato and the tripartite divisions of psyche and polis. However, with the soul's eternality being connected to eternal forms and providing a characteristically Platonic fundament for further reasoning about the arrangement of cities, even there the account is *animated* de anima, from the soul so to speak.[8] This psychologizes the social at the outset, as tends to happen in many accounts of the social manifold following after Plato that singularize the plural and individualize what is plural and manifold. Indeed this happens within the vaguely post-Kantian, quasi-Rawlsian lay notion of liberal democratic society that runs through the language of national and international orthodoxy. Society, government, and other macro-structures are supposed to be just that, *macro*-structures; they are supposed to be bigger versions of what happens with the rational form, the faculties, the psychology, and the inherent dignity of individual agents. Setting aside the different aims of the projects, consider how society, as thought in terms of a Rawlsian original position, ends up "nullify[ing] the effects of specific contingencies" between parties much like Kant's tabula rasa moral agent in a way that ends up articulating procedural justice on the social macro level in line with what happens with legislative morality on the individual micro level.[9] More to the point, Rawls freely admits that his work extends the veil of ignorance already implicit in Kant's statement and application of the categorical imperative, thereby placing his influential work within a dominant tradition that tends more often than not to seize upon some feature of the individual to explain how things are or should be for the group.[10] Of course, extrapolating one-way correspondence from the micro to the macro, from the individual to the social, makes perfect sense as a strategy for a philosophical account, and, sure, there is some manner of interplay between society and individual in such accounts, for neither Plato nor Kant nor Rawls could be so obtuse so as to claim otherwise. However, the terms of such accounts, so dominant in the Euro-American sphere, so often seem to have a characteristic arc and telos of springing from and returning to the soul, the rational self, the psyche, or something similarly atomistic as a superordinate point.

Getting back to the matter at hand, the approach here is *co*-ordinate and it requires neither putting the social above the psychic nor the psychic above the social in the manner just described. Instead, the call here is for appreciation of how human growth within either level, and on either time frame, mutually informs growth on the other. Though Butler's own work (at least her earlier *Psychic Life of Power*) tends to focus more on self, the problematic that she sets out, borrowing from Foucault, profoundly respects how the nature of disciplinary power makes it so that the putatively individual subject will is rather "the site at which the social implicates the psychic in its very formation—or, to be more precise, *as* its very formation and formativity."[11] This leaves the subject deeply relational and respecting the chicken-egg dynamic for what it is. The tack taken here supplements Butler's account with observations from Confucian philosophical sources old and new on self-cultivation as well with as insights from connected contemporary European and Chinese sources in order to bring balance to the roles of human individuals and human society in responding to Foucault's challenge. Therefore, within this project there is no single way, no single source from which to grow an account of growth. This represents, to a certain extent, a refigured appreciation of Ralph Waldo Emerson's observation regarding individual life and the broader subtext of general human experience, where he points out that,

> in the growth of the embryo, Sir Everard Home, I think, noticed that the evolution was not from one central point, but co-active from three or more points. Life has no memory. That which proceeds in succession might be remembered, but that which is coexistent, or ejaculated from a deeper cause, as yet far from being conscious, knows not its own tendency.[12]

Accordingly, and this is a point that will be drawn out as both a matter of methodological form and as philosophical content, the type of development being talked about here with both self and society is the kind of growth that cannot re-member and re-collect its own many disparate, scattered origins, articulations, offshoots, and so on.

While the nature and implications of such growth and development occurring from multiple points remains a matter for the latter portions of this work, what Emerson has to say about the embryonic and what Deleuze and Guattari have to say about the rhizomatic informs the basic method here. A straightforward account of something proceeding in succession will not do here. There are too many intertwined factors, like self and society, amidst too many overlapping fields, like discourse, discipline, and disciplines, to say that any one *must*, by its preeminent nature, come first. The rhizomatic approach undertaken here proceeds on the somewhat pragmatic, if not obvious, basis that one has to start from somewhere—since, because of the very nature of giving an account, one aspect *needs* to come first as a genuine kind of primus inter pares, first among equals, in dealing with the issues presented here. This is a book with a first page and a last page, after all. However, the "need" here is rather soft and far from properly essential. What guides this work just happens to be the challenges presented by Foucault and Butler's work on subjectivation, but it very well could be otherwise.

Now, it may be objected that this is simply a roundabout justification of laziness and sloppiness, but when honest consideration is given to the constitutive interconnections in the phenomena being considered, it is clear that a proper account should likewise be interconnected and interdisciplinary in its constitution. With discourse turning into discourses, with discipline forming disciplines, and with human growth occurring from multiple sources and on multiple levels, all foreclosing any single discourse or discipline from acting as ur-source for inquiry, a rhizomatic model simply makes sense when it comes to addressing and in some way reflecting this manifold within a philosophical account.

Intercultural Philosophy

And there is yet another sense in which an interdisciplinary, rhizomatic method is called for, and that is the intercultural nature and content of this project. As mentioned earlier, one great benefit of subjectivation theory is that it draws together a number of major views within the Euro-American tradition. This way of representing these strands in more recent continental thought lends itself to an even broader intercultural conversation with complementary approaches regarding how the self as (a) relational, (b) discursive, (c) bodily, and (d) ritually impelled subject might survive and even thrive amid social forces that are on the one hand restrictive and on the other productive, per Foucault's challenge.

In dealing with the question concerning the productive/restrictive nature of society, of culture vis-à-vis self across the course of human development, it likewise makes little sense to be restricted to *one* sociocultural horizon. Indeed, what is being addressed is the emergence of culture, which is not a linear phenomenon with all of humanity set on the same course, but rather more something akin to Emerson's embryo growing from multiple sources. There are, of course, *cultures* plural. Here, pursuant to the overall question of accounting for the productive/restrictive developmental dynamics of culture and self, two further intertwined questions emerge, with both speaking to the form and content of this project—namely, What constitutes culture generally and what constitutes *a* culture singularly insofar as such a determination can be made?

But, digressing slightly, there is the need for self-defense, not uncommon when presenting work like this to a wider audience, as questions of cultural incommensurability inevitably arise. Is comparative philosophy legitimate? Is intercultural? Is any type of global philosophy possible? Is this particular kind of project possible? Are the cultural, terminological, and perspectival differences simply too great?

Simply put, this type of talk, while well intentioned, is not fruitful. Taken in terms of contemporaneous cultures, one might ask whether Butler has license to deal with French philosophers. Is this too much distance? One might ask whether it is right to put her into conversation with Lǐ Zéhòu, who has also put out influential work on proximate topics during a similar timespan. One might ask if China itself is too far away. What about Lǐ Zéhòu's long-term residence in America?

The same question occurs with regard to anachronism and historical/cultural incommensurability. Does a contemporary "Westerner" have license to talk about Plato when his Athenian culture is really quite far away from today's world? Does Butler have the right to appropriate Aristotle? Does Lǐ Zéhòu have warrant to delve into Confucianism? The obvious answer to these facile questions is "yes," because soon the very idea of tradition and continuity would become lost in such a way that Nietzsche's sardonic quip that "there was basically only one Christian, and he died on the cross" would become the rule for philosophical, religious, and cultural enterprises in general.[13] However, glibly leaving things at "yes" and simply moving on presents problems in the long run. The gap calls for a fuller response.

In both cases, whether addressing how contemporaneous cultures talk to each other or how contemporary idioms speak to the past, something of a "sorites paradox" emerges. The sorites paradox, using the Greek term for "heap" (σωρίτης or *sōritēs*), refers to the slippery slope question of quantification. A heap might have a certain large number of straws of hay in it, but taking them away one by one, at some point a threshold is reached whereby the heap ceases to be a heap. A similar logic underlies questions concerning baldness and there perhaps being some threshold number of hairs between 0 and *n* where one becomes bald or not bald. The hourglass likewise comes to mind, manifesting the paradox over time.

What does this mean here? Well, the idea is that some point exists where things either become *intracultural*, occurring within a single proper domain, or *intercultural*, occurring between two separate cultures. This implies a threshold, a spatial, temporal, or spatiotemporal border at which this culture here ends and that culture there begins, and also a border where each becomes a proper entity, a heap unto itself, and not just subcultural detritus.

This all gets rather messy rather quick. The kind of logic often motivating these questions of cultural incommensurability is far from unassailable, dubiously tending toward false reification or what Alfred North Whitehead calls the fallacy of misplaced concreteness.[14] Whitehead holds that "by a process of constructive abstraction we can arrive at abstractions which are the simply located bits of material, and at other abstractions which are the minds included in the scientific scheme."[15] And here, in this project, culture counts as one such constructed abstraction.

Why is this a problem? Well, such abstractionism quite often becomes vicious, at least as understood by William James. He writes:

> Let me give the name of "vicious abstractionism" to a way of using concepts which may be thus described: We conceive a concrete situation by singling out some salient or important feature in it, and classing it under that; then, instead of adding to its previous characters all the positive consequences which the new way of conceiving it may bring, we proceed to use our concept privatively; reducing the originally rich phenomenon to the naked suggestions of that name abstractly taken, treating it

as a case of "nothing but" that concept, and acting as if all the other characters from out of which the concept is abstracted were expunged. Abstraction, functioning in this way, becomes a means of arrest far more than a means of advance in thought.[16]

When it comes to abstracting cultures from culture (and even the abstraction of culture as such is problematic because of the kind of interconnections already described), such abstracted cultures lend themselves to "no true Scotsman"-type thinking. Coined by Antony Flew, this refers to the all-too-common self-serving form of rather flimsy essentialism on display in the following scenario:

> Imagine Hamish McDonald, a Scotsman, sitting down with his *Glasgow Morning Herald* and seeing an article about how the "Brighton [England] Sex Maniac Strikes Again." Hamish is shocked and declares that "No Scotsman would do such a thing." The next day he sits down to read his *Glasgow Morning Herald* again; and, this time, finds an article about an Aberdeen [Scotland] man whose brutal actions make the Brighton sex maniac seem almost gentlemanly. This fact shows that Hamish was wrong in his opinion but is he going to admit this? Not likely. This time he says, "No *true* Scotsman would do such a thing."[17]

And so, this is the tendency of one to dismiss this or that derelict, untidy, or inconvenient instance as not truly Scottish, French, Maasai, Japanese, Cherokee, or whatever may be the case, since these occurrences would simply be the random noise of statistical outliers and nothing properly *essential*.

This vicious cultural abstraction happens as much with the hypothetical sex maniacs of Brighton and Aberdeen as it does with academic philosophers toiling in their particular bailiwicks. It is very easy for this kind of thinking to become self-serving or at least conforming to pre-existing biases, such that the abstraction of what belongs to this or that particular culture leaves out or downplays the parts of a tradition that its bearers might prefer to forget. And this is to say nothing of how a virulent strand of the pathetic fallacy can easily give way to retrograde racism and the ascription of specific, often none-too-laudatory, anthropomorphic characteristics to this or that portion of humanity. This happens, for example, with the regrettable typecasting of entire cultures committed by supposedly enlightened philosophers like Kant and Hegel, where whole continents are seen as representatives of this or that human attribute like "fetishism" without "an inner drive for culture" in the case of Africa, or "the dull brooding of spirit" in the case of Asia, or proper rationality in the case of a self-aggrandizing view of Europe.[18]

This "a few bad apples"-type thinking, this "no true Scotsman"-type thinking, leads not only to a bizarre insistence on some construct of cultural essence serving as the measure of authenticity in a way that is only becoming more out of pace alongside increasingly fluid notions of belonging, inclusion, and self/cultural identification amid globalization; but this narrow thinking can also lead to the real-world dangers of pernicious tribalism and national chauvinism. Though cultural incommensurability may well cause worry for good people acting in good faith, enough rotten logic lies beneath to justify calling the question of incommensurability itself into question.

Simply put, yes, intercultural philosophers and methods should indeed have to defend themselves, since critical inquiry demands no less. However, they should not find themselves initially and forever thereafter in that position of defense and haunted by the supposedly frightful specter of the culturally incommensurable, when that question is itself predicated on many less than defensible premises.

This is not to say that the abstraction of particular cultures is not useful. It is, and powerfully so, for it provides basic differentiae for breaking down the world into portions that can be grasped by finite human understanding. This is not to say that such talk will be absent from this work, since an affinity for thinking through cultures in the promotion of intercultural philosophy has already been claimed as a strength of this work. What is being said, however, is that it makes little sense to use standards like cultural/national essence in evaluating the rightness or wrongness of an intercultural conversation when similar abstractions end up becoming a matter of diminishing returns upon close scrutiny and when, in the worst-case, this language leads not just to error in dealing with particulars but also to highly questionable and potentially dangerous notions of group, tribe, and nation as exclusive.

And it is not just the logic of abstraction that makes the question of incommensurability highly problematic. The philosophical question of cultural borders soon finds itself enmeshed in geopolitical discussions of tribalism, regionalism, nationalism, recognition, postcolonial legacy, and the like. The anonymous Yiddish saying, which is sadly ironic in its connection with German, that "a language is a dialect with an army and a navy" (a shprakh iz a dialekt mit an armey un flot) comes to mind and with it the crucial realization that there is a great deal of historical contingency that works to determine the legitimacy of cultures and the success or failure of particular languages or idioms in receiving institutional imprimaturs, such as those of the academic world.

And so it is that certain nations, domains, languages, idioms, and traditions freely enter the academy and the realm of philosophy proper without any real scrutiny, while others find themselves forever groveling for admission, while there are yet others who are so faceless, "backward," and indistinct that they are not even recognized in any meaningful sense as genuine philosophical traditions—all of which makes the global state of academic philosophy similar to the stale "dynamic" of the United Nations as concerns the permanent, veto-capable members of the Security Council (China, France, Russia, the United Kingdom, and the United States, all World War II allies). Some places of thinking enjoy the privilege of simply being legitimate without mediation or bound, be they less-tangible philosophical positions or more-tangible geolocations curiously ossified within today's nation-state borders. In these places of thinking there is no need to suffer from what W. E. B. Du Bois, using the terms of Hegel's *Geist* philosophy to tell the story of *The Souls of Black Folk*, would call mediated- or double-consciousness, referring to "this sense of always looking at one's self through the eyes of others, of measuring one's soul by the tape of a world that looks on in amused contempt and pity."[19]

There is always "pure" philosophy, philosophy "proper," and then there are the subordinate domains of "Japanese" philosophy, of "Chinese" philosophy, of "Indian" philosophy, and of "African" philosophy, in addition to of the multitudes of parties apparently not deserving of even a qualified headline (and this does not even begin to address major intersections with domains of gender and class and how a kind of institutional ghettoization often occurs in these realms as well). These others are left to do some brand of "Other" philosophy, forever being qualified, which in and of itself is pejorative. So understood, the simple imputation of such boundaries through questions of incommensurability serves to bind recognition of this or that place of thinking, consigning the people on the wrong side of fortune to misrecognition, deferred recognition, or no recognition whatsoever.

Presuppositions of cultural boundaries, the presuppositions at the root of the questions of incommensurability meant to stymie intercultural philosophers ought instead to vex the voices of orthodoxy posing such questions, for these presuppositions prove to be troublesome not only conceptually in terms of the sorites paradox and the dubious assertion of hard and fast boundaries, but they also prove to be problematic in a way that indicts institutional academia and its indefensible record of maintaining the geopolitical status quo and excluding those not belonging to academia's decidedly *ivory* tower.

Nobody posing the incommensurability question feels that it is racist or in any other way untoward, but instead that it is simply a question of real separation that implies nothing in particular about inequality or exclusion. But, as African-Americans in the United States have proven with regard to the racist and exclusionary practices of so-called Jim Crow law after a great deal of struggle inside of courts and even more outside, "separate, but equal" is a myth that evaporates upon realization of the inherent injury and inequality caused by such nonconsensual exclusion.[20] Both the sorites paradox lurking behind the assertion of cultural borders and the hurtful, contradictory, and hegemonic effects of such thinking go to show that the incommensurability question ought to be heavily qualified or, being so heavily qualified and watered down, dismissed entirely.

What then is to be done with this vacuum? There has to be a way of recognizing real differences without giving into the pernicious logic of presuming separation. If more standard views of cultural orthodoxy are deemed invalid and irrelevant, then it seems like some type of intercultural philosophy would be called for. And there is a need for culture and generalizations of culture in order to talk about cultural archetypes, memory, rituals, both as part of this book, where these are major topics, and more generally. Questions quickly emerge though. How would it then make sense to talk of cultures having conversations, as happens even in this project, if the fallacy of misplaced *cultural* concreteness is taken seriously? How can things be intercultural if there are no cultures as such? How is it possible to rescue basic talk of cultures more generally and avoid somehow implying that all talk about Chinese philosophy, French culture, or American literature is in some way essentialist, racist, or nationalist?

Answering such questions is no mean task. There needs to be a type of intercultural philosophy that does not lapse into pernicious abstractions of cultures, and that still retains the ability to speak of this culture or that as the case may be. There needs to be a way of talking about world philosophy as a unity while respecting philosophical worldviews as a dynamic manifold where the constituent elements are fluid yet insistent particulars and not simply so much misplaced concreteness. In accounting for multifaceted human development, something needs to be said, even edgewise, about the emergence of any possible intercultural philosophy within this dynamic.

Perhaps the beginning of an approach to intercultural philosophy can be found by returning to Deleuze and Guattari's observations on rhizomatic method. Sensitive to the fluid nature of language and culture, they write:

> There is no ideal speaker-listener, any more than [there is] a homogeneous linguistic community. Language is . . . "an essentially heterogeneous reality." There is no mother tongue, only a power takeover by a dominant language in a political multiplicity. Language stabilizes itself around a parish, a bishopric, a capital. It forms a bulb. It evolves by subterranean stems and streams, along river valleys or train tracks; it moves like a patch of oil.[21]

And so, the particular project here of looking at the multisource, intertwined growth of society and of self through language and culture takes something of a rhizomatic approach to language and culture. However, this bears some qualification when it comes to the specific matter of intercultural philosophy.

Earlier mention was made of setting aside the extended theoretical commitments of Deleuze and Guattari. This was done, in part, because, while the rhizomatic approach that they advocate is robust and well-suited to a project like this, their own specific words when it comes to intercultural philosophy are also problematic, despite their sensitivity to the need to abandon any notion of an ideal (and putatively European) speaker-listener.

In *What is Philosophy?*, Deleuze and Guattari entertain the question of speaking of a "Chinese, Hindu, Jewish, or Islamic 'philosophy.'"[22] Leaving, for the moment, the question of the differing, but still overlapping, valences of these domains (ethnic/national, religious, ethnic/religious, and religious, respectively), an inequivalence that can perhaps be defended in terms of the rhizomatic approach, there is still the troubling claim put forth by Deleuze and Guattari that such traditions amount to protophilosophy. With a paternalism not unlike Hegel at his most regrettable, Deleuze and Guattari maintain that, in such areas, the deterritorializing introduction of the concept, seemingly from without, is required for philosophy as such to occur, to arise out of preoccupation with physical figures like mandalas in the case of Hinduism, Sephirot in the case of Judaism, "imaginals" in the case Islam, icons in the case of Christianity, and hexagrams in the case of any possible Chinese philosophy, proto or otherwise.[23]

Deleuze and Guattari's overall point, even if they are somewhat inelegant in presenting the cases of China, Hinduism, Judaism, and Islam, is somewhat more nuanced though. In their understanding of "geo-philosophy," there is absolutely nothing inevitable whatsoever about the idea of philosophy, such that what is known as philosophy, with all of its Greek roots, is likewise a contrived abstraction covering up the similarly deterritorialized growth of the tradition from multiple points. Pointing toward the Egyptian influence on the early Greek tradition, Deleuze and Guattari write:

> That which we deny is that philosophy presents an internal necessity, whether in itself, whether with the Greeks (and the idea of a Greek miracle would be nothing other than an aspect of its pseudo-necessity). However, philosophy was a Greek thing, as well as something brought by immigrants. For philosophy to be born, it required an *encounter* between the Greek milieu and the immanence of thought.[24]

This mitigation of the characterizations that Deleuze and Guattari make of Chinese, Hindu, Jewish, and Islamic bodies of thought continues in their appraisal of Kant, Heidegger, and cultural hegemony in philosophy. Without using the words "intercultural philosophy" per se, they assert that philosophy, if it is ever to expand, must grow into and with nonphilosophy, such that philosophy *must* proceed by way such deterritorialization, since the other option of philosophy forever encountering itself, a position that they attribute to navel-gazing Europeanization, is static in nature.[25] This is simply a basic point of becoming—a thing, here philosophy, if it becomes, becomes what it is not; the matter of change, be it one of appropriation, annihilation, or amelioration, is another matter though. In any case, the basic point is that for philosophy to grow and become it must reach out into what is deemed nonphilosophy. This leads them to conclude:

> For the race summoned forth by art or philosophy is not the one that pretends to be pure, but rather an oppressed, bastard, lower, anarchical, nomadic, and irredeemably minor race—exactly the ones that Kant excluded from the course of the new Critique.[26]

However, in the phrasing of this idea, Deleuze and Guattari again threaten to undermine a valuable point. Here they speak of philosophy encountering nonphilosophy, putting Indian thought in the position of nonphilosophy and promoting a dangerous idea of alterity in the process. They hold:

> The thinker is not acephalic, aphasic, or analphabetic, but becomes so. He becomes Indian, and never ends in becoming so—perhaps "so that" the Indian who himself is Indian becomes

something other than himself and tears himself away from his own agony. We become animal so that the animal also becomes something else.[27]

Now perhaps the linking of a thinker becoming Indian to becoming animal should be read as a kind of parallelism hinging on the basic idea of something becoming what it is not and *perhaps* this view can be read as falling on the "is" side of an is/ought description of the state of global philosophy and not as being reflective of any intention to actually link Indian people to animals. However, even if the rhetorical bombast is excused or explained away, there still remains the very real way in which the position of Deleuze and Guattari further commits to the error initially made in their version of the question regarding the possibility of "Chinese, Hindu, Jewish, or Islamic 'philosophy' "[28]—namely, it concedes the terms of the debate at the outset; it concedes that such things need to be talked about in terms of a possibility whose existence requires defense (thereby leading to a qualified and only partially mitigating definition of protophilosophy).

And so it is that the rhizomatic model of Deleuze and Guattari, while being useful for talking about the kind of multisource growth and development of self and society under discussion here, runs into problems as its many extended offshoots prove unwieldy. Fortunately, a positive trait of a rhizome, and one identified by Deleuze and Guattari, is the capacity for the more ungainly offshoots to be pruned and cut and for the main bulb to be transplanted for the purpose of growth in a new medium.[29] Therefore, when it comes to the particular question of intercultural philosophy, it makes sense to transplant the rhizome into a medium better capable of addressing pluralism in philosophical discourse. Taking what has been said into consideration, this calls not for a monologue or even for a dialogue, but instead for something more suited to rhizomatic growth, a polylog.

This idea of a polylog (following the German nomenclature) is the product of Franz Martin Wimmer. As might be anticipated, Wimmer joins Deleuze, Guattari, and Ames in calling for what he terms a "non-centrist view on humanity's histories of thought."[30] In his view, taking the name intercultural philosophy seriously as something of a regulative ideal for the enterprise requires taking up the presumption that particular philosophies, thoughts, concepts, lines of reasoning have developed culturally in the course of history in such a way that makes intercultural encounters natural and inevitable.[31] As such, there are likely to be philosophical resources for a given topic, which, while not relatively close, can still be closely relevant.

Accordingly, with clear emphasis Wimmer exhorts philosophers to "[s]*earch wherever possible for transcultural overlaps of philosophical concepts, for it is likely that well-grounded theses were developed in more than one cultural tradition.*"[32] With the presupposition being that multiple, diverse, culture-laden philosophical positions should emerge in the course of philosophy broadly speaking, this means aiming not at A talking *to* B or even at A talking *with* B (and B with A). Instead, the aim is a richer exploration of what should presumably be a manifold of views from different cultural traditions occurring without mediation, but perhaps with varying levels of directional intensity in the mutual engagement, as depicted below (i.e., where there is likely more engagement of French or German philosophy in America than there is of American philosophy in France or Germany).[33]

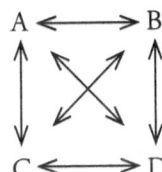 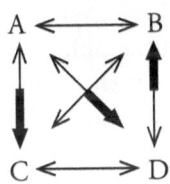 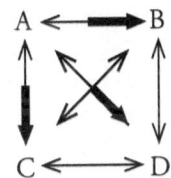

Wimmer lays out what he terms the central question for philosophy, namely, finding "the values and images of humanity that regionally delineated cultures have produced that are fruitful for present and foreseeable human problems."[34] Speaking interculturally, this task calls for reflection on philosophy's own possibilities and upon the process of globalization. Accomplishing this means taking cultural and philosophical pluralism seriously—the question as to how this is to be done remains.

There is a need, recognized by Wimmer, to get past constraining and ultimately counterproductive modes of cultural engagement, which he breaks down into three groups. First, there are monologues that are often marked by single parties displaying a one-way, culturally imperial interest in changing or overcoming the barbarisms of unfamiliar philosophies. Second, there are transitive discourses where traditions only connect through some intermediary (e.g., presuming Nietzsche cannot be in dialogue with Confucius, given the largely opposing views that each holds when it comes to society, harmony, family reverence, and the like, unless such a connection were to occur *through* Daoism on the basis of the latter's connections to both Nietzsche's thought and to Confucianism). And, finally, there is the third species, namely, dialogues that only allow certain parties the privilege of being exotic and worthy of the dubious recognition of being nonetheless capable of two-way philosophical dialogue (while still consigning problematically exotic others to the realm of the barbaric, where interest is often expressed in terms of the one-way imperialism mentioned earlier).[35]

But just because there is a desire to avoid the ills of cultural imperialism does not mean that there should be a complete abandonment of the idea of cultures being in some way distant or different. It is possible to split the difference between the logic of cultural realism maintaining that there *is* an essence to a given tradition, which might then ground imperialist claims regarding the sufficiency or insufficiency of that tradition with respect to proper philosophy, and that of cultural relativism, which asserts that, there being no such thing as cultural essence, it is impossible to make claims and ascriptions about cultures at all or to say something about them being distant or different without lapsing into objectionable forms of centrist universalism (i.e., cultural imperialism).

When it comes to finding such a middle path, Wimmer's words here are instructive. As a matter of definition, he holds that "for every tradition every other one is 'exotic': Therein lies the consequent form of polylog and of an intercultural philosophy."[36] Were other cultures not in some matter exotic, were other cultures not in some way really distant or different, there would be no conversation at all, polylog or otherwise, for a conversation at zero distance is tantamount to mumbling to oneself. Something must be conceded to the cultural realist here, just not the conclusions of cultural imperialism.

Again, Wimmer's words are helpful as he trenchantly observes that, while some manner of cultural realism vis-à-vis exoticism is needed, the fixation on cultures in intercultural philosophy goes down the wrong path. He rightly draws attention to the fact that "[it is] not cultures encountering each other in conversation, but rather people, who are culturally molded in diverse ways. Intercultural philosophy will have the task of qualitatively expanding this conversation and of basing itself not only on the mainstream majorities and their representatives."[37] So considered, the abstraction and reification of cultures, so crucial to questions of cultural incommensurability, should diminish in importance.

With it being people, real particular philosophers, talking to each other in polylogs as well as in monologues, dialogues, or transitive conversations, the question of incommensurability should not turn on whether or not cultural monoliths abstracted into forms of apparent yet errant concreteness can abide each other, but whether the conversation between particular parties *turns out to be any good.* It should not be the case that incommensurability (or commensurability) be presumed as part of an initial a priori observation about cultures made from some kind of quasi-objective vacuum, but rather that it should be something proven or disproven in the real-world results of conversations engaged in by real-world, culturally informed *people*.

The view here is that things can still in fact be intercultural, not because of cultures as such, as concrete things; rather the crucial factor is what is *inter*, the people and issues in between, with secondary priority being given to specific cultures abstracted for the sake of convenient understanding and nothing more. The question should not be whether Tradition X or Culture X is good enough for philosophy, that is, good enough for philosophy in Tradition Y, even if a large number of people in Tradition Y evince a near-pathological blindness of their own whiteness, or rather Y-ness, and treat their brand of philosophy as "philosophy as such," as philosophy qua philosophy. The question should instead be whether the issues generated in the conversation between *people* from those traditions are rich and rewarding (with the constructed nature of these traditions, as abstracted for finite human understanding, being a secondary matter). This in effect turns the question of incommensurability from one of concrete cultural entities and the quantitative judgment of formal difference along the lines of the sorites paradox to one more sensitive to the fluidity of people within cultures and the qualitative appraisal of philosophical content in terms of both similarity (overlap) and difference (inevitable exoticism).

This approach indirectly responds to the heap problem mentioned earlier concerning the definition of a boundary for when a culture becomes a culture separate from other cultures by diminishing the importance of boundaries per se. However, more is necessary for a fuller answer as to how to talk about cultures in a way that supports a rhizomatic, polylog-type approach to intercultural philosophy generally and to this project in particular with its engagement of the Confucian tradition, past and present. Fortunately, leading contemporary comparative philosopher and interpreter of the Chinese philosophical canon Roger T. Ames speaks to these issues directly.

Ames's work is useful here because his view supplements Wimmer's finding that respecting *both* the dynamic and static nature of cultures means looking for a third way apart from both simple cultural relativism and cultural realism.[38] In criticizing a type of "naïve realism," Ames points to Hilary Putnam and his description of how "like Relativism, but in a different way, Realism is an impossible attempt to view the world from Nowhere."[39] There is a false posture of objectivity that comes from attempting to view the world from nowhere, be it realism or relativist, and it ill fits a rhizomatic and genuinely intercultural approach. What are the other options then?

Instead of rejecting realism and succumbing to the kind of simple relativism that would deny the possibility of talking about cultures or philosophies in general terms, there is still a middle path. Ames advocates self-consciousness in interpretation that neither shies away from generalization nor questionably presumes objectivity. Indeed, a certain kind of self-consciousness in interpretation is needed in order to mitigate (but perhaps never quite finally eliminate) the dangers of transacting with cultural abstractions as though they are real quasi-Platonic essences. Self-consciousness in interpretation means admitting that abstractions and generalizations are like helpful prosthetics for understanding reality and that they are not to be understood as corresponding to anything *in* reality. However, self-consciousness does not need to manifest as any kind of self-restriction that would bar one from generalizing in any way whatsoever—a point well made by Ames. He maintains that

> the only thing more dangerous than striving to make responsible cultural generalizations is failing to make them. Generalizations do not have to preclude appreciating the richness and complexity of always evolving cultural traditions; in fact, it is generalizations that locate and inform specific cultural details and provide otherwise sketchy historical developments with the thickness of their content.[40]

Indeed, what Ames specifically advocates is an understanding of interpretation as, "literally, a 'go-between negotiation' " that "emerges analogically through establishing and aggregating a pattern of truly productive correlations between what we know and what we would know" and where success is measured by "accumulat[ing] and optimiz[ing] these meaningful correlations effectively in our own life situations."[41]

So understood, what is important is neither the character of Chinese philosophy in a generalized sense nor the distance or difference from some generalized view from nowhere, but instead the ability of Chinese philosophy to speak to wherever one finds oneself, in whatever physical location or philosophical position. If Chinese philosophy, however abstracted, can be helpful, then so be it, so long as one is conscious of the abstraction and construction of this entity then subsequently called "Chinese philosophy." On this point, Ames asserts, "Self-consciousness in interpretation is not to distort the Chinese philosophical tradition and its cosmology, but to endorse its fundamental premises. Just as each generation selects and carries over earlier thinkers to reshape them in their own image, each generation reconfigures the classical canons of world philosophy to its own needs. We too are inescapably people of a time and place."[42]

Rather than getting hung up on what well may be impossible if not undesirable notions of cultural purity, of purity-giving boundaries, and of pure idioms of philosophy, the call here is instead for honest, self-conscious awareness of *impurity*. These quasi-sorites paradoxes of incommensurability that are supposed to upset intercultural philosophy all in some way turn on the idea that there is some point x at which "this" culture is too far from "that" culture or at which a collection of events, discourses, histories, and so on, becomes large enough to coalesce into a culture proper. Simply put, such talk is only possible if one confuses absolute magnitudes of distance and extent with relative notions of farness and largeness (or closeness and smallness respectively). Questions of cultural incommensurability confound the ability to perceive and in some way measure the former with the ability to make judgments on the basis of the latter. Nothing about a magnitude of distance, time, or extent discloses that the quantity *is in and of itself* (too) large or (too) small; for that, the information of a superordinate context is needed. Nothing about the Chinese tradition discussed here, from either the physical or temporal distance from today's English-speaking world to the size of the philosophical tradition, determines it being too far, too minor, or too irrelevant for philosophical discussion. Quasi-sorites confusions of cultural incommensurability go away upon rejection of the idea of there being, apart from what is contrived after the fact for convenience in thinking, some pregiven point zero or some absolute outer bounds that might supply context and begin to give that point x genuine meaning.

With this in mind it possible to recognize that convergence, the kind of convergence of thought pointed to throughout this work, implies a still-remaining distance and, moreover, that this distance is OK. In language that speaks directly to this project and its concern with ritual propriety or *lĭ* as a social tool for subject life, Ames spells out what is reasonable to expect from such a convergence. He says, "You cannot say '*lĭ* 禮' in English, or in German either, although you can say lots about it in both languages."[43] The intention here in this project is to bring together voices like Butler to say something about *lĭ* in English, voices like Hegel and Nietzsche to say something about it in German, as well as voices like Foucault and Stiegler to say something about it in French in the hopes that this will add to what can be said in Chinese by the classical Confucian thinkers and by more recent figures like Lǐ Zéhòu on the general topic of the productive/restrictive character of society in the ritual formation and performance of the self.

Tied to the need for self-consciousness in interpreting and negotiating these various idioms, the key criterion for judging this kind of conversation is whether or not both nearness *and* remoteness, cohesion *and* particularity, are properly in proportion for the kind of embryonic, rhizomatic growth hinted at earlier. As Deleuze, Guattari, Wimmer, and Ames variously and diversely show, results are what really matter—are we seeing quality growth? Does developing these sources together in a way that both attends to convergent growth *and* respectfully preserves the very real differences do anything to grow and generate genuine philosophical content?

Growing the Rhizome

This work is like a tuber, like a potato. What does this mean? Per Deleuze and Guattari, "There are no points or positions in a rhizome, as found in a structure, tree, or root. [It is] only lines."[44] As such, there is no obvious point zero from which its growth might proceed, like a seed, or from which one might grasp it, like a stem. There are instead multiple sources of growth, a multisource sprawl. However, picked up from this end or that end, on the horizontal or on the vertical, on the transverse or the obverse, the potato or the ginger root, shows certain lines of growth and articulation.

True, if the goal is to break this rhizome down for understanding, one has to begin slicing and dicing somewhere, and here the contours of growth prefigure a sixfold movement. This work starts with (1) Foucault's challenge to describe society's productive/restrictive character alongside subjectivation and Butler's extension of that work before moving to a discussion of (2) autonomy/freedom in art and then transitioning to (3) the classical Confucian idea of ritual, *lǐ* 礼, which then prompts consideration of (4) subjectality, Lǐ Zéhòu's Confucian/Kantian/Marxian aesthetically driven approach to collective unconsciousness in social ritual, which in turn connects to (5) the idea of technique in appearance as developed through Hannah Arendt's notion of appearance and Bernard Stiegler's Marxian understanding of technique, technology, and memory, all of which finally links with (6) Richard Shusterman's work on somaesthetics. Despite everything said seeming to extol vagueness in terms of things in between, there is nonetheless a beginning, middle, and end to this particular account. It just happens to be that these six elements are abstracted and organized in a quasi-linear fashion for the sake of understanding (and because truly nonlinear rhizomatic writing, like that of the compilers of the Chinese classics, Emerson, Nietzsche, Derrida, Deleuze, Guattari, etc., is a bit of high-wire act that takes time to hone). In any case, there is a logic at play here.

And this is key; there is *a* logic at play here, singular. This is not the only way to do things, but this fact is far from a failing. One could find similar challenges and similar issues in other domains, only a few of which are explored here. One could in fact start things in another idiom. There is no reason why Butler's work on subjectivation *needs* to drive things here; there is no reason why her understanding of the (a) relational, (b) discursive, (c) bodily, and (d) ritually impelled subject *needs* to be in the foreground other than perhaps the pragmatic wisdom of starting where one *actually* is with resources at hand, with things familiar, and working outward, as I have attempted to do.

And such is the case with this reconsideration of the life of power, which very self-consciously casts itself as responding to Judith Butler's landmark *Psychic Life of Power*. Speaking biographically, this project results from a personal engagement with philosophy and a challenge issued well before any postgraduate work, to reckon with the seeming trap of subjectivation presented by Butler; and so it arises from what is personally most familiar and significant within the assemblage presented here. In any case, one could very well start cutting from another end of the potato or ginger root. Subjectivation, Foucault's challenge, and Butler's *Psychic Life of Power* just happen to serve collectively as the starting point for breaking things down here, but this constellation is not the beginning or the end of the issues at play. Furthermore, this project, lacking a superordinate center as it does, is also without any single basis for reconciling the myriad views under discussion; but this is not necessarily a problem. As Butler herself writes:

> I make eclectic use of various philosophers and critical theorists in this inquiry. Not all of their positions are compatible with one another, and I do not attempt to synthesize them here. Although synthesis is not my aim, I do want to maintain that each theory suggests something of ethical importance that follows from the limits that condition any effort one might make to give an account of oneself.[45]

Following this spirit does not mean engaging in philosophical relativism at the expense of realism. Rather, it means that in the process of carving up the issue here this way or that, starting from this or that end, one should get not only fairly similar bulk material by weight, but also similar natural contours, just as one might with a rhizome, like a potato or a ginger root. It would not be at all surprising to hear of possible approaches to cutting through similar issues perhaps growing from this same rhizome and yielding somewhat similar results, nor would it be surprising to hear that already this is being or has been done. Without having a given point zero, one still gets to the center of this material all the same, with the matter's complex intertwined logic of subjectivated self and social culture(s) itself providing a riddling guide of sorts.

This stands as a defense of sorts against some faceless, hypothesized questioner of interdisciplinary and intercultural work. What can be said positively for this method?

Simply put, it grows. It grows from multiple sources and can extend roots in multiple directions. It grows even from cuttings, sliced this way or that.[46] It makes multiple sprouts and points of connection germane. The hope here is that this approach, or even just certain portioned cuttings, will stand as a basis for further investigation in conjunction with other potential sources capable of growing this body of thought. This could well include looking further into the language of ritual, so crucial to this particular endeavor, and looking at voices critical of the classical Confucian approach within the East Asian sphere. This could include looking at Daoist perspectives, which tread ground similar to that of Confucianism, but which provide vastly different, and in many cases directly opposing, ideas of human development and "self"-cultivation. This might well mean looking at perspectives and practices from Buddhism, which, as a philosophical/religious school arriving from India, appropriated already extant Daoist views, notably in the development of Chan and then Zen Buddhism in China and Japan respectively. Moving in this direction might in turn lend itself to different, somewhat more well-known recent conversations involving Buddhist views on this topic of subject emergence and the productive/restrictive character of society, particularly as one sees with philosophers working within and influenced by the Kyoto School, like Nishida Kitarō 西田 幾多郎 and Yuasa Yasuo 湯浅 泰雄.

The potential outgrowths and transplants do not need to take place strictly on a cultural or intercultural axis. Disciplinary and interdisciplinary growth is possible too. With performance being a major issue here, the language of theater and theater studies connects up to this inquiry, although only a few offshoots can be explored at this time and within this space, thereby leaving plenty more to be developed in the future. Likewise, this notion of ritual lends itself to being considered in terms of anthropology and sociology. Something similar can be said too for disciplines like political theory and psychology as regards the major theme of ritually manufacturing consent, a topic with a broad body of literature (not to mention a major work under that title), only a fraction of which can be brought into play here in this particular project.[47] This also holds true for disciplines occurring *within* the traditional confines of philosophy, as, for example, ritual normativity opens up an array of possible connections to work in *both* ethics and aesthetics, only a small portion of which can be taken up here.

Ideally, this rhizome of a book, this decentralized account of subjectivation and productive/restrictive sociocultural power can, between its multiple sources, grow a sufficiently strong internal structure so as to be not only substantial in and of itself, but also capable of supporting further outward growth into the broader field and hopefully in connection to other bodies of thought. And so the ability to provoke further discussion and sustain further inquiry more than any kind of A-leads-to-B-leads-to-QED standard of proof stands as the criterion of success for the rhizomatic, interdisciplinary, and intercultural method taken up here.

Chapter 1

Subjectivation/Subjection

However, "hell is other people" has always been misunderstood. It has been thought that what I meant by that was that our relations with other people are always poisoned, that they are invariably foreboding relations. But what I really mean is something totally different. I mean that if relations with someone else are twisted, vitiated, then that other person can only be hell. Why? . . . When we think about ourselves, when we try to know ourselves, we basically use knowledge that others already have of us. We judge ourselves with the means other people have [and] have given us to judge us. Into whatever I say about myself someone else's judgment always enters. Though I speak about myself, the judgment of others always [is there] in between. This means that if my relations are bad, I put myself in the total dependence of others. And then indeed I am in hell. And there are a number of people in the world who are in hell because they depend too much upon the judgment of others. But this does not at all mean that we cannot have other relationships with others. It simply marks the capital importance of all others for each of us.[1]

—Jean-Paul Sartre

Preliminary Remarks: Butler on Subjectivation/Subjection

It is nice to talk about self and society as if these are two wholly separate things, as if there is a pure kernel of rational personality that exists prior to bodily life and social entanglement. However convenient this fiction may be, this way of thinking obscures the nature of the self as a subject within society. Personhood is deeply and thoroughly relational. It accrues and accumulates through experience. People are not gods. The Abrahamic religions hold that humans are made in God's image, but there is a limit to this—simply put, *we* are.[2] *We* are not the proverbial "I AM THAT I AM."[3] *We* are not singular, certainly not in that deep sense. *We are*, and this precedes any particular "I." *We* are plural. *We* are familial, social, and political, and it is these spheres that found the self, not vice versa. *We*, as other people, are more than just hell, since we constitute each other and our mutual constitution forms the basis of Sartre's quasi-religious, heaven-on-earth-like vision of the day when the human race attains completion in defining itself, not as the sum of the globe's many isolated inhabitants, but in terms of "infinite unity of their reciprocity."[4]

While some of this may sound appealing at first, further consideration of the present state of affairs and the dominance the former, damning definition of humanity shows this idea of relationality ultimately to verge on not only being excessively postmodern, but also rather gloomy. While *we* are in fact more than hell, for many, any greater possibility remains far from being realized. For the time being and for the most part, *we* other people are still that—hell.

And so, if "I" am deeply and completely relational, then my sense of self, my identity would not be "*mine*" per se, but would rather owe to forces beyond myself. Without an eternally self-same soul underneath it all, then it would seem that "I" stand as a fiction dictated from without. So understood, "I" do not come on to the scene as an already coherent entity, but rather "I" am made to cohere, always doing so on somebody else's terms. If that is so, then "I" truly am a subject, in that "I" am subject to the powers that set the terms through which "I" understand myself. Then it seems that "I" perpetually lose myself. Self-understanding may take the form of ego, but "I" can never have full possession of self, because that individuality has and will always be contingent on maintaining a certain place, posture, and pose in society. And so a subtle, if persistent, melancholy sets in, becoming the order of the day.

What then is to be done with this thoroughly relational mode of personhood? What is to be done with this melancholic subject? Raging at circumstance may be one answer. Flinging back the terms of subjection offers comfort, cold and temporary though it may be; but this falls well short of relief. Turning the chains that bind the subject into weapons against social powers might sound appealing. However, this answer is shortsighted and likely to yield neither freedom nor redemption for the subject, let alone contentment or happiness. Defining oneself as a lion in opposition to social power still cedes the basic terms of discourse to that power, leading to profound resentment. Even if outright redemption seems unlikely here, there remains the task of finding resources that can at least help to rehabilitate this notion of the relational subject and perhaps avoid some of its more dour conclusions.

Such a resource may exist in comparative philosophy, in exploring traditions that emphasize relationality, rather than individuality, as the basis of self. Unfortunately, while comparative philosophy is thriving, not all of its possibilities are being adequately explored. Such is the case of conversations between Chinese philosophy and the European continental tradition. It is perhaps understandable why there is not a great deal of interface between these traditions. After all, the standard (and somewhat unthinking) view goes that the former tends to emphasize tradition, family, and the like, while the latter tends toward postmodern, post-structuralist, cosmopolitan orientations. Furthermore, where there has been contact, much of it has tended to be conducted in the constrictive terms of doctrinaire Marxism (though this is starting to change). In any case, comparative work bridging these two fields has unfortunately tended to have a narrow focus, with a great deal of disparity in terms of directional emphasis, much as Wimmer's figure of polylog variants from the previous section depicts.

What is lamentable here is that these two traditions have much to say to each other, despite common assumptions that they talk past each other. In particular, Confucian philosophers, both classical and contemporary, and the thinkers drawn together by leading American philosopher Judith Butler in her book *The Psychic Life of Power* have profound connections with each other. While Butler, a longtime University of California, Berkeley, professor, and the European tradition she represents may not be as sunny about the matter as Confucians, they all nonetheless share particular insight into how the relational self arises discursively through naming, ritual, and performance.

With a career spanning back to the 1980s and with renown for her 1990s books *Gender Trouble* and *Bodies that Matter*, Butler also spends a great deal of her time addressing the subject more generally in a way that overlaps with her more specific work on gender, although by her own admission these broader efforts are "less known—and less popular—dimensions of [her] philosophical work."[5] This part of Butler's work examines in broad terms how external power forms and regulates its psychic life, with many forms of alterity animating and constraining the subject, not just sexual difference, which Butler specifically casts as "not the primary difference from which all other kinds of social differences are derivable."[6] While gender and sex have profound implications for the subject, Butler does not make these the major focus in this less popular strand of her thinking. In this context the term "subject" refers to that which characterizes being human in the world, namely, a self-reflexive, self-examining, self-critical, socially impelled, embodied agency. Here, the figure of the subject more generally represents a turning-on-self initiated by pressure from without, from what is other (with gender still nonetheless being a crucial dimension of that alterity, especially with the precariat disproportionately affected by poverty and exposure being women, transgender, and queer people).[7]

Judith Butler elucidates this idea her work *The Psychic Life of Power*, which draws upon notions like Hegel's unhappy consciousness, Nietzsche's bad conscience, Freud's melancholic ego, and Foucault's subjectivation model. Since her work deals with so many major figures at great length, comparative philosophical inquiry based on Butler's work can have wider implications, which in this project means connecting up a host of continental sources to strands in Confucian thought. At the outset, though, it may seem counterintuitive to turn to a psychoanalytic, post-structuralist gender theorist as a resource for comparative Confucian scholarship, but provided one can get past the labels and the "-isms," there are intriguing similarities as well as informative divergences.

While the connection may not be readily apparent, Butler's thinking shares many features in common with Confucianism. Though Butler looks at power with a disdain largely absent in Confucianism's strong endorsement of hierarchy, there exists a common view that power is discursive and propagates through naming, performance, and ritual. However, Confucianism has one distinct advantage—it pays distinct attention to the aesthetic dimensions of the development of the subject and to related issues that are underexplored in Butler's account. More to the point, the aesthetic dimension of discourse, particularly the Confucian idea of ritual, not only has an affinity with Butler's paradigm, but it provides a way out of its more pessimistic findings—namely, that the enduring condition of the subject is one of melancholia or rage. The argument here breaks down into two parts.

First, power, as described by Judith Butler (following Michel Foucault), is the purposive macro-level social force that animates individual persons. Power does not simply occur in psychological/moral terms, but thrives in cultural productions, artistic expression, iconographic depiction, and so on. Power thus has an aesthetic life akin to the "psychic life" that Butler identifies, and these parallel lives both reside in the sort of unhappy consciousness that Hegel describes. This means that serious, mainstream social practice and the capricious, arbitrary artworld of postmodernity mutually alienate each other, like Hegel's stoic and skeptic. This is what is examined in this first chapter on subjectivation and in the second chapter on autonomy and the artwork.

Second, power, with its basis in ritualized social norms and the establishment of "correct" discourse, can fruitfully be understood in Confucian terms, namely, the intertwined notions of ritual bearing (*lǐ* 礼) and the right use of names (*zhèngmíng* 正名). In Confucianism, both of these terms are simultaneously moral and aesthetic in nature, and this provides the basis for latter-day Marx-influenced theorists to investigate the artistic, productive forces behind social formation. Hence, an account of Chinese philosophy old and new can provide a broader account of power, address the aesthetic dimension of ritual, and point the way to attaining freedom through self-cultivation. This is what the remaining major chapters on the topics of ritual *lǐ* 礼, subjectality, technique in appearance, and somaesthetics aim to provide. This all will serve as the basis for a brief concluding section.

As for where this first major chapter will ultimately lead in terms of this larger project, Butler holds that subjects who regulate themselves on society's terms must be dealt with *on society's terms*—and negotiating this bind through art and artful ritual practice is the main topic here in this work. Why is this a bind though? For Butler herself, one's "own" body or soul is not in any way pregiven as any kind of shelter or source of prior meaning, since, for her, the embodied soul is constantly emerging through recognition and how it matters to others. This reflects Butler's more succinct view that what "matters about an object is its matter."[8] For Butler, bodies matter and subjects persist by virtue of the ritualized forms of recognition that suffuse social discourse, the result being that only rage and resignification of that discourse remain as options. However, this way of thinking perhaps does not give sufficient attention to art's complex relationship to the deterministic discursive structure that Butler identifies. This in turn problematically cuts off the possibility explored here of bodily practice itself becoming artistic and a source of freedom.

Getting back to the current topic of subjectivation, Butler proceeds from the view that a subject's identity arises from external normativity, which initiates and takes up residence within and thus initiates the inner sphere of self-consciousness.[9] Butler starts with the leading figure of nineteenth-century German idealism, Georg Wilhelm Friedrich Hegel, who sees what he terms "unhappy consciousness" as the internalization of two desires toward freedom and negation, which themselves follow from the split between what he takes to be the representative figures of what he identifies as the immediately prior mode of consciousness, that of the master and the slave.[10] For Hegel, the struggle between master and slave is motivated by the fact that self-consciousness exists only in and for itself through recognition—recognition, which in Butler's particular reading of Hegel's *Phenomenology* serves as the *only* means for fulfilling the desire to persist in one's being.[11] Reflection requires a mirror for self-consciousness in the form of another self-consciousness to recognize it.

Here, the notion of recognition drives self-consciousness and it appears in terms of the two extremes of the slave's self-negating recognition of the master, on the one hand, and the freedom that the master acquires by being so recognized, on the other.[12] However, as Butler notes in her follow-up to *The Psychic Life of Power*, *Giving an Account of Oneself*, "I can never offer recognition in the Hegelian sense as a pure offering, since I am receiving it, at least potentially and structurally, in the moment and in the act of giving. We might ask, as Levinas surely has of the Hegelian position, what kind of gift this is that returns to me so quickly, that never really leaves my hands."[13] The relationship between master and slave, recognized and recognizer, is always muddled, leaving recognition itself deeply unsatisfying. And so, as Butler's later work maintains, it is not the case "that the Hegelian subject effects a wholesale assimilation of what is external into a set of features internal to itself."[14] Instead, "the relation to the other is ecstatic, that the 'I' repeatedly finds itself outside itself, and that nothing can put an end to the repeated upsurge of this exteriority that is, paradoxically, my own. I am, as it were, always other to myself, and there is no final moment in which my return to myself takes place," meaning that vacillation between loss and ecstasy marks the Hegelian "I" who is given over to a world of preexisting normative convention that return this "I" as a subject.[15]

These desires toward freedom and negation are internalized inside of a single unhappy consciousness in such a way that neither desire dominates, thus giving self-consciousness nothing but the most fleeting satisfaction.[16] Here, the drives toward freedom in pure thought and negation respectively become forms of stoicism and skepticism—forms in between which the unhappy consciousness wavers internally.[17]

For Butler this sets up a situation in self-consciousness where a skeptical character emerges as a "watching self, defined as a kind of witnessing and scorning, differentiates itself from the self witnessed as perpetually falling into contradiction."[18] By despising the stoic part that gets drawn into contradiction, self-consciousness therefore "appears as negative narcissism, an engaged preoccupation with what is most debased and defiled about it."[19]

Self-consciousness, in such a state, exists as it does by virtue of what it hates and wishes did not exist.

What Hegel sees as the split between recognized and recognizer internalized in unhappy consciousness, Friedrich Nietzsche, working a few decades later in the German tradition, rearticulates in his notion of the bad conscience—a socially driven split of the self into tormenter and the tormented. Working from this convergence, Butler reasons that a profound unhappiness develops as social forces set up and "create" the psyche, with the social regulating the psychic sphere so that action in society takes place within norms.[20] In both cases, social forces form the layout of the mind, regulating it and negating socially unacceptable behavior.

Therefore, in Butler's reading of Hegel and Nietzsche, the social regulates the psychic, leading to an internalizing of society's value. This enables the will to be tame enough to get by in society. The self, being so constituted, does not really possess its own will, but is formed in relation to others. Hence, in explaining the relational self, Butler writes that "the 'will' is not . . . the will of a subject, nor is it an effect fully cultivated by and through social norms."[21] She suggests instead that the will is "the site at which the social implicates the psychic in its very formation—or, to be more precise, as its very formation and formativity."[22]

This turning of the self back upon the self forms the inner/outer, psychic/social threshold. Hence, according to this view, there is no movement of the pregiven self from inside of some psychic realm outward into the social world through presence or action.[23] As asserted earlier, there is no core, no eternal soul that comes prior to the social implication of the psyche, such that peeling back the onion only gets more onion and combing through the sediment of past social relationships only yields more sediment. As Adriana Cavarero reasons, this means that the narratable self becomes both the subject and object in any attempt account for one's own life.[24] As Butler describes this ambiguity of subject and object in her reading of Cavarero, "I am not, as it were, an interior subject, closed upon myself, solipsistic, posing questions of myself alone. I exist in an important sense for you, and by virtue of you. If I have lost the conditions of address, if I have no 'you' to address, then I have lost 'myself.' In [Cavarero's] view, one can tell an autobiography only to an 'Other,' and one can reference an 'I' only in relation to a 'you': without the 'you,' my own story becomes impossible."[25] So considered, "I" cannot be abstracted from relations and analyzed discreetly, but the unique exposure and vulnerability of *this* particular body sets a limit for how "I" might be substituted with any other subject body, and this means it is necessary at some point to resolve and explain things in terms of a singular life, even if the point drawn by Butler from Cavarero's reading of Hannah Arendt is correct and life stories cannot have a singular author because of the public, common nature of exposure.[26] And so, any accounting for oneself proves difficult, since describing how an "I" is formed "is not a matter of discovering and exposing an origin or tracking a causal series, but of describing what acts when I act, without precisely taking responsibility for the whole show."[27]

Hence, for Butler, this kind of self "does not stand apart from the prevailing matrix of ethical norms and conflicting moral frameworks" but is instead "already implicated in a social temporality that exceeds its own capacities for narration."[28] There is no pure self to be redeemed here, but perhaps some kind of rehabilitation beyond the problematic trappings of subject life might be possible. If subject life means being a slave to the recognition of others and the internalization of conventional morality, perhaps rehabilitation means acquiring something of the sense of nobility forfeited as a condition of surviving as a creature of ritualized norms. However, as will be discussed later in terms of Foucault and Confucianism, there is an artistic component to nobility that can come into play as a resource in this rehabilitation.

As concerns the particularly Nietzschean questions of regaining nobility, it bears mentioning here that the third yes, the holy yes, the child stage of Zarathustra's metamorphoses, is about saying "yes" to repetition in the eternal recurrence of the same. Though Nietzsche famously avoids directly stating what an affirmation of recurrence would be, casting it instead as a dance and a secret between male Zarathustra and female eternity, the stakes are sufficiently clear.[29] One must be able to bear each moment repeating eternally, including all of those cutting and formative moments of felt loss in which slave morality takes hold bit by bit. Butler does not take on this aspect of Nietzsche's thought in her theory of self, nor does she deal with rehabilitation through ritual practice. This is unfortunate, because when it comes to answering Nietzsche's challenge to affirm recurrence, what could be better than honing each gesture, each word, each action in order to raise each moment up to the level of practiced art? How could one better embrace repetition than by learning to regard the repetition of bodily action as a medium for art, as ritual, as something to be honed and made graceful in each varied scene of appearance, address, and performance?

Of course, it must be conceded that there are reasons to be wary of Nietzsche's pronouncements concerning moral artistry. First, Nietzsche's statements on the topic cannot be easily separated from his metaphysics of the will, which has been challenged by later philosophical developments (notably, Heidegger's phenomenological approach and critique), as well as the influential tradition of grossly oversimplified armchair history linking that metaphysics of the will to the rise of fascism, and so on. Secondly, and more importantly, Nietzsche's remarks on moral creativity show him at his most grandiose and least sober (fitting for the Dionysian, to be sure), to the degree that Zarathustra's third metamorphosis of spirit, the saying of the holy "yes," is withheld from the reader as an ineffable secret.[30] Hence, there is a limit on the extent to which Nietzsche's statements can be made a resource here. However, despite these limits, Nietzsche still does speak to this project and its own approach to affirming repetition in terms of the body.

While Butler may have some warrant for strictly limiting her appropriation of Nietzsche to the formation of the subject, it is still disappointing that she does not do more to follow up on this thread in Nietzsche's approach to overcoming the subject's bad conscience. Granted, Nietzsche's faith in the possibility of the will's unification and redemption would probably not serve her more lucid project. However, by rejecting this part of Nietzsche's thinking entirely, Butler throws out both wheat and chaff as she overlooks resources for what Nietzsche shows to be a genuine issue for the relational self—the role of artistry and repetition in obtaining freedom and happiness.

Foucault's Prison: Subjectivation in the Panopticon

If anything, Butler abandons the idea of freedom far too quickly and fixates on the comprehensive formation of the subject by social and discursive elements. On this point, the late twentieth-century French theorist and originator of the term subjectivation, Michel Foucault, seems particularly influential. In commenting on the docility of the body, its ability to "be subjected, used, transformed, and improved,"[31] Foucault argues that new and subtle forms of disciplinary power emerged in social organization in the seventeenth and eighteenth centuries. This approach was different from more overt manifestations of power, such as institutional slavery, vassalage, and clerical obedience. He speaks of this historical moment occurring

> *where an art of the human body was born*, which was directed not only at the growth of its abilities, nor at the intensification of its subjection, but at the formation of a relation in which the

mechanism itself makes it more obedient as it becomes more useful, and conversely. This formed a policy of coercions that act on the body, a calculated manipulation of its elements, its gestures, its behaviors. The human body entered a machinery of power that explores it, dismantles it, and recomposes it.[32]

Foucault then goes onto describe how the cold calculus works, and from this Butler draws a great deal of inspiration for her particular extension of the paradigm of subjectivation. For Foucault, the point of such disciplinary power is to increase the body's economic utility amid diminishing overt manifestations of political power by instilling obedience. And so, for Foucault, disciplinary power "inverts the other energy, the power that might result [were it associated positively with the body], and makes it a relation of strict subjection."[33]

Foucault explains how the production of power and the distribution of persons occurs through a "permanent and continuous field."[34] He calls this emerging hierarchy mechanical, not because it is deterministic, but because of how it functions in organizing power into something "multiple, automatic, and anonymous."[35] This being the case, Foucault describes disciplinary power, not as a top-down, king/subject affair. Indeed, Foucault makes clear his position that power *does not exist*, at least not as a locatable thing unto itself or as something with a deducible genesis, calling this view flawed and instead stating that power is relation, organization, and coordination.[36] And so Foucault describes this disperse agglomeration of power as manifesting through "a network of relations from top to bottom, but also to a certain extent from bottom to top and laterally," creating a circular nexus from which no party is preeminently free, with the masses taking on the task of disciplining each other so that all are held in the panopticon, being "surveillants, perpetually surveilled."[37] Here, social power takes the place of the divine in a grim twist of the Biblical exhortation to the faithful to take up "submitting yourselves one to another in the fear of God."[38]

What is the panopticon? Simply put, it is a space where all are meant to see all, where all are under surveillance—a prison. Jeremy Bentham originates the term, describing the panopticon in his nineteenth-century work on prison reform, laying out the blueprint (see figure) for a building designed for surveillance culture.[39] Decidedly less positive in his spin, Foucault contends that the ideals of the panopticon can now be accomplished without physical structures and that all subjects inhabit such a space whether they know it or not. And so it is that Michel Foucault famously describes life in a type of "virtual" panopticon—an assessment made all the more prescient with the unfolding of the digital age, the beginnings of which were only glimpsed by Foucault. On the panopticon, Foucault writes:

> Hence the major effect of the panopticon: to induce in the inmate a state of conscious and permanent visibility that assures the automatic functioning of power. So to arrange things that the surveillance is permanent in its effects, even if it is discontinuous in its action; that the perfection of power should tend to render its actual exercise unnecessary; that this architectural apparatus should be a machine for creating and sustaining a power relation independent of the person who exercises it; in short, that the inmates should be caught up in a power situation of which they are themselves the bearers.[40]

This describes how power, as deeply relational, becomes a self-sustaining machine; this mode of power can be called disciplinary. Disciplinary power, by its very nature, tends toward multilateral networks in order to produce individuals who unconsciously conspire to regulate each other, obviating the need for an overarching sovereign force to do so. Hence, rather than believing that the self emerges as a pregiven and atomic individual, Foucault utilizes a focus-field model where the individual emerges as a focal point, a site in a broad field of social relations that serve to form a sense of identity through the regimes of self-discipline mandated by society's networks of power. Focal points like this in the field of disciplinary power are thus called subjects.

Foucault then gives a historical account of how disciplinary power became anonymous and mechanized within the panopticon—an account that has a curious consonance with Confucianism. In *Discipline and Punish* he describes how in the feudal age, the sovereign's power brought with it individuality in the form of "rituals, discourse, or artistic reproductions"[41] from which the masses were excluded. In Foucault's analysis, as power has become more networked, anonymous, and mechanized, a new and unsettling mode of subjectivation has come to the great unwashed. He remarks that this type of disciplinary power functions "by surveillance rather than ceremonies, by observation rather than commemorative accounts, by comparative measures that have the 'norm' for reference, rather than by genealogies that give ancestors as landmark points; by deviations rather than by deeds."[42] While it would be difficult to read Foucault as seriously calling for a return to the feudal ages, there is some similarity to the current of contemporary

Confucian scholarship in lamenting a decreasing attention to constitutive roles and relationships in contemporary society.

For some this may call to mind the work of comparative philosophers like my mentor Roger T. Ames and his collaborators the late David L. Hall and Henry Rosemont—the latter of whom counseled me in my writings on Confucianism and Foucault before he himself passed away in 2017, shaping this very book beforehand—Foucault goes on to sharpen his attack on this mode of individualization, arguing that the individual-as-atom is a fiction. Instead, he believes that, apart from a new notion of discipline, the Industrial Age also produced a still living "technique for effectively constituting individuals as correlative elements of power and knowledge."[43]

Acknowledging the individual to be a correlative element created within power's field, Foucault thus sees that power cannot be simply treated pejoratively, for it is indispensable. He throws down a gauntlet, issuing a challenge to which Confucian scholars are well poised to respond, writing, "It must cease forever describing the effects of power in negative terms: it 'excludes,' it 'represses,' it 'suppresses,' it 'censors,' it 'abstracts,' it 'masks,' it 'conceals.'"[44]

Instead, power's production of reality and truth, for right or wrong, must be faced head on.[45] Butler's work does engage in such a confrontation to a certain extent, but it suffers from not being sensitive enough to the connection between artistic production and power. While the Foucault-inspired aspects of Butler's work have the benefit of bringing the body into the discussion, they have the deleterious effect of rooting her philosophy in an overly deterministic idea of discourse. Underscoring this are Butler's views that becoming a subject occurs as "discourses . . . imprison the body in the soul," where this discursive imprisonment can be understood in terms of "sign chain[s]."[46]

These prisons and chains are not just rhetorical whimsy for Butler, but instead they reflect her deep cynicism concerning power and the formation of the discursive subject. The subject-as-prisoner idea is made most clear where she writes:

> The "soul brings [the prisoner] to existence"; not unlike in Aristotle, the soul, as an instrument of power, forms and frames the body, stamps it, and in stamping it, brings it into being. In this formulation, there is no body outside of power, for the materiality of the body—indeed, materiality itself—is produced by and in direct relation to the investment of power.[47]

True, Butler does concede in her subsequent work *Giving an Account of Oneself* that Foucault's account of reflexivity is not in fact *so* grim, since it is not exhausted by the Nietzschean scene of punishment and since is it not simply a reduction of morality to Nietzschean bad conscience.[48] And she makes similar concessions to criticisms of her view of discourse with her more precise, needle-threading statements that "the body is given through language, but is not, for that reason, reducible to language" and that "it must be possible to claim that the body is not known or identifiable apart from the linguistic coordinates that establish the boundaries of the body—*without* thereby claiming that the body is nothing other than the language by which it is known."[49] However, the larger point remains that "for Foucault, as for Nietzsche, morality redeploys a creative impulse."[50] And so, even where she allows that subject-making may be about reflexivity arising in relation to moral codes and not just about reflexivity in the mode of punishment as described by Nietzsche and even where she speaks of the body perhaps being about more than total determination by language, Butler still paints a rather foreboding picture. For her, subjectivation is total and results in self-constitution occurring as a dark brand of *poiēsis* such that "there is no making of oneself (*poiesis*) outside of a mode of subjectivation (*assujettisement*) and, hence, no self-making outside of the norms that orchestrate the possible forms that a subject may take."[51] This leaves only "the intervention of countervailing norms," the haphazard forging of sign chains within a "matrix of relations" that "is not an integrated and harmonious network," as providing the only basis for breaking with those norms.[52]

Hailed into Existence: Interpellation

In her view, this imprisoned subject "appears at the expense of the body,"[53] in a type of "sublimation" where the "bodily remainder . . . survives . . . in the mode of already, if not always, having been destroyed, in a kind of constitutive loss."[54] This allows for the scene of "interpellation" described by Louis Althusser where the subject turns around, turning upon self, when a voice, putatively (but not certainly) that of a police officer, yells "Hey! You there!"[55] In this scene, the hail initiates a reflexive consciousness where the subject quite literally performs a turn-on-self. Here self-recognition means being almost preternaturally guilty without any actual trespass having been committed. Hence, it is irrelevant whether the hail is one of recognition or misrecognition; the hail establishes the truth of the subject as recognized and creates a "You," an "I," which is defined by turning around. This turn-on-self occurs such that "one has already yielded before one turns around, and that turning is merely a sign of an inevitable submission."[56] This inescapable bodily turn toward the voice of authority makes the subject a prison for the body, adopting what Nietzsche calls a "slave morality" for the purpose of surviving, even though the irrelevancy of the "truth" of this recognition may make the subject's place in society as this or that kind of subject frightfully precarious and always contingent on asserting and reasserting, enacting and reenacting the terms of subjection.[57] As the process occurs in a manifold of everyday encounters great and small, the turn-on-self has to be thought of as similarly manifold and extended over time. Regarding this point, Judith Butler explains that "interpellations that might be said to 'hail' a subject into being, that is, social performatives, ritualized and sedimented through time . . . are central to the very process of subject-formation as well as the embodied, participatory habitus."[58]

The subject hailed into being is characterized by a kind of unhappiness owing to all that has been lost in becoming a subject. Drawing on Butler's reading of Freud, it could be said that the melancholy of subject life represents a type of incomplete mourning that preserves as unspeakable a series lost objects, lost attachments, lost possibilities for life, and even loss in the form of minor slights, where survival implicitly demands the habitual, ritualistic repetition and neurotic reenactment of such unspeakable losses as they are thereby cancelled out and curiously preserved (*aufgehoben*) in ideals that serve as eroticized gathering sites for self-annihilating death drives in the form of the negative narcissism or the moral masochism of conscience.[59]

With this language of habitus being invoked in this way, Pierre Bourdieu enters into the discussion here despite Butler judging him negatively for tending "to assume that the subject who utters the performative is positioned on a map of social power in a fairly fixed way," a way which fails to appreciate how it is that "the performative is not only a ritual practice: it is one of the influential rituals by which subjects are formed and reformulated."[60] This criticism is leveled at Bourdieu where he speaks of "the elementary actions of bodily gymnastics" within what he calls "the logic of socialization" that

> treats the body as a memento, . . . complexes of gestures, of bodily postures and of words—simple interjections or particularly worn platitudes—, into which one simply enters, like

a costume from the theatre, for the resurgence, by virtue of evocation of bodily mimesis, a world of ready-made sentiments and experiences.[61]

Rejecting this view of identity being a costume into which a ready-made soul might slip prior to acting out a role, Butler holds that interpellation actually initiates bodily life as a kind of ritualized performance, with the origins of the self stretching out far beyond any one particular life or biographical account.

This presents a problem as the turn-on-self before a quasi-police authority of interpellation gives way to scenes of interrogation where the story of the ritual performance of this subject cannot be explained in any coherent way (without beginning to substitute in the plight of other subjects and thereby recounting subject existence as a fiction or fable). This is so because the history of the gestures and so forth being reenacted far exceeds the temporality of any one person's life and thus is beyond what any one person could ever tell, as that access to constitutive scenes of loss is itself lost in becoming subject.[62] Here on this point Butler echoes Foucault's sentiment "discourse is not life; its time is not yours."[63] And so it is that in Butler's expansion of her views on subjectivation and subjection, *Giving an Account of Oneself*, she speaks of an accusatory hail initiating the "I" into a particularly narrative form of subject life as "in fearful response, I offer myself as an 'I' and try to reconstruct my deeds, showing that the deed attributed to me was or was not, in fact, among them."[64]

Therefore, understood on these terms, Butler sees the subject's daily life as consisting of a variety of understated scenes of hailing, recognition, and quasi-interrogation, which arise "severally and in implicitly and unspoken ways, [such that] the scene is never quite as dyadic as Althusser claims."[65] This leads to the view that "subjectivity arises immaterially from a material ritual performance"[66] because of the subject's natural readiness to submit to such rituals.

Being recognized and made intelligible as a subject, it is possible for individuals to occupy the intelligible "site" of a relational subject, although this is a subject marked by opacity and for whom "early and primary relations are not always available to conscious knowledge."[67] However, the relationship between subject and individual ends up being paradoxical in a way that hinders any linear account, for as Butler explains:

> No individual becomes a subject without first becoming subjected or undergoing "subjectivation" (a translation of the French

assujetissement). It makes little sense to treat "the individual" as an intelligible term if individuals are said to acquire their intelligibility by becoming subjects. Paradoxically, no intelligible reference to individuals or their becoming can take place without a prior reference to their status as subjects. The story by which subjection is told is, inevitably, circular, presupposing the very subject for which it seeks to give an account.[68]

Misrecognition and Limited Freedom from Sign Chains

While she denies the possibility of giving a full account or making a full recovery of what has been lost in the turn-on-self, Butler allows for some small degree of novelty in subject life.[69] Freedom and change come obliquely into Butler's work where she describes the signs that make up social discourse and grant the subject recognition and social legitimacy as always carrying "the risk of a certain misrecognition" in the "performative effort of naming."[70]

Thus Butler looks to the idea of a "sign chain" as explored by Foucault and Nietzsche.[71] Here Butler makes limited room for novelty by describing how gaps occur as language is used, allowing for reversals of signification and possibilities beyond the original constraints on normative terms.[72] For Butler, this is so because, while it may be persons that confer recognition, the normative terms of recognition far outstrip the individual person, such that,

> if I understand myself to be conferring recognition on you, for instance, then I take seriously that the recognition comes from me. But the moment I realize that the terms by which I confer recognition are not mine alone, that I did not single-handedly devise or craft them, I am, as it were, dispossessed by the language that I offer.[73]

This introduces a gap that might be exploited between the terms of discourse and the subjects taking up that discourse, where the lack of clear ownership and origin makes reappropriation possible. One may think of the widespread reappropriation of the slur "n-----" as "nigga" in African-American youth culture or of Butler's own example of how "drag allegorizes heterosexual melancholy" and what is inevitably lost in becoming gendered by "reversing the terms of signification."[74] And, of course, since "it is not just the catcall or the insult or the slur that constitutes an interpellation within the scene of address; every pronoun has an interpellative force and carries with it the possibility of misrecognition," there is the possibility of misrecognition and resignification in much more subtle and even intimate encounters.[75] Whatever the particular circumstances may be, such resignification often plays out in rage when the turning of the self back upon the self becomes too severe to bear and threatens the life that the subject posture was originally supposed to guarantee.

This is the rage that comes upon examining the costs and benefits of subject life and realizing that one has given up so much for what in many cases turns out to be only a meager place in society, where one's small purchase on legitimacy is unstable and even this is capable of being revoked at any time. This calls to mind Malcolm X's "joke" about what to call a black PhD. Answer: "n-----."[76]

Giving up so much and receiving only the most precarious recognition, it is easy to see how the ego might come to rue something like an ego-ideal, how "I" might come to despise everything that has been lost and idealized in submission to subject life upon recognizing the gap between the kind of recognition "I" was supposed to receive with a PhD and the sad, paltry, ever-vanishing reality of still always being suspiciously and pejoratively black.[77] Nonetheless, in Butler's view, rage-filled resignification against social ideologies and ego-ideals, including (one imagines) even the rage of the firebrand Malcolm X, does not take place in any way that such that "an autonomous ego exercises autonomy in confrontation with a countervailing world."[78]

This, however, is a paltry and unsatisfying notion of freedom, based solely on the inability of the terms of social discourse to fully determine subjects. More to the point, this idea of discourse flattens all signs, all cultural productions to a structure of intentionality, where freedom only occurs in the gaps between the intent and the use of language and signs. This view overlooks the possibility that art may present a different, if not greater freedom to the subject, as it is not easily reducible to such purposive, intentional structures. This in turn leads to two further prospects that will be explored later in this book: (1) the possibility of a constitutive relationship between art and the normative social environment and (2) the possibility of making the best of quotidian repetition through rearticulating and honing what is given in normative subjectivation/subjection in a kind of ritual artistry of the body.

Kantian Responses to Subjectivation/Subjection

In this regard, this approach is somewhat akin to the one taken by contemporary American religious studies professor David Kyuman Kim in his 2007 work *Melancholic Freedom*. His work and my project each apply a branch of Kantian aesthetics to the problem of subjective agency as laid out by Butler and Foucault before her. Kim, who in passing mentions the analogues to contemporary discourses on agency in the Confucian tradition, looks to regenerate the subject in order to flourish after melancholy has been in some way overcome.[79] However, for him, the solution to this riddle lies in the cultivation of imagination through religious experiences of the sublime.[80] Instead, in the project undertaken here, it is beauty, and not the sublime, that is the focus of the account.

What Kim has in mind, though, is not just the Kantian sublime per se, but a specific reading of moral perfectionism carried out by the towering nineteenth-century American transcendentalist Ralph Waldo Emerson, who takes a Kantian problematic of disjointed and fragmented subject-object experience as a challenge to be met by *re*-membering and actively realizing the diverse subject/object members of experience as an immanent divine unity, thereby changing the nature of the "self" in self-reliance. Kim notes the clear difficulty of applying such a notion of cultivating self-reliance to Butler's project, given her descriptions of the problems facing subject life, which ultimately leave perfectionism as something of a pipe dream, an unreachable ideal within her scheme.[81] Kim sets the stage well:

> Through his perfectionism, Emerson could entertain the ideal that self-reliance and the idea of trusting oneself only requires the gamble of being misunderstood. In making the case for the strenuous life of the melancholy of difference, Butler is effectively showing how the interpellated/subjected self is in a state of being in which the possibility of agency must measure and weigh the costs of becoming an agent beyond mere misunderstanding, that is, where the performative quickly turns from parody to the critical detachment of irony, and finally falls to a dire choice between conformity and the risks of social death. Performative agency is, in the end, melancholic freedom.[82]

Conscious of the gulf, Kim nonetheless sees a reason to take up Emerson's approach to the Kantian sublime in response to Butler's problematic, for, as he puts it, "Butler shares Emerson's investment in the notion of possibility as a moment and instance in which a self can thwart the power of conventions and subsequently overcome the self called into being (interpellated) by power."[83] For Kim, an ambivalent view of power, like the one coursing through this account and proceeding from the initial challenge from Foucault, replicates the structure of the sublime, "the mixture of awe and fear" in a way that allows Althusser's pejorative hail to be read also positively as a *vocation*, the sublime issuing a call for the cultivation of the self.[84] This leads Kim to a quasi-religious, quasi-Kantian response, advocating a very specific "piety to the ideals of integrity and an attunement to the conditions that enable possibility."[85] And so Kim's location of this piety is in the body, which, in Kim's description of Butler's account, "is a sublime limit that exceeds language even as it demands language to name it [where] the dialectic between the sublime body and language echoes [Stanley] Cavell's notion of becoming intelligible to oneself and the Emersonian idea of 'the next self.'"[86]

Without disagreeing with this approach to the sublime and still taking Immanuel Kant's *Critique of Judgment* as a similar point of departure for the expansion of the self, the initial argument here in this work is that, in addition to what Kant terms the sublime or what Cavell describes as an ecstatic relationship to text, beauty in artworks can serve as a model of freedom, as a source of meaning for moral subjects, and as a basis for the kind of specifically artful bodily self-cultivation that responds to Foucault's formidable challenge. By starting with Kant and drawing together voices already made part of the conversation by Butler, such as Hegel and Nietzsche, much in the fashion that she herself does in her own work, a recurring insight becomes clear—namely, that artworks, in some way, exhibit something like the spontaneity so lacking in normative subject life ritually performed for the sake of recognition and survival.

Kant on Purposiveness and the Artwork's Negative Freedom

Admittedly, it is odd to start an account of artistic, body-oriented spontaneity with a figure as staid as Kant, especially given how the strength of his emphasis on the autonomy of the imaginative subject comes at the expense of both the artwork and the artist. It may seem stranger still to begin with Kant when his description of artworks and freedom are so bound with his metaphysical edifice. Nevertheless, there is an insight, somewhat passed over by Kant himself, that, though artworks are not free like human beings, that they *do* possess some measure of freedom *with respect to the determination of the subject's intuition*, a measure that sets them apart from generic things.[87] Were this not so, the experience of beauty would cease to be extraordinary. Before going further, though, more needs to be said about how Kant understands the freedom of human subjects and his oblique characterization of the lesser freedom belonging to art objects.

The sort of freedom that Kant cares about with respect to moral action is autonomous in character. Autonomy concerns the ability of practical reason to furnish laws and determine conduct as a matter of reason's own form. As understood by Kant, reason thus considers purpose and sets forth ends in a manner that in no way falls under nature's determinate structures. In other words, the causality of the rationally considered "ought" differs in kind from that of the phenomenally apprehended "is." As such, genuinely autonomous choice determines interaction with objects in the world without being determined by them. Hence, in Kant's schema, acts in accord with reason occur spontaneously with respect to the causal structures of the physical world.

Reason, as exhibited by rational agents in this schema, thus provides a ground for respect. This respect involves treating persons as "ends in themselves" and not merely as middle terms in vast causal chains.[88] Extending such respect to other rational agents follows from the form of practical reason. Respect is thus incumbent upon moral subjects as a matter of duty, and consideration of the subject's own existence as an end in itself.[89]

Kant claims that there is some manner of analog relationship between aesthetic judgment and moral reasoning, though the details on the link are lacking.[90] If there is some sort of analog relationship, then notions *like* freedom and respect should appear in judgments of beauty. Of course, artworks are not the same as free rational agents, but, as his account of beauty indicates, there is reason to believe that they have some measure of freedom and spontaneity. This is key, as Kant provides an initial impetus to the view set forth in this project that, while artworks may not be other people, they are still "Other" in a way that can prompt and form reflective self-consciousness.

Kant denies that aesthetic judgment and the ascription of beauty belong to the object. Instead, he looks to what the art object occasions—the subject's consideration of ideas. Ideas, in this usage, express something idiosyncratically Kantian. As a terminological point, they refer to "the representation [*Vorstellung*] of imagination that occasions much thinking without though a determined thought, i.e., a concept, being adequate to it, which consequently no language can fully reach and make understandable."[91] Such ideas arise not capriciously, but are "given by the nature of reason itself."[92] Ideas thus differ from the concepts of morality, which *can* determine ends. Nevertheless, ideas still initiate a sequence of experience that is similarly free from objective determination.

Freedom in aesthetic judgment is thus independent from determination in nature, where the sensual and phenomenal aspect of art objects should be of only subjective interest, but instead interest is broadened as it is directed toward the ideas of reason represented, however inadequately, in aesthetic experience. Because ideas do not determine which intuitions belong to them, the presentation of ideas by art objects has no fixed course, unlike what is set forth by the concepts of pure practical reason. According to this view, beauty is found subsequently in the "richness" of the form of the subject's reflection upon ideas, and not in the object per se. Kant calls this flexible and open mode of reflection a "free play of our cognitive powers."[93]

The aesthetic ideas of free play, though indeterminate in nature, still possess certain necessary features. Chief among them is the "enlivening of cognitive faculties," which takes place as imagination connects sensations.[94] Since these faculties, in their play, belong to a common form, subjects can give expression to, and quarrel about, the beauty of art objects. Observers can thus describe the presentation of ideas and their unpredictable stimulation of thought, even though the specific consideration of ideas may vary from person to person.[95] Along with other ideas, beauty may in fact be in the eye of the beholder, but commonalities in the eye, the senses, the body, and the rational faculties allow for some type of conversation about such ideas to occur.

What then does the artwork do? Well, it serves as the starting point for imagination's sequential representation of ideas. Ideas, as unbounded, contrast here with pure concepts determined categorically by reason. Poetic art thus consists in "the capability of aesthetic ideas to show their entire measure," with the poet making sensible these rational ideas, even as they outstrip causal determination in nature and set up a free play of faculties with its own independent sequence.[96] Is there any way, though, in which the art object itself surpasses causally determined phenomena too? The judging subject might be free to reflect upon a play of faculties, but does no degree of freedom belong also to works of art?

Kant gives clues that the object enjoys some sort of freedom, though he does not follow up on this line of inquiry. Specifically, he speaks of aesthetic attributes "*of an object*" (emphasis added), which "express the bound consequences and the affinity for other [concepts] of an object, whose concept cannot be adequately presented as an idea of reason."[97] Kant then goes on to differentiate an artwork's symbolic attributes from the cosmological and theological ideas that it occasions in imaginative free play.[98] Aesthetic attributes *of the object* thus "furnish" (*geben*) aesthetic ideas belonging to the imagination of the subject.[99]

The object, and not the subject, therefore manifests something exceeding conceptualization through the phenomenal world's cause-and-effect relationships. It follows, then, that the object must itself be free in some fashion from that overarching determination. This realization of the art object's freedom represents a Copernican turn for Kantian aesthetics, by changing what is at stake with the key to Kant's paradigm of disinterested reflection—"freedom." However, to recognize the object's freedom, description in the same terms as free human agency will not suffice. Applying "freedom" so univocally makes the term border on meaninglessness. How then is the object's "freedom" to be understood?

For Kant, freedom in the form of play and the consideration of beauty on the part of the observer in no way negates the possibility that the artwork is also, in some limited manner, free. Kant develops the resources with which to describe such limited freedom in his first *Critique*. At issue is Kant's distinction between the cosmological and practical senses of freedom.[100] Here the contention is that the former is the sort of freedom belonging to the artwork, insofar as it presents ideas unconditioned by cause-and-effect sequences.

By cosmological freedom Kant means "the capacity of a state to begin from its self, the causality which does not stand under another cause, which would determine it temporally, according to the laws of nature."[101] Such freedom is spontaneous with respect to determination of events by prior causes. Such spontaneous, cosmological freedom refers only to independence from natural sequence, but it falls short of practical freedom and the consideration of natural sequence in terms of an "ought" capable of determining ends.[102] Elsewhere, Kant uses the language of "negative freedom" to describe freedom lacking any self-sufficiency of form; and this less grandiose language seems more suitable to ascribe to art objects, even though cosmological freedom is ultimately the issue.[103]

In Kant's eyes, a fuller, more attractive sort of freedom belongs to humans, in the form of "the autonomy of pure practical reason" of free agents who are able both to follow moral dictates and experience beauty without conditioning by nature.[104] Autonomous freedom eclipses the lesser, negative freedom in Kant's work, to the detriment of his aesthetics and his ability to appreciate an important relationship to morality. However, Kant does well to recognize the role of spirit in art.[105] He makes it plain that aesthetic attributes belong to *objects* (and *not* the subject).[106] Kant speaks of aesthetic ideas, rooted in aesthetic attributes, and how an aesthetic attribute "occasions (*veranlaßt*)" the imagination's free play in language while he also assiduously avoids speaking of a subject's representing for itself (*sich vorstellen*) those attributes.[107] Furthermore, his distinction between natural and artistic beauty relies on the premise that art objects are purposive in a way similar to, but independent of, the purposiveness and determination of objects in nature.[108]

It is worth pointing out here that beauty and sublimity complement each other. The key is the sharpening of reflective judgment in terms of "free" objects. Both beautiful and sublime objects point to a different purposiveness residing in ideas outside of the confines of conceptual language and the causally determined objects of those concepts.

Despite these insights, Kant fails to connect the art object's spirit and independent purposiveness to negative freedom. He does not turn to the thought that the ability of the objects attributes to "occasion" and "evoke" aesthetic ideas in imaginative play indicates freedom from causal determination. Whatever the reasons, this oversight disallows comparison of regard for the negative freedom of artworks and respect for the autonomous freedom of rational agents.

Nonetheless, with Kant there is the germ of a thought that grows in the subsequent German tradition and beyond, namely, that artworks are artworks to the extent that they are free from wholly causal structures. For Kant, the particular spin is that this freedom consists in the art object being more than a mere physical, and thus determined, stimulus in its provocation of the observing subject. On this score, freedom is not just connected to art, but is its sine qua non. It is not quite the more robust type of view in phenomenology linking art and logos (λόγος), but the *germ* of the idea is *there*, even with Kant—artworks speak. At the very least, in Kant's view the artwork has some freedom from natural purposiveness and the determinations of practical moral reasoning.

Hegel on the Artisan and Recognition

Though Kant does not take up this line of reasoning, perhaps the artwork's mode of freedom then can be a model of sorts for human freedom. Working in the decades after Kant, Hegel moves the discussion in this direction, particularly where he maintains that the artwork is not only free, but that it *expresses* freedom and that, most crucially, this expression gives artistic self-consciousness a new way to recognize itself. This is part of Hegel's work that goes beyond the master-slave and unhappy consciousness stages of the *Phenomenology* that are at the heart of Butler's project. Butler appears to have little interest in basing her theory in the entirety of Hegel's broader account (and for good reason).

However, Butler does recognize some resources in Hegel's earlier work, particularly with respect to the aesthetic dimensions of her project that have emerged in her work following *The Psychic Life of Power*. In this earlier work of Hegel's, perhaps somewhat unexpectedly, religious worship becomes something greater when, by means "of song, or of motions of the body," overly ponderous, concept-laden rhetoric objectively and beautifully becomes a dance through rules.[109] Butler's description of this intriguing turn by Hegel takes on an almost Kantian quality at this point, where she writes about how "dance seems to be singled out grammatically, evincing that moment when bodies come alive in a rule-bound way, but without precisely conforming to any law."[110] In Butler's view, dance, particularly of the group variety seen in Bacchanalian revelry of interest to Hegel, invokes the aesthetic domain in a way that centers on social motion, thereby allowing him to start "to imagine those who neither seek to possess others as their property nor hold on to their personhood as property," a form of relation that "deadens."[111] This specific understanding of dance, in Butler's words, is Hegel trying to imagine "love that goes beyond the dyad and property."[112] Identifying Hegel's "wish to separate what is animated and animating from the world of property," Butler goes on to describe how "what Hegel seeks through the idea of animating law (or enlivening form) is something close to a dance, the dance of lovers (not presumptively dyadic), understood as a rhythm between a finite series or sequence, understood as spatially elaborated time, and what cannot be captured within its terms, the infinite."[113]

Though it is brief, though it casts dance as something of a poetic surrogate, and though it is made within the restricted context of her reading of Hegel's early writings on love, Butler's formulation here nonetheless indirectly points to the core insight to be explored later in this project. What is key is how, in artful practices like dance, bodies can *begin* to become animate with at least some manner of purposiveness beyond the purposive structures that impel and compel the subject's normative turn-on-self. The further hope is that this animation, this movement, might be capable of telling a story outside of the finite terms of personal narrative, terms that could never hope to give a full account of the subject's manifold emergence anyways. The ultimate course of this effort will be linking this understanding of dance to yoga, meditation, martial arts, and similar practices through more amenable philosophical approaches to the body, like those of Confucianism and the more recent project of somaesthetics. This will form something of a response to the burgeoning aesthetic implications of Butler's own ongoing project on her quasi-Hegelian terms.

Returning to the matter at hand, of course the examinations of the master-slave and unhappy consciousness dynamics contain some of Hegel's most compelling insights, and, more to the point, these sections develop Hegel's approach to Butler's main concern—the development of self-consciousness as a turning of the self upon the self. With it being fairly obvious that the final stages of Hegel's narrative of spirit would sit uneasily with Butler's project (i.e., religion and the Prussian-style state), it is little wonder that she brackets off her own appropriation of Hegel.

However, by truncating her analysis of Hegel, Butler closes herself off to certain resources that could help with the unsatisfying implication of her work that the subject's psychic life must be one of either latent, low-grade melancholia or passionate, self-protective rage. In his description of art as another late stage of consciousness, Hegel broaches the topic of freedom in a way relevant to Butler's project.

In his later writings, namely, in the sections from later in *The Phenomenology of Spirit* than those of particular interest to Butler, Hegel returns to the idea of art growing from religious impulses. However, Hegel explains in a sadly predictable fashion that unconscious and primitive cultic impulses to fashion crystal talismans and the like in the "East" grew into more conscious and refined artistry in Greece. Setting aside some of the obvious problems with this analysis (e.g., the incongruously late arrival of art in Hegel's historical exegesis, the easy assumption of a clear cult/religion dichotomy, and the repugnant views of Asia and Africa), Hegel's take is useful because it further extends notions of work and freedom from the less metaphysically laden master-slave and unhappy consciousness narratives in terms of specifically artistic labor.

Hegel starts by condescending to the traditions of India and Egypt, among others, pointing out, much like Deleuze and Guattari, that their works need something external to breathe life into their fashioned crystals, obelisks, and pyramids. Hegel does, however, stress that even the artistic impulses that he deems to be underdeveloped nonetheless accomplish something profound—they begin the encounter of self-consciousness, in the guise of the artist, with self-consciousness as made manifest in the artwork. Hegel writes, that as the artwork acquires an intelligible form and significance, "[the work] comes closer to the working self-consciousness and that this [self-consciousness] arrives at knowing how it is in and for itself."[114] Hence the artwork, even in its cultic representation of natural forces, acts as a kind of model for self-consciousness.

At this stage, for Hegel, art's ability to model and mirror self-consciousness is lacking. In both cultic works and the "religious" abstract art coming from the Hellenic world there is nothing animate or autonomous in itself. These abstractly religious Hellenic artworks bear meaning, yes, but only contingently. The artwork "is not yet speech," as it needs an artisan to bring together and resolve the riddle of its opposing sides, its natural material and its intelligible character.[115]

In resolving a particular instance of the riddle of physical nature and intelligible character in the single, individual artwork, the artisan acquires self-knowledge, which is mediated not by another party (like the master), but by the artisan's own production. Unlike the portions on the master-slave and unhappy consciousness dynamics from Hegel's account, in these later sections labor is neither alien nor alienating. Whereas consciousness earlier becomes unhappy, since neither the slave's labor nor the master's desire can offer either party the recognition and freedom from contingency that each desires, here the stakes for labor are rather different. Instead of work and desire being set off as each other's limits, as is the case during the master-slave stage, work and desire are brought into unity through an artisan fashioning the artwork.[116] The artisan's work ceases to be a foreign thing, ever in danger of acquisition and annihilation by uncontrollable outside forces, and instead becomes familiar and congenial. And so, in this iteration, self-consciousness moves past the unhappiness earlier described by Hegel, by acquiring a new basis for positive self-recognition and understanding as the artisan crafts the artwork and the artwork builds the artisan's self-understanding.

Of course, the artwork is still not yet speech, at least not living speech; it is not determinate. It may bring new, nonalienating knowledge to self-consciousness; however, as Hegel makes clear it is "not by itself really an animated thing."[117] For Hegel, the process of its coming to be must still be added to the physical artwork in order to make it animate, autonomous, and alive in a way that can bring robust, if not yet fully reciprocal recognition to artisan and artwork. However, even when the agent artisan or the observer steps back in thinking and yields to the artwork's own activity, the act of withdrawal and yielding still sets the agent apart from the thingly nature of the artwork, such that "the artist finds out, then, in his work, that he did not produce a reality like himself."[118]

The key point here is similar to the earlier creative appropriation of Kant. If read through a certain lens, Kant and Hegel bring insight to the idea that, while artworks do not possess the full autonomy of thinking and acting human beings, they do still take on something of a life of their own. So considered, Kant and Hegel both can be seen as contributing to the view that art expands human self-consciousness by showing how something formed and created can still nonetheless exhibit spontaneity similar to what is sought amid the perils of subject life. The further point is that the expansion of self-consciousness brought by art, however partial, nonrational, and indeterminate it may be, is still an expansion and thus still of value.

While the remainder of Hegel's discussion of art and artistry gets more into his idiosyncratic, and for the purposes of this project, irrelevant notions of religion and the "Absolute," there is something valuable in the foregoing inquiry into self-consciousness and artistic labor. So the approach taken here is indeed a truncated, piecemeal approach in the manner of Butler. But just as Butler expands upon Hegel's insights into the formation of unhappy consciousness, so too is it possible to take these remarks on artistic labor and reapply them within a larger project outside of the strictures of chapter-and-verse Hegelianism. Put another way, there is little reason why Butler should be a slave to Hegel's timeline for the development of consciousness and there is good reason to take those portions that deal with contingency, dependence, labor, and self-recognition and deal with them nonlinearly, that is, explaining the *concurrent* development of self-consciousness both through socially alienating experiences of otherness and through art and aesthetic experience. When Hegel's narrative is dealt with this way, then it is only natural to bring art into Butler's account, since exploring the capacity of artworks may point to some measure of freedom within self-recognition.

Nietzsche on the Artistically Creating Subject

Butler's work on subjectivation/subjection, though considerable, does perhaps show the need for this line of thought to give greater attention to aesthetics and art. This shows itself again when considering how Nietzsche, following Hegel, provides his own description of artworks providing novel contexts for self-recognition. Butler demonstrates her acumen in clearly elucidating

Nietzsche's approach to the troubling emergence of the moral subject, but she does not seriously take up his views on artistic spontaneity and how they may point to a way of dealing with the subject's predicament. Though she does make great use of both Nietzsche's remarks on the formation of bad conscience through debtor-creditor transactions and his idea of sign chains, Butler abstracts these insights from what is perhaps the most seductive aspect of his thought—his views on the artistic creation of self and truth.

Butler's sensible, sober approach is perhaps necessary, since the Dionysian side of Nietzsche is sometimes too intoxicated and incoherent to be philosophically useful. She goes to great lengths to avoid importing any deus ex machina into her narrative of self-development, and so audacious statements on redeeming the past and turning "all 'it was' " into "so I willed it!"[119] probably go a bit too far for her. Nietzsche's more heady writings, like *Thus Spoke Zarathustra*, hold out the possibility of grandiose, cosmic spontaneity and new beginnings that would overly complicate, if not outright contradict, Butler's meticulously framed project.

However, Nietzsche's statements on art and the self are not all bombast, and there are several spots where Nietzsche's work finds a middle ground lacking in Butler's recent appropriation of his work—namely, a description of freedom that is not fanciful, but is instead consistent with common views of how people experience artistry and creativity. In fact, in his brief, yet profound, essay "On Truth, Lies, and the Extramoral Sense," Nietzsche takes up the basic idea of a founding turn-on-self in a way quite similar to how Butler would describe it more than a century later. His account diverges, though, where he theorizes, rather lucidly, how artistic creativity points to a way out of the self-as-social-prison.

Sounding very much like Butler, Nietzsche begins this underappreciated essay by giving a description of socialization and of the growth of powerful, yet deceptive, systems of discourse. Proceeding in a somewhat Hobbesian fashion and highlighting the urge for self-preservation from a war of all against all, Nietzsche holds that stable social life requires a social contract, and, with that, conventions for identifying what is "true" and what is a "lie."[120] He then considers the liar and concludes that the general sanction against lying is not because of the deception per se, but because of how it tears the common social fabric. And so, with his characteristic misanthropy, Nietzsche observes:

> What they hate at this stage is basically not the deception but the bad, hostile consequences of certain kinds of deceptions. In a similarly limited way man wants the truth: he desires the

agreeable life-preserving consequences of truth, but he is indifferent to pure knowledge, which has no consequences; he is even hostile to possibly damaging and destructive truths.[121]

Toward the end of this initial section, though, we see areas where Butler diverges from Nietzsche. Here, Nietzsche looks in the direction of art for resources not already determined by oppressive linguistic structures. However, what is noteworthy about what follows, is not how it points to artistic creativity as a way to resolve the riddles of self, as might be expected. Beyond speaking directly to Butler's project and anticipating her appropriation of Foucault's notion of subjectivation as the formation the imprisoned subject, Nietzsche writes here in a more deliberate, clear, and, frankly, useful manner about "redemption" of the self through artistic creativity than elsewhere in his corpus. And this gives a firmer basis for reassessing the role of artistic creativity and aesthetic experience in Butler's account of the subject.

For Nietzsche, this type of "redemption" consists in getting past the idea that language delineates the world in a necessary way and realizing that artistic creativity stands as the way out of these confines. For him, the unstated and ultimately faulty premise behind language as a whole is that it corresponds to some grand notion of truth, which then problematically serves as the basis for social regulation. He speaks of metaphor becoming hard and fixed, becoming ossified, and in so doing conditioning the belief that for each image, for each object, there is some necessary and hard-wired nerve impulse.[122] In this regard, the will to truth becomes the basis of enslavement to a normative order and a further ossification of the self.

Therefore, redemption is not some recovery of original and self-stable essence, for that would merely replicate the structure, so familiar in the philosophical tradition taking after Plato, of willful pursuit of permanent truth. Instead, Nietzschean redemption consists in remembering. This means remembering that the stony metaphor-world of common language was itself once artistically created and that a kind of extramoral artistry can dissolve it, rendering language and thought fluid.

And so, using imagery very similar to that of Foucault and Butler, Nietzsche sardonically identifies the "security" of the everyday subject as being a prison of self-consciousness. Unlike Butler though, Nietzsche points to artistic creativity as the means of escape from this prison of subject life. He writes:

> Only by forgetting this primitive metaphor-world . . . only through the undefeatable belief that this sun, window, and table

might have a truth in itself, in short, that one forgets oneself as a subject, and indeed an artistically creating subject, does one live with any calm, security, and consistency: if one could get out of prison walls of this belief for a moment, then "self-consciousness" would immediately be gone.[123]

Butler sets out more-or-less the same dilemma regarding the prison walls of self-consciousness, with the body becoming the normative subject's skin-tight prison. However, she does not go further and explore the role of either aesthetic experience or artistic creativity in escaping or even refiguring the walls. The argument of this book is that both in aesthetic experience, that is beholding artworks as an observer, and in moments of artistic creativity there is access, however oblique, to new modes of meaning and order less determinately chained to social power. Art thus points to powers beyond power and to creativity beyond normativity.

Art as Another "Other" and Novelty in Self-Recognition

Hence, the artwork can also serve as an "Other." Art can also set up a turn-on-self and initiate the encounter of consciousness with itself. Art, having an intentionality that exceeds determination in discourse, serves as a jumping off point, if not for freedom and simple redemption, then for nobility and a more complex type of ongoing rehabilitation. The encounter with art, be it in terms of Kant's observing subject, Hegel's artisan, or Nietzsche's moral artist, affects human subjects and points to something beyond the chains of bindingly familiar language and pejoratively ordinary experience. Thus, while they may not be agents per se, artworks can nevertheless in some way act as free provocateurs of aesthetic experience. Going along with that, just as the freedom of other people sets up a Hegelian struggle for recognition, so too might the different-in-kind freedom of artworks set the stage for an alternate mode of self-reflexivity.

Giving attention to the artistic, creative grounds of language, gesture, symbol, and so forth, helps in remembering that what dominates in social discourse is itself contingent, which is to say that power is contingent. This is the first part of a response to Butler. The second part lies in giving artful attention to ritual performance in a way that goes one step further and shows that the *particular configuration* of power's psychic formation of the body and banal repetition of its own norms is also contingent. There must be a two-pronged attack exposing the contingency of signs as well as the contingency of bodily gestures. However, neither aesthetic experience nor artful attention to ritual fully redeems the subject, not in the sense of recovering a pure, unsullied self. Nonetheless, they do help the subject to become less passive and a bit more agent. Artful life destabilizes the necessity of social normative structures, and focusing on the artful, aesthetic side of ritual subverts the most important vector for power—imprisonment in the body.

Putting forth this idea does not mean committing to the strong and definitional claim from the analytic school of New Criticism that artworks are artworks to the extent that they stand independently, to the degree that they speak apart from the artist's intention, or insofar as they spark spontaneous acts of the imagination. Whether artworks are in some way magical with quasi-autonomy on an ontic level or whether that magic is constructed through the kind of recognition that drives subjectivation (as an institutional theory of art more typical of the analytic school might hold), most people have in fact been jarred and captivated at some point by artworks, particularly as they seem to surpass the individual artist and take on a life of their own in provoking aesthetic experience.

If it is admitted that there are at least some artistic phenomena that are not bound by intentional schemas and that beget such profound experiences, then it becomes clear that discursive sign chains fail to exhaust the possibilities of the subject's psychic life. Moreover, if such candidate artworks speak in a way that exceeds the deterministic trappings of discourse so considered, then it would seem that they open access to different modes of otherness and recognition. Seeing oneself in terms of artworks is much different than seeing oneself in terms of discourse and other people. Whereas the collective otherness of society is likely to make concrete demands (like sublimating baser instincts, accepting baseline moral norms, etc.), artworks, despite being other, do not make such restrictive claims upon the subject—this is Kant's core insight into how artworks provoke a particularly free brand of play. As such, the mode of self-reflection initiated by artworks is much less likely to lead to the angst and melancholy that accompanies the socially impelled turn-on-self. Hence, it is worth asking if and in what way experiencing art might be a resource for the ills of social life.

Works of art provide an alternate path to the recognizer/recognized dynamic in the Hegelian portion of Butler's account of the self-reflexive subject. It may be direct, such as the temple space at Delphi with the injunction to "know thyself" or like the demand of Rainer Maria Rilke's

"Archaic Torso of Apollo" that "[y]ou must change your life"—charges that one seldom hears put so starkly in the course of daily life.[124] It may be indirect in the way that works of art—even pieces as inscrutable as René Margritte's nondepictive depiction of a pipe, Marcel Duchamp's urinal, or Tracey Emin's "My Bed"—can prompt reflection on the nature of purpose and the relationship between subject and milieu. Everyday bodily subject life may be disperse and manifold in nature, but if art and artistry can be found there, if the challenge of art can be met on the very terms of subjectivation, then perhaps subject life can expand beyond what at times are unhappily familiar confines.

Conclusion

Taking stock of things so far, the claims being made are as follows.

1. The subject is (a) relational, (b) bodily, (c) discursive, and (d) ritually impelled, where (a) constitutive relationships born of passionate attachment to others form the (b) body as a skin-tight prison—a body that, upon being (c) hailed into social life, is compelled to live out life as a series of (d) ritual performances of normativity in order to obtain recognition and survival. This is subjectivation and subjection.

2. The subject, so considered, is at the mercy of certain threads of purposiveness linking signs, language, discourse, cultural productions, and so on, to the continued enactment of a certain mode of (a) relational, (b) bodily, (c) discursive, (d) ritual subject life for the purpose of survival. Therefore, in order to begin to respond to this dilemma, the purposiveness animating subjectivation must be in some way subverted. Exposing weakness in sign chains and resignifying the terms of subjectivation may be one response, but it offers little in the way of freedom.

3. Squaring purposiveness with an idea of genuine subject freedom requires rethinking signs, language, discourse, cultural productions, and so on. Without getting bogged down in trying to apply a transcendental schema to subjectivation theory, the basic Kantian notion of freedom surpassing purposiveness in the artistically beautiful and religiously sublime can be helpful, if only to *start* to think through these issues and to reassess untapped resources linking art and self-consciousness in some of the philosophical paradigms that influence subjectivation theory. Here in this project the specific interest is in the first aspect—art and artistic beauty—and how

some of the major sources behind subjectivation theory work to link art, self-consciousness, and freedom in ways that call for further examination.

And so, with points 1 to 3 in mind, the investigation now turns to looking at how this might provide new ways of thinking through subjectivation, particularly as art and artistry can radically call into question conventional purposiveness and usher in new modes of recognition for the subject. Hence, the goal will be to see how a certain notion of autonomy in artistry can be a resource for dealing with subjectivation's sadly necessary basic dynamic of recognition, passionate attachment to continued existence, and formation of ritual bodily life.

Chapter 2

Autonomy and Appearance in Artful Ritual Practice

> What strikes me is the fact that in our society, art has become something which is related only to objects and not to individuals, or to life. That art is something which is specialized or which is done by experts who are artists. But couldn't everyone's life become a work of art? Why should the lamp or the house be an art object, but not our life?[1]
>
> —Michel Foucault

Preliminary Remarks: The Modern Alienation of Art and Practice in the Unhappy Artworld

For a litany of reasons, not to be argued here and well-explored elsewhere, schools of thought from the Euro-American sphere do not tend to draw everyday practice and art together. Indeed, the maddeningly persistent view that art and craft are in fact separate is partly to blame. When the art/craft and art/practice dichotomies are considered in terms of their Platonic-Abrahamic-Cartesian cousin, mind/body dualism, it can hardly be surprising that the associated dominant tradition has foreclosed the idea that artful bodily craft can save the soul. After all, art and craft must be separate; art must be intellectual and disregard everyday bodily practice; and something as lowly as the body could never ennoble the soul, right? And so, be it because of money, elitism, technology, or other factors, art, particularly of the high or fine variety, exists at arm's length from everyday social practice, having been vetted by critics and confined, like the mad, to high-security institutions. But is there actually anything preventing art and artistic beauty from being resources for subject life?

However, art, so understood, is supposed to be intellectually enjoyed in the quiet repose of museum or the staid confines of the conservatory or concert hall. The world is not supposed to intrude upon the art and the art is not supposed to bother the world, at least not the world of the everyday. It has hardly helped that the "artworld" (following Arthur Danto's influential use of the term) has become a world unto itself.[2] The artworld, being awash with skepticism and irony, and contemporary society-at-large, being steadfastly serious and purposive, mutually alienate each other in a way that bears at least some similarity to Hegel's unhappy consciousness dynamic. It is no wonder, then, that art and artistry are seldom taken seriously as possible ways of improving conditions for any kind of (a) relational, (b) discursive, (c) bodily, and (d) ritually impelled subject.

It is worth recalling that it has not always been so; it has not always been the case that the institutional artworld and the broader world of institutional power have been at odds, nor has it always been the case that art and practice have been estranged. Just as subjectivation and the machinations of power are epochal, according to Foucault, being tied to economic and historical factors, so too should the relationship between art and the artworld on the one hand and power-laden social practice and power on the other be seen as similarly epochal.[3] There is in fact a great deal of evidence pointing to more conciliatory, if not convergent, conceptual arrangements between art and broader social practice occurring throughout much of human history. How is this to be understood, both in terms of the current state of affairs and in terms of how earlier epochs related art and power?

Speaking first and in roughly Hegelian terms to what might be called unhappiness in contemporary culture, on one side there is the serious, stoic purposiveness of everyday social practice, which is to say the seriousness of power in its many guises. Roughly speaking, this corresponds to bourgeois society with its widespread and naive idea of freedom as resting in things like human dignity and rational agency in a manner not unlike Hegel's description of stoic-stage self-consciousness as being "withdrawn into the simple essence of thought."[4] With liberal democratic order accompanying industrialization and now globalization, labor and everyday life has become more and more compartmentalized and abstract in nature, leading to an increasingly atomic and formal notion of freedom that has proven "unsatisfying in life" due to, as Hegel might put it, the revelation of pure thought as being void of content.[5] Thus, stoicism, in effect, points to a condition prevalent in industrial and postindustrial, liberal, democratic settings, namely, a grudging discontent with freedom merely being formal and on paper, with very little content and very little with which to content oneself.

Such cultural stoicism is, by its very nature, uncomfortable with anything that might call into question its guiding principle, the inherent essential dignity of the rational self, which is cashed out by Hegel as the notion "that consciousness is a thinking being and something that has only essence for itself or that is true and good for it [itself]."[6] Such stoicism will be vexed by anything threatening the idea of freedom as pure freedom of thought. Just like Hegel's stoicism, this kind of cultural stoicism withdraws into spaces of "pure" contemplation of "free" expression in quiet repose, placing cultural endeavors in museums and concert halls and behind a velvet rope. This calls to mind Pierre Bourdieu's definitive statement on art and culture serving to promote social distinction, where he describes how

> the denial of inferior, gross, vulgar, venal, servile, and in a word natural enjoyment, which constitutes how the culturally sacred includes the affirmation of the superiority of those who know how to find satisfaction in sublime, refined, disinterested, gratuitous [for its own sake], distinguished pleasures forbidden to the simply profane. That is why art and artistic consumption are predisposed to replicate, whether or not with volition, whether or not with knowledge, a social function of legitimizing social differences.[7]

With a quasi-Hegelian logic at work, the antithesis of cultural skepticism springs from and opposes the prior thesis of stoicism. How does this come about?

The spaces for putatively "pure" contemplation cease to be spaces, they cease to be pure and devoid of content. The spaces become filled out, if not by things as artifacts, then by the intentionality of consciousness itself. The empty space becomes a *thing* unto itself. It becomes a museum as such; it becomes a concert hall. Pretty soon these full-blown institutions, in striving to be spaces of pure thinking, instead start to be about the border *around* the space. Instead of being about the open invitation of the inspirational muses into the museum, the museum becomes pejoratively institutional as a set of border walls. The institutions of art eventually metastasize into an artworld hostile to both bourgeois conventions and, somewhat infuriatingly, to its own unachievable aims of providing freedom in contemplation.

With institutional space turning in on itself, the artworld has become decidedly skeptical. The artworld has started to regard its own icons as material, leading art to become less iconic and more iconoclastic, more often fetishizing or breaking sacred images than creating them. Art in this mode, being somewhat maddening, has become beset by what twentieth-century investigator into the psychology of art Robert Solso labels as a kind of cognitive dissonance, becoming less about icons or even quasi-icons like Leonardo DaVinci's early sixteenth-century masterwork *Mona Lisa* (*La Gioconda*) and more about the cheeky snark of Marcel Duchamp's 1919 piece *L.H.O.O.Q.* ("which, pronounced letter by letter in French, means 'She's got a hot ass,'" as Solso explains), which insouciantly depicts the Mona Lisa with a moustache, or the type of media savvy in the age of mechanical reproduction on display in Andy Warhol's 1963 work *Thirty Are Better Than One*, which sees an array of Mona Lisas set as thirty tiles.[8] Being so overwhelmed by such irony, art cannot help but become skeptical of everything, including itself. Art becomes simply another thing to be negated by art.

And so it is in postindustrial, liberal, democratic spheres that people are left to contend with the discontents of purely formal freedom and thereby to wrestle with the dynamic described by Hegel where *all* freely thought premises can be drawn into living contradiction by self-consciousness operating at skepticism's zenith (or nadir, depending on one's perspective). This kind of skepticism takes childish, impish delight in the negation of the stoic's empty formal freedom, thereby living out a negative, non-end-determining kind of freedom, as opposed to how the stoic posits and determines ends, but only on paper. Whatever free thought the stoic might have can be easily undermined. Any premise can be turned on itself and have its conceptual basis subverted in a way that contradicts supposedly "free" thought by drawing attention to the impurities lurking within putatively "pure" freedom. Any attempt to give naive rational freedom real, lived form can be interrupted by the labor of the toiling artisan, who, not being driven by a notion of "pure" freedom of thought and its attendant aversion to labor, experiences a genuine connection with the material necessaries for life. This is the basic point of Hegel's master-slave dialectic—the master eventually becomes a slave to desire and the slave eventually masters the material fulfillment of desire, if only for a time.

Carrying this logic forward, paradigms or media of pure, free expression can be subverted by the laboring and now thoroughly skeptical, artisan. The basic means of expressing pure thought can undergo upheaval (*Aufhe-*

bung) upon the skeptical laboring artisan drawing attention to the folly of presuming such purity.

Such skepticism befits straight-line-eschewing, deconstructivist architecture in the vein of leading Austrian firm Coop Himmelb(l)au's incendiary manifesto arguing that "architecture must burn!"[9] Such skepticism accords with music like that of John Cage's silent anti-composition *4'33"*. Such skepticism suits visual artworks like *The Treachery of Images*, René Margritte's depiction of a pipe accompanied by the provocative claim that "this is not a pipe." Such skepticism takes the closest thing to a priori pure notions behind media—that architecture should stand, that music should make sound, and that pictures should depict—and calls each enterprise into question using nothing more than the medium, the material at hand. Such skepticism negates, but it may be a matter of taste whether such negation is determinate and offers anything of artistic value. At any rate, art (or at least this brand of art) seems to be about making the absurdities of convention manifest as a prelude to a larger rejection of convention generally speaking, very much including the most basic conventional premises of abstract symbolic communication.

On this score, the now-skeptical artworld, so disdainful of bourgeois notions of pure rational freedom, can be regarded as embracing an exclusionary velvet rope meant originally to secure such purity in the stoic contemplation of cultural and artistic works. What emerges in the artworld is something of an inverted version of the church/temple space—a place of repose and a repository of art. Meanwhile, on the other side of the rope, the stoic side of society will be vexed by anything threatening its idea of freedom being pure freedom of thought. Such stoicism well describes the hostility of society at large to postmodern, post-structural, deconstructionist, or deconstructivist idioms of art, all of which tend to call into question conventional, formalist, bourgeois notions of freedom. So understood, the alienation of the artworld and the world at large is a mutual affair and one that brings an unsettling symmetrical unity to this species of unhappy consciousness in and of late-stage postindustrial, liberal, democratic, capitalist culture.

And so, this kind of medium-subverting art offers interesting parallels with the plight of the unhappy subject life as understood by Butler. This kind of art, falling under the loose heading of "postmodern," addresses Foucault's and Butler's common project of resistance and its aim of undermining harmful power structures in the prevailing discourse. However, there is the tendency in this mode of art, much like in Butler's endgame for subjectivation, towards nihilism, if not outright rage. It thus makes sense to ask whether or not there might be a way past this, if there might not be a way to for subjects to appreciate art and for art to appreciate and add value to subject life.

The Early Human World: The Historical Link between Art and Ritual Practice

It was not always that art, as a superlative rising over and above common discourse, was sadly and misleadingly cast as irrelevant in the development of normative subject life. Just as subjectivation is epochal, so too are art and the artworld. Just as subjectivation is an ongoing, changing phenomenon that reached a critical juncture with the advent of the Industrial Age, so too is art. And just as subject life has a deep history calling for the kind of anthropology and archaeology of knowledge advanced by Foucault, so too does art history, similarly and broadly construed, offer a resource for charting the course of the artworld now.

Of course, there was not always an artworld set off from the "real world." Commenting on the lack of an artworld as such for early humans, Danto writes, "It would . . . never have occurred to the painters of Lascaux that they were producing art on those walls. Not unless there were neolithic aestheticians."[10]

There was not always a question of purity surrounding cultural production. The question of purity in cultural production only arises with the transition from consciousness to self-consciousness in the withdrawal into the notion of the self as pure thought. Put another way, only with *self*-consciousness does one ask if "I" really, truly, purely am this and/or that. So what is the situation, then, with respect to art when humans and human societies are more marked by consciousness of things external than by the kind of existential introspection that comes with self-consciousness?

Looking at early human societies provides an occasion for understanding art as being profoundly constitutive of humanity as such and of the kind of ritual life that marks the human subject. The work of twentieth-century psychologist Joseph Lyons is instructive here, particularly his argument *against* "the view that cave paintings were produced as central items in an elaborate group ritual [and the assumption of] the prior existence of rather complex societal and religious patterns, with all the symbolic and imaginative developments presupposed by this view."[11] Looking to examples of cave art like that of the site at Lascaux, Lyons uses the language of gestalt theory to look at framing and the small number of species that, like humans, appear capable of setting off one portion of the experiential field within a frame apart from the wider whole.[12]

Lyons sees this framing as something that humanity developed through appreciation of the accident of resemblance. This is something known by anyone who has had the pleasure of staring at clouds and seeing what the formations look like. In Lyons's account of early humans, the focus instead is on rocks looking like this or that object (often animals).[13]

The human capacity for seeing-in, which allows for seeing a duck or a rabbit in figures like the duck-rabbit discussed by Joseph Jastrow, Wolfgang Köhler, and (most famously) Ludwig Wittgenstein, is crucial to the growth of decreasingly physical and increasingly abstract forms of symbolic communication.[14] Being able to squint, whether in reality or just figuratively, and see an ox in a ox-like rock sets up every other advance in symbolic communication including being able to perceive a corresponding sound in the printed letters "ox" (or on a digital screen through a mish-mash of 1s and 0s conveying that text string) as well as being able to call to mind an actual, real ox from that sound or from those characters. How so?

In becoming symbolic, the hypothetical rock in question became different than all of those other rocks and other things, at least within the early observing human's field of sense. This marked this rock as special, as different, as a proto-icon, thereby drawing a type of abstract, nonphysical frame around the resemblance-bearing rock. The key is that humanity at some point made a leap into the realm of symbolic abstraction, where, by carrying a rock that looked like an ox or buffalo, or the like, it was possible to quite literally convey an object without actually physically carrying an entire animal.[15] Such physical conveyance of meaning in the form of bearing found objects eventually gave way to symbolic conveyance through "objects" fashioned by means like painting and musical performance, both of which can be spatiotemporally distinguished from the everyday within much less abstract frames or stages (e.g., the cave paintings at Lascaux).

With this, not only was symbolic expression born, but also, in addition to this feat, monumental in all senses of the term, a kind of magic was genuinely accomplished. Starting with found objects and proceeding to manipulated and fashioned objects, symbolic and artistic objects have made the absent and *the desired* strangely manifest. One way or another, such artworks have traditionally possessed a special power, and in Lyons's reading, this magical power follows from such artworks in a way that gave rise to early ritual practices. He writes:

> In place of the claim that art arose in the service of magic, we have now proposed a reversed sequence, to make the argument psychologically sound: that art arose first, in an apperceptive and perceptual leap forward, and that magic developed as a set of practices taking full advantage of the viewer's participation in the unreal world of represented objects. Ritual practices, and perhaps even forms of sympathetic magic to insure success in the hunt, would then have emerged within a short time—and may have been developed by later generations of viewers who had already lost track of their ancestors who had produced the first paintings.[16]

And this quote speaks to the theme of sedimentation, the way in which a ritual practice can grow, accumulate, and take on a life of its own over time, here with "magic" in ritual practice cast as emerging *from* art.

Of course, such early human rituals bear only passing connection to what Butler is talking about with ritual performativity, right? The way in which these early human rituals use artworks to mediate desire for (and *object*-consciousness of) absent peoples, places, and things *obviously* could never have anything to do with the modern human subject marked by unhappy *self*-consciousness and the neurotic ritual reenactment of an underlying dynamic of desired objects, absence, and melancholy, right?

But this is wrong. The unhappy consciousness that marks subject life amid postindustrial postmodernity is unhappy because access to origins is lost; and as much as Hegel's *Phenomenology of Spirit* stands as an account of individual spirit on a psychological level and of the development of humanity on a world-historical level, so too does the Hegelian "loss of a loss," so crucial to Butler's account, bear reading on these multiple levels of the life of the self *and* the historical art of society. Subject life is not *just* driven by the personal experience of constitutive loss foreclosing access to personal origins, but it is also impelled by what has been lost, foreclosed, and preserved in ideal forms as part of humanity getting to the stage of subjectivation itself. Hence, for both *The Psychic Life of Power* and therefore for this account, expanding the notion of loss past this or that particular subject is more than appropriate. Art provides *one* context for doing so.

Arendt on Purposiveness, Appearance in the World, and Art

Of course, without a time machine it is a bit difficult to verify Lyons's account of large-scale rituals of social order emerging as a consequence of the magic of art. Likewise it proves difficult to buy into the rather general account given above of a skeptical and destabilizing artworld resulting from quasi-religious institutions like museums, reflective of a certain bourgeois notion of pure, almost-stoic freedom of thought. Giving these stories any real scrutiny renders their collective explanatory power a thing of diminishing returns.

However, the narrow correctness of these conveniently generalized narratives is not at issue here per se. What matters, and what shines forth independent of any particular view of history, is the superlative enduring quality of artworks. Speaking on what this means more broadly, Hannah Arendt addresses the issue directly in her magnum opus, *The Human Condition*:

> Whether this uselessness of art objects has always pertained or whether art formerly served the so-called religious needs of men as ordinary use objects serve more ordinary needs does not enter the argument. Even if the historical origin of art were of an exclusively religious or mythological character, the fact is that art has survived gloriously its severance from religion, magic, and myth.[17]

Though she decries the link between art and mytho-religious magic in her own description, Arendt sees artworks as exemplary with regard to survival through the ages, thereby ascribing a kind of magic to them. Arendt speaks of the consummately and "intensely worldly" quality of artworks in comparison to things generally. Her words here sound very much like those of Kant on nonpurposive purposiveness in artistic beauty, particularly with her own description of how separation from everyday use makes artworks durable over and above change and corrosion in nature.[18] Arendt goes on to conclude that when it comes to artworks "their durability is of a higher order than that which all things need in order to exist at all; it can attain permanence throughout the ages. In this permanence, the very stability of the human artifice, which, being inhabited and used by mortals can never be absolute, achieves a representation of its own."[19]

Now, it might be objected that putting subjectivation theory into conversation with this phenomenological viewpoint is problematic, given the former's more personal, psychoanalytic scope. However, Arendt's phenomenological approach is rather helpful because the convergence that she draws between *Schein* and *Sein*, between appearance and being, points to a possible resource beyond interpellation for addressing subjectivation to be addressed later (indeed Butler's references to Arendt and Adriana Cavarero on the topic of exposure seem to indicate that her thinking is moving in this direction).[20]

Now, recall that in Butler's understanding, subjectivation/subjection is a comprehensive process. For her, there is no such thing as a bodily remainder that might aid the subject, since the body as such is "destroyed" in the constitutive loss that founds the subject body within the normative bounds of a skin-tight prison. This is what leads her to deny the existence of an unconscious psychic remainder inhering in either body or mind, arguing specifically against Mladen Dolar broaching the question of "love [being] what we find beyond interpellation." Butler argues against anything occurring beyond the dynamic of interpellation and subjectivation, since the setting up of the field of conscious and unconscious psychic life occurs on the basis of a passionate attachment to continued existence preceding any particular love, which thereby frustrates any attempt to claim an interior space that might be prior to power relations.[21] This basic logic holds for Butler generally speaking, since in her view there is nothing beyond interpellation and the passionate attachment to authority that precedes each and every actual social encounter and context for self-recognition.

However, Arendt can still add to this discussion, since she points to something genuinely beyond interpellation, namely, the very manner in which appearance on the scene occurs. She makes the strong case that appearance is coextensive with being, writing, "Everything that is, must appear, and nothing can appear without a shape of its own; hence there is in fact no thing that does not in some way transcend its functional use, and its transcendence, its beauty or ugliness, is identical with appearing publicly and being seen."[22]

And so, plugging this into the logic of subjectivation, one shows up on the scene prior to each and every hail into social existence, prior to each and every passionate attachment in ongoing subject life. Subjectivation seems to exploit the necessary publicity of human life, the seeming compulsion of *having* to appear on the scene and do so continuously in order to be and persist in being. One cannot be constantly hailed into existence by perceived authorities, by the putative police officer, or even by petty slights, unless one is compelled to be there (as *Dasein*), thrown into the scene out on the street with a readiness and perhaps eagerness to be so hailed.

However, Arendt's point, and one that is well taken when it comes to subjectivation, is that being-as-appearance can be refined. Everything may have to appear publicly in order to be, but some things are better at doing so. This is what artworks, as nonpurposive and durable things do; they appear, and thus exist, in a fuller way. Arendt draws both a distinction and a continuum between artworks and things, writing:

> For although the durability of ordinary things is but a feeble reflection of the permanence of which the most worldly of all things, works of art, are capable, something of this quality—which to Plato was divine because it approaches immortality—is inherent in every thing as a thing, and it is precisely this quality or the lack of it that shines forth in its shape and makes it beautiful or ugly.[23]

Now, the idea being presented in this project, following Arendt, is that basic appearance on the scene takes place before and beyond the processes of interpellation and subjectivation driven by passionate attachment. Appropriating a tangent of Arendt's logic and adding a twist of Butler's notion of subjectivation/subjection, the idea here is that artworks have the almost magical potential to call into question core notions of presence and absence in a way that can disrupt the basic logic of preserving oneself through preserving what is absent and lost in an idealized form within the locus of self-castigation called conscience.

And so, by paying attention to artworks in general and refining one's own bodily life and appearance on the scene in terms of art more specifically, a subject can then become something of an artwork with a life of its own and with a timeframe and sense of purpose (*Zweckmäßigkeit*) far surpassing that of mortal life. The particular suggestion here is that, if the body is always undergoing subjectivation and always having first to appear, then the body—with its basic appearance, presence, comportment, and countenance always being formed by the "objective" world—can be similarly refined in terms of how it appears on the scene, perhaps also taking on a life of its own and finding a different sense of mortality and purpose beyond what has been inculcated in the course of subject life. Put yet another way, if appearance is in some way beyond the dynamic of interpellation and subjectivation as a condition of the possibility of its occurrence, then why should art, as the apex of appearance vis-à-vis endurance, not become a model for the subject body in its struggle for survival amid a host of normative demands? If either art or the artful body can in some manner surpass subjectivation, even if just momentarily and in fits and starts, then why should the senses of time, durability, and purpose at play in art not alter the nature of subject self-recognition?

Bringing Art and Novel Recognition into Play in Everyday Encounters

A certain parity needs to emerge here. For, just as subjectivation is not necessarily about master and slave, stoic and skeptic, creditor and debtor, or even about the judging subject and the apprehended artwork, but is instead about a complex process of small-scale everyday, ritual, bodily acts of recognition, so too is there a corresponding need for art to challenge and refine subject life as part of a more subtle and manifold process. Any attempt to apply this idea of recognition through art to subjectivation will ultimately have to reckon with the rather intractable and imprisoning nature of subjectivation, where recognition and misrecognition occur throughout subject life in the panopticon of the everyday, sedimenting in the subject's enduring disposition, psychic *and* somatic. Recognition through encounters with a variety of other subjects sets up the recognized body in terms of habit, gesture, and performativity. Put another way, though it might happen in an assortment of less grandiose contexts, recognition through other subjects boils down to something like Althusser's scene of interpellation with the police officer yelling, "Hey, you there!"—one way or another, even in these more subtle encounters, the neck, like the psychic posture, turns.

And so, if art is a different type of other and if it is to be brought into play as something that could change the stakes of recognition and thus of subjectivation, then art, under whatever bounds, determinations, and definitions that might apply, must lead to real-world changes in *bodily* subject life. There must be practical effects on bodily gesture, comportment, and the very physical manifestations of the turn-on-self.

There is a path for this. Exposure to art—through observing, creating, composing, criticizing, interpreting, and so on—points to how meaning can occur, and to how meaning, as portioned out by conventional discourse, is not what it is because of any type of overriding necessity. Put simply, art exposes contingency.

This can be thought of as a natural corollary of prevailing definitions of art—whatever art is, it arrests attention, standing out as art, not nature, per Immanuel Kant, or with art securing poetic justice such that the artist *earns* the initial right to attention, as leading American pragmatist Stanley Cavell put it before his 2018 passing.[24] If art captures attention, it does so by being extraordinary, by rising above the din of mere signs. In capturing attention in this manner, art is not merely *subject to* recognition; rather, it issues a *claim for* recognition. This changes the stakes.

And so, if the bad conscience, the social psyche trapping the body, is a horrible artistry, then working to reclaim the body through art makes sense. If the moral discourse forming the bad conscience and trapping the body is a fiendish artistry, then why not fight it with art? If what is sometimes the wretched art of conventional language has the power to bind, then what prevents art from having the power to loosen those strictures of recognition? However, if artistic power is to be brought to bear, there must be a medium—but what? It needs to be something present at hand and not a deus ex machina, and, moreover, it needs to change the stakes of bodily imprisonment through recognition.

And so the solution to this problem of acquiring recognition outside of the normal confines of subjectivation is clear—the body must *itself* become that artful medium and become meaningful on its own terms. If the body can become artful and acquire whatever limited "magic" it is that artworks bear that allows them to disrupt conventional structures of purposiveness, then the body can become a different kind of other. One's body can, over time, become a source for a less pernicious and less imprisoning form of recognition, which might do at least something to counter the prevailing and entrenched form of recognition that drives subjectivation encounters. What is needed then is a theory of bodily appearance, of bodily presence, of bodily performance, of bodily practice, and one that does not ascribe any undue and inexplicable creativity or spontaneity to the body or to art, but which nevertheless develops a serious account of the possibility of a certain kind of subject freedom.

If this is the case, if the concession can be made that art goes past common discourse and offers novel, less power-laden modes of recognition, then it seems only natural to turn to the artful and aesthetic aspect of those performative rituals crucial to the emergence of the subject in subjectivation. And so, the first step becomes developing a way of talking about art as a different type of other that allows for different modes of recognition. The second step then becomes turning the body into a different type of artful "Other" and thereby developing a different manner of *self*-recognition. However, the language for doing so is somewhat lacking in the European and American sources driving subjectivation/subjection theory.

Despite this state of affairs, there is a resource, and one that speaks to the steps previously laid out, for changing the stakes of recognition through an appreciation of art and then of the artful body—and that is the framework of music, ritual, and body offered by the still growing and changing enterprise of Confucianism. Classical Confucianism may not have anything akin to Butler's extensive and often bewildering psychoanalytic apparatus. Nevertheless, Confucianism, especially as reworked by some of its more recent advocates, adds a great deal to the discussion, since it emphasizes the aesthetic side of ritual and social discourse in the formation of relational persons in a way quite amenable to Butler's own work. Moreover, Confucianism does this according to the steps previously laid out, with a compelling account of self-refinement through art and self-recognition through artful bodily ritual that self-consciously avoids bringing supernatural or otherwise unwarranted notions of creativity into play.

And so, in line with Sartre's insistent remarks at the beginning of the last chapter, the argument turns to Confucianism's sensitivity to the importance and possible benefits of constitutive relationships with other people in the tradition's characteristic fusion of decor and decorum in artfully cultivated ritual practice. This in turn grounds an examination of contemporary work extending this model of freedom into the sphere of the ritual and bodily technologies of the subject, which not only responds to Foucault's challenge, but attempts to change the stakes for subjectivation as well.

Conclusion

Following up on the main three points previously argued, the case made here can be summarized as follows.

4. Art can be a resource for thinking through subjectivation. However, there are factors that prevent it from being taken seriously as something that might speak to self-consciousness in the everyday. There is the idea that art is extraordinary and that its place is away from the ordinary in quasi-religious institutions like museums, where a pure and nearly stoic freedom of thought might be possible. Further removing art from the everyday is the skeptical character that has grown inside the insular institutions of the artworld, one that takes impish delight in being both iconoclastic and inaccessible. It might have been the case at one time that art and artworks were constitutive for the rudiments of self-consciousness and ritual social behavior for

early humans, but, as it stands now, art is generally not seen as a resource capable of going past the superficial to affecting real change in subject life.

5. However, art should be seen as a resource in this way, for the appearance of both artworks particularly and of things generally is in some sense beyond interpellation and subjectivation. Art points to a fullness of appearance and being that endures with a sense of time different than that of everyday things, since artworks surpass conventional notions of purpose and use. Understanding the appearance of the body in this way, as something that can take on a life of its own through skill and technique in the development of a sense of proprietary nonconventional purpose, has value for subjectivation. The artful body thus represents a possible way of altering how recognition and survival work in subjectivation.

6. Art and the artful body may be underdeveloped as topics in dominant Euro-American literature, but this is not the only possible source. As arguably the most influential philosophy of East Asia, Confucianism presents a compelling historical approach to early human development that shows how spontaneity in the artistic performance of bodily ritual, broadly construed, allows for rethinking the relational self, where the formation of the self does not occur strictly through a negative relationship to normative structures imposed from without, but also occurs positively through artful rituals in the service of personal cultivation.

And so working on the basis of points 4, 5, and 6, this project thus turns to Confucianism with its classical vocabulary of ritual and music before connecting to contemporary work on the species-level aesthetics of ritual in the theoretical platform of subjectality advanced by Lǐ Zéhòu, the notion of the political space of appearance developed by Hannah Arendt, the approach to technique taken up by Bernard Stiegler, and Richard Shusterman's more practice-oriented paradigm of somaesthetics.

Chapter 3

Confucianism and *Lǐ* 禮/礼

Ritual Propriety, Music, and the Arts

> A careful reading of the *Analects*, however, uncovers a way of life carefully choreographed down to appropriate facial expressions and physical gestures, a world in which a life is a performance requiring enormous attention to detail. Importantly, this [ritual]-constituted performance begins from the insight that personal refinement is only possible through the discipline provided by formalized roles and behaviors. . . . It is only with the appropriate combination of form and personalization that community can be self-regulating and refined.[1]
>
> —Roger T. Ames and Henry Rosemont, Jr.

Preliminary Remarks: The Relational, Discursive, Bodily, and Ritually Impelled Person in Confucianism

Confucianism and its central idea of or ritual propriety or *lǐ* 禮/礼 (the traditional and simplified characters, respectively), might seem like an unlikely resource for dealing with the issues brought up by the idea of subjectivation, but further reflection shows the potential of this approach.

Consider what has been said about subjectivation so far. Subjectivation's conclusion of rage and reappropriation in reaction to threats to the subject is unsatisfying. Subjectivation stands in need of a better historical apparatus for talking about the development of ritual and performativity on a species level. A broader account of subjectivation ought to address art and its strange, quasi-autonomous purposiveness with respect to everyday discourse and then connect this idea of art and artfulness to bodily gesture.

Such resources exist, even if they appear to be far from subjectivation as a topic of theoretical, academic inquiry, Confucianism being a case in point. Originating from sayings made circa 500 BCE by a wandering scholar/political advisor named Confucius (Kǒng Zǐ 孔子) in the cultural context of Ancient China's Warring States period, the still-living and still-developing school following his teachings can nonetheless genuinely speak to the issues raised by subjectivation theory, questions of incommensurability aside.

Stemming from what Karl Jaspers calls the "axial age," the approximate time period during which Plato, Aristotle, and Buddha were also active, Confucianism set the stage for ensuing philosophical traditions from East Asia, furnishing a great deal of basic vocabulary, with its notions of role-based ethics, ritual, and familial relations proving particularly influential in the long run.[2] In China, this axial age was a period of strife, known as the Warring States period, where the core of the nation as it is now known, centered between the Yellow (Huang) River in the North and the Yangtze in the South, was a loose collection of small fiefdoms controlled by warlord kings. In his day, Confucius was little more than a roaming mid-level advisor, giving his brand of counsel to various courts of the day in the hope, not to be realized during his own lifetime, of this chaos giving way to a type of social harmony modeled on the Chinese golden age brought about by mytho-historical sage kings like Yáo 尧 and Shùn 舜. In this regard, Confucius appropriated and extended legendary accounts like the canonical *Book of Changes* (*Yì jīng* 易经) and its commentary tradition concerning the creative employment by these sages of language, ritual, and music for the purpose of social harmony.

However, Confucianism is not just about ur-history. Today, Confucian precepts permeate everyday social conduct in mainland China as well as in what preeminent Confucian scholar Tu Wei-Ming calls the four mini-dragons—Hong Kong, Singapore, South Korea, and Taiwan—in addition to Japan (as well as throughout each respective diaspora).[3] Being so widespread and long-lasting, subsequent epochs have seen Confucianism reinterpreted in light of a series of Daoist, Buddhist, and, more recently, Marxist influences and critiques, such that, rather than being a philosophical antique, Confucianism thrives as a living tradition and one that is taking on ever greater importance as East Asia continues to rise.

Nevertheless, even while properly respecting Confucianism as a living, dynamic enterprise, it is necessary to acknowledge a clear conservative tendency within the school. This body of thought, called *rújiā* 儒家 or "the school of advisors" in Chinese, does in fact bear marks of a war-weary political advisor's characteristic emphasis on stable harmony in statecraft and family, all of which might seem inherently repressive and at odds with the emancipatory aims of subjectivation theorists like Foucault and Butler. Well before Foucault and Butler, Karl Jaspers was sensitive to the possibly coercive nature of the distinct conceptual contribution from Confucianism under discussion here, the notion of ritual propriety (*lǐ* 禮), writing that

> morals create the spirit of the whole and are then again animated by it. The individual only comes into existence through the virtues of the collective of humanity. *Li* mean the constant education of all. They are the forms belonging to all spheres of existence in which proper attunement consists—earnest participation in affairs, trust, respect. They conduct humans by way of something common through which education is acquired and becomes second nature, such that what is common is felt and experienced as its own being and not as compulsion.[4]

The ambiguities regarding the Confucian idea of ritual propriety presented here are telling, with Jaspers casting ritual *lǐ* as an empowering brand of social education, on the one hand, and as perhaps masking widespread normative coercion, on the other, in what is commonly *experienced* as something other than compulsion. But this perhaps is the nature of disciplinary power described in subjectivation theory—being repressive and productive in the social implication of the psychic, as Butler might put it, or with the "individual only com[ing] into existence through the virtues of the collective of humanity," per Jaspers.

And so, what is important here is the significant overlap and telling divergences in the conceptual vocabulary for talking about person-making, especially where, like subjectivation, Confucianism offers an (a) relational, (b) discursive, (c) bodily, and, most importantly, (d) ritualistic notion of self. Moreover, this approach can rise above merely addressing the dilemmas of subjectivation to actually contributing meaningful solutions to the problems posed by subjectivation theory, with what David Kyuman Kim identifies as Confucianism's exemplary feature, namely, "the pride of place it grants to self-cultivation and the continuity it seeks between the different realms of the ethical life."[5]

As for (a) relationality, Roger Ames sees that "the Confucian project begins from a recognition of the wholeness of experience and the constitutive nature of relationality that is entailed by it. Moreover, because each person and event is constituted by an interdependent web of relations, what affects one thing affects all things in some degree or other."⁶ Such relationality needs to be distinguished from individuality, where relations exist but are merely superficial to the self, on the one hand, and collectivism, where relations not only exist but also obliterate the particularity of the self, on the other. This is what Ames and his longtime collaborator Henry Rosemont do as they describe the external relatedness of standard models of the individual self in contradistinction to a "focus-field" model emphasizing deeper correlational constitution (one might think of how atomically individual billiard balls with hard and fast borders relate to each other externally, while waves on the ocean are constituted *through* relations to other waves, as focal points of insistent particularity within the "field" of the sea). The following provides a visual depiction.⁷

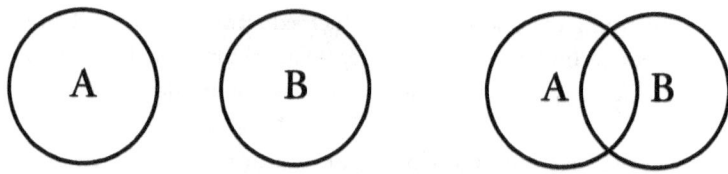

This leads Ames and Rosemont to emphasize that, within their reading of Confucianism, they are speaking of "unique personhood, *not* individualism."⁸ On this understanding, personhood still obtains in a meaningful way; there still is particularity. However, it is not any kind of particularity, haecceity, quiddity, or this-ness that would derive from some atomic psyche, eternal soul, or the like. Instead, such particularity emerges from real-world integral relationships with others, where one finds oneself—or rather one engages in the lifetime process of finding oneself as a kind of focal center for what is familiar—an idea expressed in the Confucian notion captured in the title of the canonical volume the *Zhōngyōng* 中庸, rendered with some poetic license by Hall and Ames as *Focusing the Familiar*.⁹ On this score, rather than being anything singular, a priori, and superordinate, the source of the particularity of the self is instead experience in all of its manifolds—a notion that lines up well with subjectivation theory.

On the other hand, there is the need to define such relationality in opposition to collectivism. There is the very real sense, in which the rights-bearing, atomic individual is neither part of the classical Chinese worldview nor of the classical Confucian worldview. Perhaps this difference and associated apprehension over Chinese and East Asian history lead to the fear that Confucianism ends up being nothing more than a complex justification of subservience to political superiors for the sake of a stifling brand of social "harmony." This is a notion that has been recently expressed in China itself with a good deal of fervor during the end of the imperial system in the early twentieth century and again during the Cultural Revolution following the rise of the Communist Party on the mainland, post-1949, where Confucianism was widely condemned for its role in perpetuating a specific mode of regressive, counterrevolutionary Chinese feudal subservience. And so there is a genuine worry.

In any case, even though it is rooted in the mundane, the comparison by Roger Ames of the greetings "every*one*, please stand up" and the corresponding Chinese phrase "*Dàjiā qǐng zhàn qǐlái* 大家请站起来" or "*grand family*, please stand up" illustrates a concerted emphasis on collective structures within the Chinese and, by extension, the Confucian worldview.[10] However, this does not make Confucianism collectivist per se, despite there being a clear stress on the self as understood in terms of social roles. As Roger Ames and another of his longtime collaborators, the late David L. Hall, explain:

> The identification of the person with roles is not in any sense a collectivist understanding. It is not a philosophy of self-abnegation in which "selflessness" is taken as a primary virtue. There is a very real sense of personal identity and self-realization, though one distinctly at variance with Western views. The roles defining the person are ritually enacted.[11]

They go on to explain the difference as principally residing in a distinction made by Confucius himself, between societies governed by law (where, in a Confucian, understanding, a failure has already occurred if overt coercion is needed) and societies governed by exemplary excellence and ritual practice, with Euro-American societies falling somewhat more into the former category and post-Confucian societies falling somewhat more into the latter.[12] As concerns a specifically Japanese context, this corresponds at least superficially to the popular distinction made by Ruth Benedict in *The Chrysanthemum and the Sword* between cultures emphasizing guilt and cultures emphasizing shame, with Japan being categorized in terms of the latter.[13] Despite this difference, Confucian views on society should not be seen as collectivist, for what is being stressed is not a denial of the self, but rather the value of appreciating the self as an ongoing project of situating of the self primarily in terms of roles—an idea that, again, is not too far from subjectivation theory.

Continuing this thread, similar to how Butler believes a "field of power relations . . . forms and frames the body . . . [and] brings it into being" through discursive speech acts, gestures, and hailing, Confucianism has its own view on (b) discourse being integral to personhood.[14] In a very deep sense, naming, or *míng* 名, provides one's lot in life, rendered by the nearly homophonous term *mìng* 命, and this indicates some manner of discursive determinism.[15] Hence, naming and the legitimate, normalized use of language together serve to ground social power. This is perhaps best captured in the *Analects*, the collection of sayings attributed to Confucius that stands as the central tome of the school bearing his name, and its passage concerning the so-called "rectification of names" (*zhèngmíng* 证明). Here Confucius puts forth that naming is the basis of speech, which in turn allows people to take care of everyday matters, through which ritual propriety and the arts, both deeply connected to the body, flourish, all of which ends up establishing social order.[16]

Key here is a connected statement on the rectification of names from another major *Analects* passage—unless titles are fulfilled in action, unless "the ruler rules, and the political ministers minister, fathers father, and sons 'son'" (君君, 臣臣, 父父, 子子), social structure is for naught.[17] Though a bit incongruous and anachronistic, Yeats' "Second Coming" springs to mind:

> The falcon cannot hear the falconer;
> Things fall apart; the centre cannot hold;
> Mere anarchy is loosed upon the world[18]

Conversely, things hold together to the extent that reciprocal relationships might obtain such that the falcon *can* hear the falconer, which is to say, when parents parent and children can still hear and respond effectively as children. Accordingly, the emphasis is not on abstract, universal ideals but on finding harmony in common real-world roles.

To achieve this type of harmony, Confucianism advocates education. But rather than using syllogism, reason, and Socratic inquiry, the method here employs a (c) body-oriented approach to self-cultivation through (d) ritual and musical performance in service of heightening awareness of social roles and the correct use of discourse. With sufficient and studied practice, attention to ritual can lead to a habituated, almost instinctive, sense of appropriateness. With ritual practice deeply embedding a sense of appropriateness, proper distinctions can then be made within language.[19]

This idea brings in another interesting point of connection to Butler's work, namely, that speech acts and hailing regulate the patterns and rituals that undergird social life. However, the twist is that, whereas Butler sees the subject as being formed and ultimately imprisoned by social rituals, Confucianism is far more sanguine about this prospect, particularly in its emphasis on the aesthetic, artistic side of ritual vis-à-vis self-cultivation.

For Confucian thinkers the watchword here is *lǐ* 礼, and this term, often translated as "ritual propriety," may represent the most significant point of connection with subjectivation and its approach to the intersection between ritual performativity and normativity. The importance of this idea of *lǐ* is perhaps only matched by the level of frustration that it begets in translation. Ames and Rosemont, in elaborating their view of relational personhood in Confucianism, go onto explain that

> persons are not perceived as superordinated individuals—as agents who stand independent of their actions—but are rather ongoing "events" defined functionally by constitutive roles and relationships as they are performed within the context of their specific families and communities, that is, through the observance of ritual propriety (*lǐ* 禮).[20]

It is clearly important, being a cornerstone of the notion of the relational self, but what exactly does this term *lǐ* mean? In its grander sense, *lǐ* refers to ceremony, particularly in the mode of ritual sacrifice, which indeed is indicated by the traditional form of the character (禮) depicting an altar (示) and a sacrificial vessel (豊). This is a convenient, if not coarse, translation, doing little to convey the role of *lǐ* both in the extraordinary and in the everyday. On the one hand, *lǐ* deals with ceremony writ large, particularly in the mode of ritual sacrifice. This broad notion of ritual includes not only ceremony but also the normal ways in which we show respect or deference, by using honorifics like "Professor" or "Officer." It extends far, stretching all the way to the varying subtle and silent glances that we use everyday to recognize family, friends, acquaintances, coworkers, bosses, subordinates, and so on. Hence, the term *lǐ*, which does not fully conform to English-language terms, either singular or plural, is often translated not just as ritual, but also as propriety.

However, *lǐ* also refers much more subtly not just to etiquette, but also to comportment, in daily life. Moreover, *lǐ* is often mentioned alongside cultural products, especially music, as something that gives one bearing, or, as *Analects* 8.8, 16.3, and 20.3 playfully iterate and reiterate, "knowledge of where to stand" (*lì* 立). Perhaps more instructive, here are the words of Xún Zǐ, who declares in his eponymous work's chapter on self-cultivation (修身) that

> [self-cultivation] suits living in times of success and is beneficial when living in poverty. This is ritual and being trustworthy.... That which arises through ritual thus runs through governance. If not arising through ritual, then it will be disordered and promote negligence.... If food and drink, garments and clothing, home and hearth, action and rest arise through ritual, then they will be harmonious and ordered.... If one's countenance, bearing, sense of propriety, and hurried steps arise through ritual, then they will be refined. Thus, a man without ritual will not live; an effort without ritual will not succeed, a nation without ritual will not be peaceful.[21]

And it is not just that this understanding of ritual *lǐ* concerns life; it also concerns death and loss, and here there is curious resonance with Butler's own understanding of how the rituals of subject life reenact and preserve scenes of constitutive loss in idealized forms. Within Confucianism, mourning serves not just as an exemplary context for *lǐ* in the sense of ritual propriety, rather mourning rites are *constitutive* of life in the everyday, of one's actions, and of sense of self, particularly in how such rites preserve experiences of loss on both a personal and a cultural level. Though there are a number of sources just from the *Analects* giving special attention to mourning, consider the core Confucian text, the *Zhōngyōng*, and its formulation of engaging in ritual and music on behalf of the dead, extending their affections, and taking up the affairs of the dead as though they were living and the absent as though they were present.[22] As the preceding passage of the *Zhōngyōng* makes clear, this notion of ritual propriety is not just limited in space to mourning proximate family members, since such deferential mourning extends to high ministers and to the imperial ruler, the so-called "son of heaven"; and it is not just limited in time, since this mode of ritualized life also extends back in time to early kings and *their* employment of rites of ancestral sacrifice.[23] Hence ritual propriety understood on these terms serves to bind rulers, ministers, fathers, and sons (and presumably women too, one hopes) to each other in a series of historically grounded analogies of family and state, where everyday ritual behavior makes present a network of histories of idealized loss and absence. This cashes out in real-world terms not unlike those of subjectivation where, in keeping with the core notion from the *Analects* of the "rectification of names," people constantly negotiate specific analogic roles like those of ruler, minister, father, and son in reference to ritualized ideals and hence in reference to ancestral mourning rites on a grand scale.[24] And so, despite not having the specific language of conscience, attachment, foreclosure, and the like, this notion of ritual *lǐ* makes explicit rather early on in Confucianism a constellation of thought similar to what Butler and her European sources have only more recently developed. The key here is the idea of everyday action ritualizing, idealizing, and preserving objects of loss on a cultural level far surpassing any one single person.

With so much conceptual richness and with this background dynamic of preservation and idealization (and even if mourning rites per se are not the focus of this or that given discussion), *lǐ* is difficult to nail down with a one-word translation. This proves especially difficult here, since what *lǐ* captures indeed cuts across a number of the behaviors, contexts, scopes, and realms at play in this interdisciplinary inquiry into human development.

Working in a manner that generally can be called rhizomatic in his engagement with classical Chinese sources, Roger Ames thus eschews more literal definitions of the one-to-one correspondence variety. He instead takes what he calls a "paronomastic" approach, using "definition by phonetic and semantic associations," where typically in "paronomastic definitions . . . a 'thing' reverts to an 'event,' a 'noun' becomes a 'gerund,' indicating the primacy and categorial nature of process. For example, the way (*dao* 道) is defined as 'treading (*dao* 蹈),' exemplary person (*jun* 君) is defined as 'gathering (*qun* 群),' excellence (*de* 德) is defined as 'getting (*de* 得),' and so on."[25]

When it comes to the particular idea of ritual propriety, Ames turns to the standard Chinese *Shuowen* lexicon, which "defines *lǐ* paronomastically as *lü* 履: 'treading a path.'"[26] Understanding ritual propriety in the vein of *lǐ* as being especially attuned to process, event, and the path trod in the everyday, Ames turns to the somewhat less appreciated descriptions of Confucius's actions because of what they draw attention to concerning "the slightest gesture, the cut of one's clothes, the cadence of one's stride, one's posture and facial expression, one's tone of voice, even the rhythm of one's breathing."[27]

With *lǐ* encompassing a variety of ritual phenomena, from the subtle to the grand, it is necessary to borrow vocabulary and conceptual support from the complimentary notion of *yuè*, or music, and to explore the explicit wordplay-based, paronomastic definitions underlying the idea of music in Confucian texts.

Performance, especially performance of musical and dance works, is key for understanding the general idea under discussion, since performance focuses and distills the subtle everyday gestures that belong to *lǐ*. In fact, descriptions of *lǐ* by Confucian thinkers often accompany remarks on music (*yuè* 乐). While *lǐ* provides orientation in ordinary contexts, participation in music/dance performance emphasizes ritual gestures and provides a novel context for learning where to stand. Confucius puts these terms together, playing with the identical Chinese characters used to render enjoyment and music, and says, "乐节礼乐," that enjoyment of music and ritual is a basis for self-improvement.[28]

A Background Vocabulary of Music in Reference to Ritual

Before getting into the specific view of ritual, music, and body-conscious social life that Confucianism offers, it is best to first look at the context of ancient China more broadly. The classical Chinese lexicon is key here, particularly as concerns harmony and rhythm. In both classical Chinese and contemporary Mandarin, their respective counterparts, *hé* 和 and *jié* 节, have noteworthy etymological connections.

Hé 和 signifies not just "harmony," but togetherness in a sense more general than anything having to do with music per se. Though originally having a culinary basis in the blending of flavors, this notion of harmony later came refer to sonic harmony.[29] This idea of harmony became so ingrained that it has come to stand for association itself, signifying the operator "and" in contemporary Mandarin, with the more specific use of connecting two nouns (i.e., "Wang and Chen," "apples and oranges," but not "walking and chewing gum").

Classical Chinese thinkers stress that harmony differs from and exceeds sameness in a way that brings together disparate elements, be they different tones in music or different people in society.[30] This sort of harmony is far from incidental, as seen in the syncretic philosophical compendium *Lü's Spring and Summer Annals*. Its passage "Great Music" contains a description of sound accompanying the emergence of bodily forms in the cosmos, bearing the type of harmony from which the first sage kings would fix principles for social flourishing, according to the cannon.[31] In fact, this idea connecting sage kings to sound is contained within the Chinese language itself, as explained in the following etymology from the later Táng dynasty:

> A sage (*sheng* 聖) is one who sounds (*sheng* 聲) and who communicates. This means hearing sounds and knowing circumstances, communicating with the heavens and the earth, and apprehending the myriad of things.³²

Likewise, Roger Ames and Henry Rosemont link the graph for sage or *shèng* in Ancient Chinese (聖) to sound where they argue that the character "suggests that the sages have the 'ears' (*er* 耳) to hear what is valuable to hear, and on that basis communicate or 'manifest' (*cheng* 呈) their vision of what will be."³³ And so, as will be shown, this kind of emphasis on sound and harmony generally guides the later emerging Confucian understanding of the music and the social rites attributed to those sage kings.

The term for rhythm, *jié* 节, is similarly complex. The character, having originally signified a bamboo joint and division, has a mereological connotation. From this sense of part and whole, a word family grew to include terms not just for musical rhythm and celebratory rites, but also for moral integrity, regulation, restraint, and control, all of which underlie this type of harmony's social and normative component. *Jié* and its associated terms thus point to an awareness embedded in the Chinese language of a deep structural relationship between music, rites, and social normativity.

Beyond the basic vocabulary of music, classical China had a number of canonical works on music that also prefigured more particular theoretical approaches to music and rite, especially within the Confucian canon. There is of course the *Book of Songs*, the compendium of lyric poetry that stands as one of the five classics upon which scholars like Confucius based their studies. The lyric poems themselves are the source of aphorisms and sentiments later taken up and expanded upon by Confucian scholars. They give the tradition a good deal of its direction, being used to sum up and justify Confucian arguments, somewhat akin to Socrates's use of myths of the underworld to drive his rational arguments home.

The connection between music and social order can be seen more directly in another of the five classics, the *Yijing* (popularly known as the *Book of Changes* or *I Ching*) and its description of how "ancient kings took up composing music to revere virtue, enrich the emperor, and to recall ancestors."³⁴ Moreover, yet another of the five classics, the *Book of History* (*Shūjing* 书经), also conveys the idea of music being tightly bound to social order. Here, the pertinent example is the court of Shùn 舜, later idealized by Confucius and his followers. Kuí 夔, the celebrated court musician for the mytho-historic leader Shùn, is credited with bringing order through his music, such that "when [he] strikes the stone, when [he] claps the stone, beasts dance and all of the officials assent harmoniously."³⁵ All of this is to say that, between terminology, ancient poetic verse, and the founding social myths of China, a common thread persists—music and rite, rather than merely being products of society, also actually produce selves and society, setting up social life as such.

Ritual and Music in Confucianism

The Confucian school, growing from these roots, thus offers a wide-reaching framework for rites and music, and this has the benefit of exposing the relative paucity of work on this topic within mainstream Euro-American philosophy. The most important notion here is ritual, or *lǐ* 礼 (traditionally 禮). This idea of *lǐ* occupies a conceptual space largely missing in dominant English-language terminology. It serves as the point of connection between music, standing in for the arts in general by way of synecdoche, as well as the social formation of persons. Additionally, this Confucian notion of *lǐ* expresses a bodily sensibility often missing in Euro-American approaches. This all cashes out in how *lǐ* serves as the pivot point between music, or *yuè* 乐, and the Confucian vision of bodily self and society. First, though, more needs to be said about *lǐ* specifically.

Confucian thinking turns on a link between the traditional terms for ritual propriety and the body—*lǐ* 禮 and *tǐ* 體. The phonemes are related, and the characters contain the same sacrificial vessel component on the right, *lǐ* (豊), with the left part of *tǐ* indicating bone or skeleton, *gǔ* 骨, in connection to the body. Leading present-day Chinese philosopher Cheng Chung-ying holds that, rather than referring to something like a singular static physical corpus, *tǐ* "refer[s] to groups of people organized for special purposes, and even to concrete things in the world . . . [and] to anything that has a definite form and style of organization, such as types of writing styles."³⁶

This view, where self-cultivation through *lǐ* occurs with *tǐ* as the dynamic qualitative process of organizing bodies, thus provides further conceptual background to the Confucian notion of musically centered rite. With such rich connotations, it quickly becomes clear that the richness of *lǐ* vexes translation. Responding to this, renowned contemporary Confucian scholar Tu (Dù) Wei-ming 杜维明 catalogs the English-language renderings of *lǐ* and includes "'ceremony,' 'ritual,' 'rites,' 'propriety,' 'rules of propriety,' 'good custom,' 'decorum,' 'good form.'" More to the point, Tu himself understands *lǐ* as "an authentic way of establishing human-relatedness" and as "the movement of self-transformation, the dialectical path through which man becomes more human."[37] Tu explains that the notion of *lǐ* "includes virtually all aspects of human culture: psychological, social, and religious," such that "in the Confucian context it is inconceivable that one can become truly human without going through the process of 'ritualization,' which in this particular connection means humanization."[38]

Likewise, comparative philosophers Roger T. Ames and Henry Rosemont, Jr., also call attention to the varied meanings and broad applicability of *lǐ*, describing this complex term as "a social grammar that provides each member with a defined place and status within the family, community, and polity."[39] It is on this conceptual basis that Confucian texts mention *lǐ* as part of a conceptual dyad alongside *yuè*, or music, as giving one bearing. Speaking to this point, Confucius repeats a bit of wordplay in the already mentioned dictum that *lǐ* give "knowledge of where to stand" (*lì* 立), and this addresses how the idea of *lǐ* connotes *tǐ* as a process of organizing bodies in social space-time.[40]

Accordingly, the concept of *lǐ* eludes capture by a one-word translation, since, per Confucius, it describes how things large and small arise.[41] Confucius again acknowledges the difficulty in general of speaking about *lǐ* (and music) where he asks, "In talking about *lǐ*, how could I just be talking about gifts of jade and silk? In referring to music how could I just be talking about bells and drums?"[42] Similarly, exaggerating *lǐ* and focusing on its grandiose elements by simply calling it ritual without qualification greatly misses the role of this social grammar in everyday contexts.

Xún Zǐ 荀子 on Ritual *Lǐ* in Regard to Distinction and Difference

The foregoing shows the broadness of *lǐ*, which can be difficult to comprehend. Fortunately, Xún Zǐ, perhaps the most extensive and exegetical thinker of the early Confucian tradition, offers a very useful framework for understanding *lǐ*. Riffing on the ambiguity in English, it could be said that, for Xún Zǐ, *lǐ* work to distinguish.

In the first sense, *lǐ* establish hierarchical and deferential relationships, where superiors are recognized as distinguished persons. For Xún Zǐ, *lǐ* "take common belongings for use, take the eminent and humble as prime for refinement, take disparity for distinction, take the lofty and the weak as necessary."⁴³ In his view, *lǐ* are part and parcel of how distinguished persons refine themselves, such that "*lǐ* trim what is long and extend what is short, do away with excess, add to the deficient, reaching to the refinement of love and respect, so that the beauty of conduct flourishes."⁴⁴

Secondly, *lǐ* also distinguish between things, because ritualized propriety exaggerates and clarifies the different roles that all people play, thereby aiding appreciation of distinctions within language and social life. For Xún Zǐ, being nurtured by ritual helps in becoming "fond of distinctions," so that "the eminent and the humble have rank, young and old are treated differently, the poor and rich each have different degrees of importance" with "distinctions between the noble who serve the noble and the vulgar who serve the base, the grandeur of the great, and the pettiness of the small."⁴⁵ In this sense, *lǐ* establish the terms of polite society by separating and focusing constituent parts of the social scene. Though not specifically dealing with Xún Zǐ and how *lǐ* distinguish, David L. Hall and Roger T. Ames describe how in this regard Confucian thought anticipates major themes in Jacques Derrida's neologism *différance*, the process of deferring and differing.⁴⁶ When thought along these lines, understanding the many senses of *lǐ*, grand and subtle, comes down to a common process—the continual and stratified coemergence of the singular and plural, of self and society.

Xún Zǐ on Ritual and Music

The centrality of *lǐ* within Confucian social thinking also makes music, or *yuè* 乐, a major topic, because musical performance focuses and distills the more disperse occurrence of social rites. Accordingly, Confucian thought treats *lǐ* and *yuè* as a conceptual pair corresponding to ordinary and extraordinary, onstage contexts for learning where to stand. Furthermore, music elevates ritual, bringing aesthetic pleasure and emotional enjoyment to *lǐ*. It is worth noting again here how Confucius puts these terms together, playing with the identical Chinese characters used to render joy (*lè* 乐) and music (*yuè* 乐), in the idea that joy accompanies ritual and music.⁴⁷

Xún Zǐ voices a similar sentiment at the beginning of his discussion of music, where he is less coy with his wordplay in directly stating "music is joy, being inevitable in human feeling."⁴⁸ The following passages then form the basis for his argument that music plays a necessary role in social life because of its connection to *lǐ* and to his particular theory of human emotions. This was necessary for Xún Zǐ because a general opposition to the Confucian understanding of music was a major platform of the competing Mohist school. Its leader, Mò Zǐ 墨子, believed music, despite its pleasure, to be ultimately superfluous to statecraft as well as a diversion of valuable materiel, and energy.[49] Moreover, Mò Zǐ held that music's common appeal distracts people from their proper and particular domains, taking the politician away from governance, and the farmer from farming.[50] Therefore, for Mohists, ritual and music are to be condemned.

Xún Zǐ targets the Mohists because of their failure to realize that, though ritual might divert from other supposedly more necessary ventures, the regulative value of ritual for those other ventures is profound. In Confucianism, there is a very real sense in which personal and social investment in music and social rites helps to secure social roles. It may not be something that pays off financially, but for Confucians, the wider social economy flourishes to the extent that "the sovereign reigns, ministers minister, fathers father, and sons 'son.'"[51] For Confucians like Xún Zǐ, this valuable knowledge of where to stand in social roles depends on rites and music, which therefore means that they cannot be superfluous, contra Mò Zǐ.

And so, Xún Zǐ goes to great lengths to claim that not only is music a worthwhile pursuit, but that it is integral both to statecraft and to self-cultivation, with a social value rooted in the nature of emotion. Here, Xún Zǐ presents what could be called a "hydraulic" view of human emotionality, meaning that in his view there must be suitable outlets for expression, lest pressure build.

Note that this is somewhat different from how music's social power might be seen now, that is, as being able to articulate social critique, protest, or general dissatisfaction. The conservatism of Xún Zǐ and classical Confucianism would preclude music that might breed anarchy. And it is precisely the specter of social chaos that necessitates room for at least some expression of emotion, even in this strict view. Xún Zǐ makes this clear where he declares, "people have affectionate and hateful feelings, but without joyful or angry ways of responding, there will be disorder."[52] So, contrarily, when a regime is attuned to the people and makes available appropriate musical outlets for emotion, joy is possible. This shows that, for Xún Zǐ, the equivalence between music and joy is not a given, but rather something to be achieved.

As regards the founding of personhood through musical/ritual self-cultivation, though, Xún Zǐ goes into greater detail, giving real content to this notion of joy in music, declaring that performing music clarifies the will; cultivating ritual perfects conduct. The ear and eye become acute, blood and bodily energy harmonize and balance, movements and customs transform and change, everything under heaven becomes tranquil, and everyone together enjoys what is beautiful and good. Thus it said: music is joy.[53]

This passage points to another related characteristic of music, namely, its ability to bring people together. In this regard, music affects the physical constitution of individual bodies, and, with that, the quality of how those bodies are spatially and temporally ordered in the social scene. This can be seen where Xún Zǐ describes how courtly music brings together the high and low and sets up deferential relationships between fathers and sons, older and younger brothers, and so on.[54]

This shows that the Confucian notion of ritual and musical self-cultivation is tightly connected to social stability, particularly as Xún Zǐ describes it. This may be in tension with the now commonplace notion of music being a vehicle for protest and of having the capability to engender radical critique of fixed social structures (and this being thought of as a good thing).

Likewise, there are internal critiques from within the Confucian tradition against Xún Zǐ and his approach to ritual/musical self-cultivation. The point of contention here is his particular way of taking the background of earlier Chinese thought on *hé*, cosmic harmony, as being related to music and ritual flourishing in humanity's terrestrial realm. Xún Zǐ argues that cultivating *dào* 道, which would include self-cultivation through ritual and music, means realizing the *difference* between humanity and the heavens.[55] For him, the establishment of ritual propriety comes from idealized mytho-historical sages like Yú 余, who, despite being granted no special favor by the heavens, set forth the rites and established society in a grand work attributable to forces external to human nature, work that joins inborn nature and external artifice and thereby unites the earth and the heavens as well.[56]

On the face of it this might not seem to be cause for worry, but here Xún Zǐ arguably violates a major tenet of classical Chinese and Confucian thought, namely, that the heavens and the earth are one, both in the last passage cited and in his controversial statement that consummate personhood means realizing the differences between the heavens and the earth.[57] This has the effect of making the court musician as well as the sovereign conducting society's rhythm into heralds for something like a transcendental *dào*. This is not unlike the notion, commonplace in post-Hellenic thought, that genius speaks to the artist from without, from beyond. In Confucian terms, this unorthodox approach is troublesome because it indicates the sort of oppositional dualism that the Euro-American tradition has been trying get past for centuries and that Chinese philosophers usually are keen on avoiding.

Despite this, Xún Zǐ is key for the notion that takes hold in the ensuing scholarly Confucian tradition—namely, that rites and music articulate cosmic harmony. This is what Erica Brindley has in mind where, in her exhaustive account "Music, Cosmos, and the Development of Psychology in Early China," she writes that "Xunzi's idealizations of music foreshadow what becomes normative in many later writings: a belief in the power of music to complete and fulfill cosmic operations."[58]

Putting aside (for the time being) the particularities of how Xún Zǐ stands in relation to the wider Confucian tradition, it is nonetheless clear that ritual *lǐ* and music are united and that this unity is central to the Confucian worldview. Put simply, whereas *lǐ* distinguish and separate, musical performance harmonizes and unites. Xún Zǐ expands on this, stating definitively that "music has harmonies that cannot be changed; ritual has principles that cannot be changed. Music unites; ritual differentiates. The unity of ritual and music conducts the human heart/mind. Music's emotionality deals with change at its most basic level."[59] This all fits with the later definitive statement in the historical chronicle, the *Book of Han*, which records Confucius saying that "to fix the governance of the people there is nothing more proper than ritual and to move custom there is nothing more proper than music," and his conclusion that "the two go together with each other."[60]

Moving the Classical Confucian Framework of Ritual and Music Forward

Recall the notion of harmony, *hé*, mentioned earlier and the stress on it not being mere sameness, but rather the melding of different particulars. Ritual and music, *lǐ* and *yuè*, affect this type of social harmony. *Lǐ* distinguish, while *yuè* unites. *Lǐ* stratify, thinning the air and setting up hierarchical social power. Musical performance intensifies ritual propriety while also bringing a commonly thick aesthetic element and emotional sensibility into the mix. In the Confucian vision, *lǐ* and *yuè*, rites and music, act together both to cultivate individuals and to foster social harmony.

However, observers of China's present or past may be wary of the term "social harmony," and with good reason. The PRC has at times used the idea of social harmony, with all of its Confucian resonances, as a rationale for authoritarian acts. This most definitely includes control of music, both through widespread censorship and the heavy-handed promotion of propagandistic "red songs" in the state media apparatus (e.g., the campaign led by former Communist Party up-and-comer Bó Xīlái 薄熙来 before his fall from grace in 2012). This view of music, rite, and social harmony was also tied up with the historical conservatism of imperial authorities, indeed to the point of being stifling.

With these types of thoughts in mind, Tu makes it very clear in his description of *lǐ* that he sees genuine problems occurring when this view of rite (and by extension, music) goes unchecked. For him, absent an internal sense of moral right to go with the external sense of performative rite, "*lǐ* becomes empty formalism . . . degenerat[ing] into social coercion incapable of conscious improvement and liable to destroy any true human feelings."[61]

That a certain coercive notion of rite and music has sometimes found a place in Confucian-influenced societies in no way negates the value of Confucian insights into the way in which *lǐ* and *yuè* are key to the development of self and society. The notion of rite and music described in the Confucian texts can be part of critical frameworks attempting to conceptualize how power enforces and propagates particular visions of "social harmony." However, it must be noted that, as regards modern sensibilities generally and the queer-friendly, liberationist views of thinkers like Foucault and Butler in particular, there are serious conceptual differences with Confucianism, particularly as concerns the heavy emphasis of the latter on ritual *lǐ* in support of a model of family stemming from the Warring States period (somewhat downplayed both here, admittedly). What must be remembered, though, is that classical Confucianism, despite its various anachronisms being sometimes difficult to square with the modern era, still carries with it a set of insights that is of immense value. Confucianism still provides conceptual material for a living tradition with its own apparatus for calling power and prevailing social harmony into question.

And so, the contemporary Chinese sphere has also seen a trend of critically engaging and reformulating the Confucian worldview while also retaining features like its notion of body-oriented self-cultivation. Perhaps one of the most important figures here, especially for English-speaking audiences, is Lǐ Zéhòu 李泽厚, whose work draws on several sources, including Kantian aesthetics, Marxian materialism, and classical Chinese social thought. With his extensive critical apparatus, Lǐ appropriates a great deal of generally Confucian vocabulary in his Marxian approach to what he calls the humanization of nature, where all human endeavors, all human artifice, including music in connection to ritual *lǐ*, play a deeply constitutive and historically sedimented role in human life, singular *and* plural.[62] This Marxian-Confucian view shows in his formulation that aesthetic experience first emerges "as the laboring skill harmonizes with the rhythms of nature."[63] With this in mind, Lǐ surveys the Chinese and Western traditions and finds that

> Chinese sages transformed and rationalized the power of the shamans into rites and rituals and interpreted these powers as manifested in music and poetry to be constructive. Western scholars considered the powers of the muses attractive and powerful, but whimsical, and a threat to humans' most treasured faculty: reason.[64]

Though there is a dearth of Euro-American resources for dealing with such topics, there is nonetheless a genuine *need* for a way to speak about rites, repetition, disciplines, and norms as part of a continuum alongside musical performance and the arts. Even though classical Confucianism accepts the terms of power far too readily for today's more critical projects, such endeavors still nonetheless stand to benefit from listening for consonances (and revealing dissonances) in how less familiar traditions explain social power in terms of rite and music. Though it is in a different voice, the Confucian framework of *lǐ* and *yuè* can nonetheless help contemporary philosophers from around the world in articulating a more comprehensive framework for dealing with the social nature of music, particularly as concerns the possibility of body-oriented self-cultivation.

Utilizing the insights of Kant and Marx along with a Confucian framework of *lǐ* and *yuè*, Lǐ Zéhòu presents a very illustrative and useful case in point here with his notion of subjectality. His work and its examination of the process of human development on a species level stands as a welcome complement to the respective approaches of Foucault and Butler to human development on more of an individual level in subjectivation, not just because of his historical sense (which, to be fair, Foucault and Butler share in various ways), but because of his attention to the aesthetics of ritual in human development.

In any case, Butler herself points to the need for an account of subjectivation that exceeds the self, which ends up sounding close to Lǐ Zéhòu's species-level approach to subjectality where she concludes, "Indeed, when the 'I' seeks to give an account of itself, an account that must include the conditions of its own emergence, it must, as a matter of necessity, become a social theorist," a sentiment echoed where she observes:

> We are not mere dyads on our own, since our exchange is conditioned and mediated by language, by conventions, by a sedimentation of norms that are social in character and that exceed the perspective of those involved in the exchange. So how are we to understand the impersonal perspective by which our personal encounter is occasioned and disoriented?[65]

Conclusion

The following builds on the argument being developed and summarizes what has been said here about Confucianism and ritual propriety or *lǐ* in anticipation of the theme of the sedimentation of normative ritual.

7. Confucianism offers an (a) relational, (b) discursive, (c) bodily, and, most importantly, (d) ritualistic notion of the self. It may not deal with the self-turned-on-self that is the subject, but there are many similar ideas at play. In this regard it lines up with subjectivation theory in terms of several major features.

8. Confucianism, unlike major Euro-American idioms, pays a great deal of attention not only to ritual but also to the deep, constitutive relationship between the arts and ritual. *Lǐ* and *yuè*, ritual and music, thus speak directly to the issues raised earlier. Here, basic, physical presence/appearance in the world and getting along with others corresponds to *lǐ*, while physical presence/appearance finding fuller expression in the arts corresponds to *yuè*.

9. Confucianism is a living tradition, and this framework of ritual and music continues up into the present day. Confucianism furnishes the background vocabulary for several recent approaches that relate to subjectivation. Perhaps chief amongst these is subjectality, a Confucian-Kantian-Marxian platform developed by Lǐ Zéhòu that uses this consonant vocabulary to examine sedimentation in the development of collective unconsciousness on a species level, thereby offering a complement of sorts to subjectivation's platform for dealing with the formation of consciousness on more of an individual level.

Therefore, taking the classical Confucian background captured in points 7 and 8 and extending this per point 9, a look at the development of species-level collective unconsciousness will help in bringing bodily cultivation to bear on sedimented and often unconscious norms, possibly changing the basic stakes of subjectivation. This calls for first turning to Lǐ Zéhòu and his notion of subjectality in human-species development as a prelude to considering other contemporary viewpoints.

Chapter 4

Subjectality

As humans, we began working together with tools to produce food and shelter for survival. Some of these practices became rituals and, as such, they became rites. The rituals were not just habitual and efficacious ways to do something; they became the correct way. Then language described and reflected these rites, and we learned the good and bad ways to act. Morality emerged. Mores became codified into laws, and laws became the social structures of institutions. From this perspective, institutions are codified ritualized group behavior, far more complex than primitive ritualistic behavior but a natural evolution of it, and they shape human psychology. In the future, I think science will discover the major distinctions between animal psychology and human psychology, and how much debt humans owe to the history of culture.[1]

—Lǐ Zéhòu

Preliminary Remarks: Collective Unconsciousness in Species-Level Subjectality and "Individual" Consciousness in Subjectivation

As has been mentioned, *lǐ* means ritual propriety, broadly connoting a social grammar encompassing everything from the subtly ritual-habitual to grandiose formalities and with relevance to musical theater and the coordination of bodies in the everyday in the basic ordering of leaders and subordinates as such.[2] *Lǐ* is a way of talking about social choreography.

And it is here that an element of myth operates in the Chinese account and in the account that leading contemporary philosopher Lǐ Zéhòu advances. There exists a long tradition within Confucianism of ascribing the establishment of language, music, and social order to mytho-historical sages like the much-lauded Yáo.³ Here it is worth again recalling Lǐ Zéhòu's observation that

> Chinese sages transformed and rationalized the power of the shamans into rites and rituals and interpreted these powers as manifested in music and poetry to be constructive. Western scholars considered the powers of the muses attractive and powerful, but whimsical, and a threat to humans' most treasured faculty: reason.⁴

With the constructive power of the arts so understood, Lǐ Zéhòu blends Kantian, Marxian, and Confucian precepts to detail not only how bodily, ritual self-consciousness arises through social forces, but also how unconscious social forces emerge as ritual technologies sediment over time.

This is the meaning of "subjectality" as understood by Lǐ Zéhòu, and this neologism addresses the historical roots of subject life and the use of collective cultural psychology as a tool in defining and refining human society. Subjectality is the term that he crafts to describe ritual's formative role in human social life and its artful use as a tool for human survival. Briefly, Lǐ uses Marx's statements on the "humanization of nature" and the "naturalization of humanity" to explain how shamanistic art, music, and rituals were tools for social cohesion operant in the early material economy of humanity's formative transactions with nature in pursuit of survival.⁵ Moving forward historically, Lǐ Zéhòu sees Confucianism as being particularly apt (but not exclusively so) at describing and formalizing the cultural/psychological edifice sedimented in subject rationality.⁶ Here sedimentation is meant in a way similar to Pierre Bourdieu's statement on bodily habit, or *hexis*, occurring such that "social necessity becomes [second] nature, converted into [sensori]motor schemes and bodily automatisms."⁷ Commenting on how the sedimenting of habit over time occurs in ways that outstrip any particular human being, Lǐ's own view traces the psychological construction of human nature to the history of tool usage, social interaction, and shamanic rites, with "the sediment of the human species (in its historical totality) [becoming] for the individual, the sediment of the rational for the sensuous, and the sediment of the social for the natural," concluding that "human beings alone possess some structure of cultural psychology."⁸

And so, working in terms of the sedimentation of ritual, discursive, bodily practice, Lǐ Zéhòu reworks the Confucian notion of "being inspired by poetry, taking a stand with *lǐ* [rites], and finding perfection in music"⁹ in describing the ritual formation of humankind's suprabiological body, thus making "noumenal humanity"/"Jung's collective unconsciousness" an object of labor, and thus aesthetically structured as a source of internal freedom.¹⁰

This does not ascribe to human nature any kind of robust and spontaneous goodness, as happens with simple readings of Confucianism and Mencius. Summing up his own view on human nature, Lǐ Zéhòu maintains, "Human nature is neither divine nature (since man has physical needs to maintain physical existence), nor animal nature (since man has the capability to control physical needs). Instead, it is the interwoven synthesis of the two aspects already mentioned."¹¹

And so, Lǐ Zéhòu loosely and somewhat implicitly follows the mainstream Confucian reading of the tradition's secondary sages, Mencius and Xún Zǐ, in his examination of what it is that distinguishes the human species from animals.¹² Here Lǐ reads the mainstream Confucian tradition quite narrowly, using insights particularly from Mencius to address how humans are naturally good at artifice.¹³ This means that humans have a capacity for building, cultivating, and ritualistically organizing *tǐ*-bodies in society, culture, and technology (in the dual sense of *techne* as art and craft). Here, Lǐ Zéhòu reads the sedimentation of artifice on a species level, albeit with his own particular notion of subjectality and the formation of Jungian collective unconsciousness.¹⁴ For Lǐ, we are "adept" at artifice, at society, at culture, at artfully crafting techniques and technologies, from early shamanic rites to more developed and doctrinaire religions, governments, and regimes of discipline and punishment, to organize and order what for him is a distinctly material collective unconsciousness.

Working with the Confucian sage's employment of ritual and bodily self-cultivation, Lǐ Zéhòu casts the sage as an exemplar figure for understanding the proliferation of the dual processes that Marx calls the "humanization of nature" and the "naturalization of humanity," where collective unconsciousness accrues and develops.

Lǐ Zéhòu holds that "the different formal structures, various proportions, balance, rhythm, and arrangements, which set out rules for so-called formal beauty, were first so by way of the labors of human beings as they labored on and operated tools."¹⁵ And it is in this regard that Lǐ sees labor and the organization of labor as primarily aesthetic, for, as he writes, "Aesthetic experience arose first from daily labor. It is the feeling of form combining with a feeling of success, as the laboring skill harmonizes with the rhythms of nature."¹⁶

Such aesthetic experience, shaped by daily labor, is deeply material and it accrues over time into a sometimes-opaque mass of historical practice in the course of sedimentation. And it is here that something like the language of forgetting enters the picture, albeit in terms of Jungian archetypes, of mytho-historic figures in the vein of Yáo, the Confucian tradition's ur-sage and bringer of ritual propriety. Lǐ sees these Jungian archetypes and the development of collective unconsciousness primarily in terms of sedimentation, writing that "the unconscious is not any so-called 'dim' animal instinct, but is a kind of nonconscious sedimentation achieved through conscious human exertion."[17] And so, Lǐ grapples with early human technical development vis-à-vis survival and mortality. It is here, with death, that, despite the lack of explicit phenomenological bearing on Lǐ's part, those familiar questions of authenticity, *tekhnē*, and time appear.

Writing more generally on the topic of mortality within the Confucian tradition, Lǐ writes:

> If life has significance and value then this allows the individual to end naturally without needing dread or grief, this is exactly the life-and-death ideal pursued by Confucian thinkers. If there must be grief, then that grief will really be about the very short span of life—time is too quick, and too short for understanding the value and meaning that one's life has. . . . And so, on the one side, there is a weighty lamentation of human life's impermanence, life's short span, and on the other a solemn historical feeling and a striking sense of purpose.[18]

He goes on to speak of emotionalized time in terms of attachment to existence and the course of humanity's historical development, describing how "time, in the passage of human history, takes on accumulated emotional, affective significance, with the perception of [time] attached to human life and of rigid, objective [time] differing, [and] becoming entangled in feeling and emotion."[19]

Claiming "emotionalized time" to be fundamental to the character of Chinese art and Confucian aesthetics, Lǐ then links emotionalized time, oriented toward death, to something akin to Heideggerian authenticity, writing:

> If time lacks emotions, then it is just a mechanical framework and identical blankness. If emotions lack time, then they are nothing but animal instinct and empty life. Only [with emotionalized time], looking forward (future), states of affairs (present), and memory (past), only then is there genuinely vital human life.[20]

Lǐ Zéhòu's Confucian, Kantian, and Marxian account of the development and proliferation of human technology points to authenticity being found in a specific mode of social artistry hearkening back to the sage. Understood in terms of this project, this means making conscious both the "forgotten" sediment of collective unconsciousness and the dynamic through which such sediment accrues and loss is preserved through ritualized normative idealization in response to the challenges of survival. Here, Lǐ Zéhòu points to authenticity being found in emotionalized time, where emotion emerges through a certain relationship to human mortality transacted through ritual techniques. In the project of this book, this idea underscores how ritual serves as a pivot of sorts between time as a *phenomenon* and measured by clocks and time on a *phenomenological* level situated between birth and death as subjects act in conditioned, patterned ways in order to secure recognition and continued existence.

Lǐ Zéhòu's reading of subjectality therefore demands that this authenticity be located, at least to some extent, in what might be called the position of the world observer in evaluating human mortality on a species level. Having an authentic relationship to death (i.e., one where future expectation and present state of mind are tempered by past memory) requires an ongoing attempt to unearth unconscious historical sediment and make it available as material for future conscious exertion. Such sediment far outstrips any personal-level giving an account of oneself. This line of thinking thus calls for something of an anthropological and archaeological sensibility in order to begin to come to grips with the long course of ritual technique running from the shamanic to the postindustrial age.

It is here in considering artful human development along the lines of Lǐ Zéhòu that Immanuel Kant comes back into the discussion, albeit obliquely. A specific reading of Immanuel Kant by Hannah Arendt and put into conversation with Lǐ Zéhòu's own work on Kant can point the way to what may be an unlikely account tying together aesthetics, art, purposiveness, human history, and the world observer. The key lies in a notion that only comes out in Kant's later political writings, particularly in the decidedly aesthetic turn made in his consideration of the historical progress of peace. The upshot is that thinking through Butler's notion of subjectivation in terms human-species survival can help in developing a notion of hope that draws from Lǐ and Arendt with the goal of doing something to mitigate, if not ameliorate, Butler's endgame of rage for the plight of particular oppressed subjects.

However, before bringing this idea of species-level hope to the general overarching problematic of society as productive/restrictive in subjectivation, what is first of issue is the connection of global events (here dealt with in terms of world progress toward peace) to aesthetics.

Within the constellation of thought including Kant and Lǐ (and not so much Butler or Foucault), this has to do with the way in which the ideals of beauty and international right (serving as a marker for human progress) both allow for a specific type of rational public quarreling reflecting private impressions and interests. To boil it down, there is no science of the beautiful; matters of beauty cannot be settled by dispute (*disputieren*), being instead a matter of quarrel (*streiten*).[21] So it is as well with international right, right?

Kant and the World Observer

True, the major image of Kant and international right is that of his work *Toward Perpetual Peace*. Much like the kind of mainstream free-market liberalism that has suffered a series of major rebukes at the beginning of the twenty-first century, Kant treats international peace as inevitable, as a natural and necessary consequence of the purposive arc of world history and the need of people to engage in trade, agreement, common cause, and the like.[22] According to this view, the world is arranged with resources distributed in such a way so as to "conspire" to lead individual nations, pursuing their own interests, to seek cosmopolitan interest. As such, something like a permanent congress of nations is supposed to form, guaranteeing perpetual peace for a mix of reasons owing to both nature and human constitution.[23] This makes it such that international right *should* prevail, owing to nature in the same way that gravity should prevail over raindrops, which is to say as an issue resolvable by rational, demonstrable dispute (*disputieren*).[24] Thus, in *Perpetual Peace*, there is a science of human events insofar as there is a science of events more generally. However, *Perpetual Peace* does not exhaust Kant's thinking on the subject, and his later shift proves intriguing for how he goes on to regard human progress toward the ideal of international right more in terms of the ideal of beauty and nondemonstrable quarrelling (*streiten*) over the beautiful.[25]

Kant strongly rejects his earlier optimistic assessment of *Perpetual Peace* in his later *Metaphysics of Morals*, where he writes, "[If complete establishment of perpetual peace and ending war] also always should remain a pious hope, we certainly do not thus lie to ourselves with adoption of the maxim to work unceasingly towards it; for this is duty," and where he goes on to decry approaches (like his own earlier view) that "see [reason's] basic principles [as] thrown in with the other animal species to the same mechanism of nature."[26] Rather than endorsing a permanent UN-like organ and seeing human progress toward international right and peace as a "real" thing, really extant in the purposive structure of nature, as is the case in *Perpetual Peace*, in this later work Kant instead treats international right terminologically as an ideal, insofar as it is a feature of its common rationality that allows humanity to strive to approximate what is not real in nature.[27]

Arendt's Remarks on Kant

Hannah Arendt's insightful reading of Kant's political philosophy proves instructive here. She ties this shift in Kant's view toward international right and peace being matters of judgment to the French Revolution, which "awakened [Kant], so to speak, from his political slumber."[28]

Ultimately, the reign of terror and its despotic, decidedly nonpublic "legislation" of rebellion would receive Kant's scorn. This is significant because of the connection to a diminishment of Kant's optimism with regard to reason and prudence leading to perpetual peace and to an emphasis on the theoretical publicity of right, all of which Arendt links to the powerful idea that social/political life, and indeed progress of humanity toward some approximation of peace, is a spectacle open to *observation*.[29]

In Arendt's reading of Kant, "publicness is already the criterion of rightness in his moral philosophy" and morality then is "the coincidence of the private and the public."[30] Thus, right and peace, being public, ought to be observable in world affairs. Arendt rather smartly reads Kantian judgment as being something common to humanity (which follows from the condition of possibility of genuine nondemonstrable quarrel) and she sees judgment as having an underlying structure of purposiveness.[31] Hence, progress toward peace, an ideal approximating the purposiveness of nature vis-à-vis human cultures, natural resources, and so on, resembles striving toward beauty, an ideal where purposiveness without a purpose is the goal. Arendt realizes this and draws out the implications.

Arendt is thus right in claiming that, for Kant, judgment must boil down to the observer and not to the object.[32] The world observer, and not the observed human world, is the key to any judgment concerning progress. And so, similar to how Kant raises intellectual taste above spirited genius in the consideration of the aesthetic attributes of artworks, Arendt holds that he similarly promotes the observer's vantage at the expense of the human spectacle itself and of any particular human genius therein.[33] Just like with judgments of beauty in art objects, the observation of human progress, and not necessarily the deeds of particular actors, serves as the locus for the ideal of peace. Curiously, it is the primacy of the observing perspective that may in fact be the reason for believing in the progress of humanity in the first place, despite its purposiveness very likely not being anything real, an idea cashed out by Arendt as hope.

Arendt describes hope for a better world and the possibility of human progress as a sine qua non of action in Kant's schema, though she herself sees the idea of progress as historically contingent.[34] Such hope is not about certain, unblinking faith in progress, in peace, or anything of the sort, and indeed Arendt catalogs Kant's use of the term hope in describing the French Revolution and then describing the remaining "pious hope" for perpetual peace in his later thinking, even after the dashing of his earlier and grander claims of such progress being beyond dispute. Here, hope belongs to the post-*Perpetual Peace* part of Kant's thinking, to the aesthetic turn where hope drives what is decidedly the *approximation* of the ideal of peace in consideration of *the* question of human progress—What should the world look like?

Of course Arendt's own approach to Kant, hope, and the idea of the world being a stage is not all smiles and sunshine, as she holds that "the alternatives for Kant are either regress, which would produce despair, or eternal sameness, which would bore us to death."[35] And hence it is that hope, which in Arendt's specific reading of Kant means *measured* belief in progress toward approximating a quarrelsome notion of peace, stands as a transcendental dictate *compelled* by the condition of the possibility of observing the human world. Hope is not something that comes after the fact for the merely optimistic. Rather than being about any kind of audacity coming after the fact of experience, watching humanity brings with it a *necessity of hope* a priori. It is beyond dispute that watching this world in which we ourselves live means in some way hoping for the world to improve, even if in setting up the arc of world history as an ideal concept without a real-world object we cannot help but quarrel about what that improvement might mean.

However, if the idea of viewing the human saga as a saga, as something *like* an artwork, represents an achievement of Kant (a point well argued by Arendt), then there is still more to the story. Even in Kant's approach to beauty, heavy as it is on the observer perspective at the expense of the art object's materiality, these other and perhaps lesser moments still exist. Setting aside the merits and drawbacks of Kant's emphasis on the individual rational judging subject, this account should not end with the world observer any more than Kant's does with the art observer and beauty in art objects. Hence there is the need to develop an aesthetic approach to human progress that accounts for the material object, here meaning the natural world.

Lǐ Zéhòu and Kant

The assertion here is that the work of Lǐ Zéhòu, one of China's most influential voices on Kant and aesthetics, speaks to this need by adding a much needed account of world observation in terms of the material dimensions of human survival within the broader environment to Kant's notion of the world observer vis-à-vis human progress in approximating an ideal of peace. Lǐ Zéhòu blends Kantian, Marxian, and Confucian precepts to situate the root of beauty, not in object artworks or in individual subjective imagination. Instead what matters in his account of beauty is the localized cultural sediment formed by human understanding and imagination on a species-level as it accrues and surpasses the natural necessaries of survival.[36] What does Lǐ mean by sedimentation?

Using sedimentation to refer specifically to "structures in process," Lǐ responds:

> By *sedimentation* (*jidian*), I mean that human nature, which is a cultural psychological construction of uniquely human capabilities, was formed from the historical processes of using tools, social interactions, and the rituals of shamanism. What is human has been sedimented into individuals, the rational into the sensuous, and the social into the natural. Simultaneously, the humanizing of the animal sensory organs of primitive beings and the natural psychological structures acquired the qualities of human nature.[37]

Lǐ goes on to say:

> As humans, we began working together with tools to produce food and shelter for survival. Some of these practices became rituals and, as such, became rites. The rituals were not just habitual

and efficacious ways to do something; they became the correct way. Then language described and reflected these rites, and we learned the good and bad ways to act. Morality emerged. Mores became codified into laws, and laws became the social structure of institutions. From this perspective, institutions are codified ritualized group behavior, far more complex than primitive ritualistic behavior but a natural evolution of it, and they shape human psychology.[38]

It might seem as though Hegel would be the natural point of connection for this historical, materialist, quasi-Marxist approach to human development. However, for Lǐ, "in certain respects, Kant was more perceptive than Hegel," bemoaning the latter's ceding of philosophy to epistemology and engaging in a kind of panrationalism that proved an "unhealthy influence on Marxism," a perspective befitting Lǐ's primary focus on Marx's 1844 *Paris Manuscripts* and his seeming disinterest in later Marxism and its more pronounced Hegelian influence.[39] Instead, Lǐ points to "Kant's great accomplishment [and how it] lay in raising the problem of subjectivity in a comprehensive manner," using Kant's clear distinctions as a framework for his own inquiry.[40] Summing up Lǐ's engagement of Marx and Kant, is Jing Wang (Wáng Jǐng 王瑾), who writes:

> On the one hand, he recognizes that Kant is the true philosophical predecessor of Marx, for Kantianism prefigures the materialist thesis of the irreducibility of being to thought; and yet on the other hand, Li Zehou is eager to foreground the idealist framework of Kantian epistemology (to examine the "subjective psychological structure of human subjectivity" in terms of the Kantian triple inquiry into epistemology, ethics, and aesthetics) as a priori for the rejuvenation of Chinese Marxism.[41]

Therefore in his influential Chinese-language work on Kantian philosophy, *Critique of Critical Philosophy: A Commentary on Kant*, Lǐ adopts major portions of the Kantian framework while at the same time significantly reworking its premises and orientation. Summarizing this early work, Lǐ writes:

> I repeatedly emphasized the determining function of human practical activity in molding man's whole psychological structure and processes. While practical activity progressively enlarges its

field and content following the advance of history, the foundation, though not the totality, of this practical activity is in the use and making of tools.[42]

This is what leads to Wang's comment that

> the Kantian influence is palpable in this definition as Li Zehou bestows upon reason an a priori synthesizing capability to order and constrain phenomena. . . . [But] the question that plagues Li's mind is certainly not the same that plagued Kant's: How is knowledge possible? Whereas Kant is concerned about the nature of the *restriction* of human knowledge, hence the ultimate inadequacy of the human mind to grasp the 'things in themselves,' Li is preoccupied with the *application* of human knowledge. A different question is raised: How can we produce knowledge for practical utilization?[43]

Lǐ goes so far as to shake the foundations of the Kantian edifice of epistemology by claiming that "the origin of mathematics is not analysis or induction but rather the basic practical activity of man."[44] This same basic argument carries over to ethics, where Lǐ talks about "moral heritage" likewise being a sediment of practical human activity such that "the individual's morality only exists by virtue of man's [self-aware], conscious, rational control, and this belongs in the realm of the establishment of man's subjectivity. Just as there is rationality sedimented in the sense intuition of epistemology, so there is sedimented in man's sensibilities of emotion, will, and wish."[45] This logic of sedimentation also applies to what Lǐ sees as the historical development of proportion, balance, symmetry, sense, taste, and the domain of art and aesthetics in general.[46]

However, and this is crucial, it is only in aesthetic experience where the sedimented character of human practice *shows itself freely* in sensuousness without being conditioned from the outset.[47] With the conditions of the possibility of *using* knowledge rather than of knowledge itself driving things here, what emerges is an aesthetic, material emphasis on the historical practice of the whole of humankind. The question of the world observer thus returns.

Here Lǐ speaks of the collective "Big 'I'" and the individual "small 'I,'" arguing that the locus of beauty cannot rest in the individual subject (genius or observer), since judgment and the apprehension of beauty is itself the ongoing sedimentation of historical practice, which takes place on a level of species purposiveness beyond "individual accident."[48] He mitigates this species focus somewhat by talking about residual Jungian archetypes sedimented in collective unconsciousness and the power of individual artistic genius to attune to this background hum, which Lǐ, specifically following Kant, identifies as a common sensibility. However, what truly matters in Lǐ's take on Kantian purposiveness is the overall trend of human social practice.[49]

For Lǐ, beauty's root resides not in art, but in the practice of the human species elevating survival and the relationship between humanity and nature beyond necessity.[50] For example, this means making it so that "eating is not merely due to hunger but becomes dining; the relationship between the two sexes is not merely one of copulation but becomes love."[51] Thus for Lǐ progress points to the general tendency toward increasing aesthetic practice, an expansion of aesthetic activity, and rising aesthetic appreciation that characterizes "the unceasing progress of the two parts of humanized nature [inner faculties and external world]."[52]

This approach to sedimentation allows for both the historical contingency and the felt necessity of cultural traditions, which is certainly not the case with Kant's more regrettable writings on human progress and racial determinism.[53] For Lǐ, freedom and beauty are best understood as occurring where human understanding of form overcomes natural necessity, sedimented on a species level, but locally and without presuming a general, universally valid form of understanding as such. Beauty in human progress thus remains a topic of open quarrel, like the beauty of art objects as understood by Kant. Thus the existence, nature, and end of any possible beautiful human progress remain open for discussion, being like matters of taste.

However, simply discussing the issue and being engaged in the issue of human progress presumes something of the would-be world observer; it presumes hope that the observed world might in fact progress. This is where Arendt and her reading of hope come back into the conversation.

Hannah Arendt and Lǐ Zéhòu on Kantian Purposiveness in Human Affairs

True, in her *Lectures on Kant's Political Philosophy*, Arendt does not take up Kant's thinking within a project as creative as that of Lǐ Zéhòu, given her more restricted task of expository lecturing. Nonetheless, her approach to purposiveness in human events within the framework of Kantian aesthetics ends up proximate to Lǐ's concerns. Moreover, her conclusion that hope is a condition of the possibility of world observation coincides with, yet crucially diverges from, Lǐ's location of beauty in the formal sedimentation of humankind's surviving and thriving.

However, what Lǐ issues as a quasi-ethical injunction with the "should" of scientific dispute, Arendt approaches more in terms of the "should" of aesthetic quarrel—there *should* be progress. For Lǐ, this means that technology and the humanization of nature should advance and neither stall nor go backward, since retrograde motion is by (his) definition "not a human ideal."[54] For Arendt, it means that human progress toward peace should advance forward even toward a hazy and indistinct goal, since this broadly Kantian notion of observing human purposiveness implies hope. The former "should" puts the human world on a level similar to that of physical objects, things with a demonstrable course and trajectory that *should* move this way and that. The latter "should," meanwhile, is more in the direction of nondemonstrable claims of beauty that one *should* find a particular object beautiful; it has more the flavor of "If I were you, I would also hope; *we should hope*."

Therefore the argument here is that, while Lǐ Zéhòu takes up Kant's terms with regard to purposiveness in the ongoing sedimentation of human practice, more could be added to his account by considering the implication of *hoping for beauty* brought by observing human purposiveness.

Arendt does this, in part, by looking at Kant's intellectual biography and then interrogating, in quasi-Kantian fashion, the conditions of the possibility of world observation of human purposiveness. In the end, she finds hope for an engaging, interesting, and *forward-moving* human spectacle to be one of those conditions.

Hannah Arendt's language, at least in her lectures on Kant, stops short of the next step, given her narrower remit there, but it is possible to imagine Lǐ Zéhòu advocating hope for a specifically *beautiful* human spectacle, and indeed the necessity of such hope. Even if world events dash ambitious disputative claims regarding human progress toward anything like perpetual peace, as they did for Kant, it might nonetheless be a necessary condition of human experience, each individually and all collectively, to hope for beautiful human practice to prevail.

What is to be drawn from such hope? Though it may be oblique, such hope, expressed on a species level can do something to improve the melancholy and rage marking subjectivation on an individual level. The seeds of hope that can be found in Lǐ Zéhòu's work on subjectality are particularly noteworthy here because of the way that his aesthetics-based understanding of the perspective of the world observer connects to the formation of the field of the conscious and unconscious enacted by ritual normativity in subjectivation.

Even if Arendt's specific reading of Kant is somewhat narrow in scope, this is provocative when plugged into her larger philosophy, particularly her positioning of life and "natality" as counterweights to notions of being-toward-death more commonplace in phenomenological discourse, and especially when this considered in terms of species-level survival and mortality. Instead of death, this notion of natality refers to the other side of the coin, to what is nascent, to what is initial and initiative, to the "new beginning inherent in birth" without which being and being-toward-death would be impossible.[55]

Using Arendt's wider framework, the Kantian notion of progress toward peace can be broken down into (1) deindividualized somatic labor undertaken by the group for the survival of the species, (2) work on artifacts that commemorate and give a sense of endurance to human labor, and (3) action that founds and preserves the political bodies that organize work and labor, thereby "creat[ing] the condition for remembrance, that is, for history."[56] For Arendt, all three—labor, work, and action—"are rooted in natality in so far as they have the task to provide and preserve the world for, to foresee and reckon with, the constant influx of newcomers who are born into the world as strangers," with initiative action in the political realm making it so "natality, and not mortality, may be the central category of political, as distinguished from metaphysical, thought."[57]

Connecting all of this back into Arendt's more focused reading of human progress toward peace on Kantian terms can help in fleshing out the meaning of hope vis-à-vis world observation. Hope, so considered, really does spring eternal. Action in the political realm always carries with it a sense of new beginning, since "without action and speech, without the articulation of natality, we would be doomed to swing forever in the ever-recurring cycle of becoming."[58] And so taking the view of a world observer with respect to the species-level sedimentation and development of humanity indicates how nascent creativity might be possible on a macro level and this may situate hope for locating embryonic growth for oneself within the micro level of one's own subject life.

With that said, however clear it might be that subjectivation and subjectality complement each other, there still nonetheless remains the question of what precisely is to be done with this convergence. Nonetheless, some initial directions suggest themselves.

First, with all of its connection to art observation, this talk of world observation points to the value of using Arendt's insights into the political to reassess how appearance works more generally in connection to recognition, the panopticon, and Butler's notion of subjectivation. Second, the move from theory to practice requires a juncture and a decisive turn in the form of memory with regard to ritual; but this must not just be about the kind of individual memory that common wisdom maintains is held in the head; instead, given the topics under discussion, what is important is the kind of species memory of sediment that lives in the bones.

Conclusion

Building on the argument established so far, subjectality's role in the argument is well summarized in the following points.

10. Subjectality complements subjectivation. Subjectality addresses how tradition accrues and becomes unfamiliar to itself over time. Lǐ Zéhòu employs Kantian, Marxian, and Confucian premises in describing the emergence of bodily, ritual self-consciousness through social forces and how unconscious social forces form through the historical sedimentation of ritual technologies of the self. His idea of subjectality thus deals with species-level sedimentation and the development of collective unconsciousness, whereas the idea of subjectivation places the emphasis a bit more on the side of the individual development of self-consciousness.

11. Subjectality requires something of the perspective of historical world observation. The perspective of the world observer brings certain other requirements along with it, namely, a broadly aesthetic perspective on species progress and a kind of tempered optimism regarding human development. This in turn may ground genuine hope for the plight of subject self-consciousness, with this prior hope being in some way accessible within the unconscious historical sediment of humanity's social and political life.

Taking points 10 and 11 seriously thus means developing an account of appearance, memory, and ritual technique with the goal of making the unconscious hope, aspiration, and creativity sedimented in human tradition somehow conscious within the subject's everyday conduct.

And so, now the inquiry turns to Butler's own words on appearance and how they connect to Arendt's notion of the political space of appearances. So understood, appearance, far from being secondarily superficial, shows itself to be of primary importance to how subjects emerge as subjects, thus making appearance a crucial part of the technology of subjectivation.

Following this up and connecting technology to memory, both Lǐ Zéhòu and contemporary French phenomenologist Bernard Stiegler variously and independently connect the sedimented rituals of bodily life that are initially performed for survival to the idea of memory in the collective unconscious.

This framework and its combination of the views of Arendt, Lǐ, and Stiegler in turn provides the basis for understanding bodily self-cultivation, particularly as presented in Richard Shusterman's work on somaesthetics, as a practical response to the pitfalls of subjectivation that aims to change the basic stakes involved. However, before making that practical turn to responding to subjectivation through an appreciation of bodily aesthetics on an individual level, more needs to be said about the framework for understanding appearance, memory, and technique.

Chapter 5

Technique in Appearance

> We do not make up the thing, and neither does the thing induce our consciousness. We are bound together, from the start, and in partially unknowing ways; if the object solicits me, I provoke it in turn, and if I provoke it, it answers back in some way or another. I am already in relation to this thing I seek to know before I find myself knowing it.[1]
>
> —Judith Butler

Preliminary Remarks: Apprehension, Appearance, and Concern

Here in this quotation Butler is talking about the *apprehension* of relational subjects and objects on a very general level through Alfred North Whitehead's relational process ontology and his language of *prehension*, which for him is "the activity whereby an actual entity effects its own concretion of other things."[2]

These considerations lead Butler to return to something akin to Althusser's scene of interpellation, where the self is hailed into guilty existence as subject when a police officer yelling "Hey, you there!" leads to a literal and figurative turning of the self upon the self. She writes:

> Someone calls me a name, but the name is already circulating in my world before I turn to answer that, yes, that is me, or no, you have made a serious error. I understand the name before I am constituted by it, and that gap works to produce a certain critical relation to the language to which I belong, prior to any consent I might give.[3]

She goes on to talk about how language in the discursive environment and the environment more generally "acts on me, but [how] the 'me' is not a passive surface or recipient. There is surely some passivity involved in being acted on, but it is also what enacts me, sparks my action, informs and prompts an agency that comes to be mine."[4] This is to say that one finds oneself thrown into a complex world before acting, conditioned by factors human and nonhuman, such that in Butler's 2012 work she flatly states that "the performative theory of action has to be resituated in a relational understanding of living organisms, human and nonhuman, to understand both what sustains life and what imperils it."[5] The previous examination of Butler's views on the performative aspect of micro-level subjectivation alongside Lǐ Zéhòu's reading of ritual in Marx's human-nature dialectic stands as an initial foray in this direction, pointing to the benefits of also situating the performative theory of action in terms of sustaining life on a species level.

Returning to her reading of Whitehead, for Butler, the most striking feature in his oeuvre is the idea that "the basis of experience is emotional," where "the basic fact is the rise of an affective tone originating from things whose relevance is given."[6] What precisely does this mean though?

After his beginning in mathematics and his early twentieth-century collaboration with Bertrand Russell to produce the landmark *Principia Mathematica*, Whitehead intentionally positioned his philosophy of process in opposition to mainstream analytic metaphysics and its most basic terms. As a result, his interrelated emphases on occasions over entities, events over things, and becomings over beings require a shift from conventional thinking and dominant vocabulary. Naturally, this complicates the task of parsing the already-vexing premise that "the basis of experience is emotional." Fortunately, though, what Whitehead has in mind, for all of his idiosyncrasy, is something that should be familiar to mainstream phenomenologists—care or concern for being. Whitehead goes on to elaborate:

> The Quaker word "concern," divested of any suggestion of knowledge, is more fitted to express this fundamental structure. The occasion as subject has a "concern" for the object. And the "concern" at once places the object as a component in the experience of the subject, with an affective tone drawn from this object and directed toward it. With this interpretation the subject-object relation is the fundamental structure of experience.[7]

Somebody well-versed in phenomenology might read this and think that, although there is some superficial similarity between this view and that of Martin Heidegger on the being of Dasein as care, Whitehead is only speaking about beings concerned for particular beings within the frame of experience and not about any loftier, more properly Heideggerian concern for being writ large.[8] However, such a view risks both misreading Whitehead and missing out on his convergence with the more familiar ideas of Heidegger on concern.

Whitehead is *not* talking about how an already extant subject comes to prehend and apprehend an already extant object through care, but rather how subjects and objects emerge as differentiated beings through relations of care or concern. True, Whitehead is more interested in "how it belongs to the nature of a 'being' that it is a potential for every 'becoming,'" with "the *being* of a *res vera* . . . constituted by its 'becoming,'" than he is in something like Heidegger's approach of raising the question of the meaning of being in response to this "most common and most empty concept."[9] Nevertheless, despite the difference in style and aim, Whitehead is using these terms "subject" and "object" to describe what emerges after the fact, and so in a sense what Whitehead and by extension Butler are each talking about is something like Heidegger's notion of concern for being prior to differentiation into particular beings and the emergence of the everyday ego. Hence, the notion that "the basis of experience is emotional" should make at least some sense to those familiar with phenomenology. Using this as a starting point helps in understanding how constitutive subject-object relations are driven by an emotion of concern. In terms of the platform of subjectivation advanced by Butler, this could be said to coincide with the desire to persist in being as type of a felt vulnerability, susceptibility, asymmetry, and insufficiency.

Returning to subjectivation and the would-be subject's felt vulnerability, the infant being recognized and gendered certainly *feels* profoundly helpless, and this is *felt* and picked up on by the family and doctors who hear the cry and coax the infant to acting out the role of a good little boy or good little girl, where the infant then interprets (and often misinterprets) the enigmatic noises hailing them into being this and/or that.[10] Likewise, the person walking on the street *feels* vulnerable and the police officer *feels* vulnerability, sensing a weakness or at least an openness in those on the scene before any hail or turn is made. Panoptical prisoners each *feel* that they could be called to account prior to any one of the thousands of everyday and often innocuous calls to act out roles and rituals for the sake of recognition in the course of subject life. These feelings of concern, on all of these hypothetical and paradigmatic levels, mark the formation of the boundary between object world and subject ego from its very inception and they suffuse the ego's more particular feelings, inclinations, volitions, and so on. Here, relevance is felt and experienced emotionally in the unknowing connections that come before the emergence of any particular subject or object (or with existential concern occurring before any "will, wish, bias, and drive" [*Wille, Wunsch, Hang und Drang*] as Heidegger might say).[11] For Butler, this emotional relevance conditions the apprehension of objects as being relevant or irrelevant to life and to continued existence, which amounts to the apprehension of bodies potentially being recognized and thus mattering.[12]

After Butler's *Psychic Life of Power*, there has been an explicit and increasing emphasis on the aesthetic in her approach to subject life. Her engagement with Whitehead and the emotional basis of experience in her essay "On This Occasion . . ." stands as an initial step in this direction. This trend has continued with her more recent work *Senses of the Subject*, which has seen Butler further this aesthetic turn, as can be seen where she speaks of "the threshold of susceptibility that precedes any sense of individuation," which remains inscrutable, since "I say that I am already affected before I can say 'I,' I am speaking much later than the process I seek to describe."[13] In language that recalls her formulation of the body as a type of unintelligible Aristotelian prime matter beyond language that then is stamped and brought into being in the form of discursively given norms, Butler further describes this felt susceptibility, writing, "norms form us, but only because there is already some proximate and involuntary relation to their impress; they require and intensify our impressionability."[14]

Butler goes on to clarify with more precision her terminological notion of susceptibility, writing:

> The unwilled character of this dependency is not itself exploitation, but it is a domain of dependency that is open to exploitation, as we know. Further, susceptibility is not the same as subjugation, though it can clearly lead there precisely when susceptibility is exploited (as often happens when we consider the exploitation of children, which depends on an exploitation of their dependency and the relatively uncritical dimensions of their trust). Susceptibility alone does not explain passionate attachment or falling

in love, a sense of betrayal or abandonment. Yet all those ways of feeling can follow, depending on what happens in relation to those who move and affect us and who are susceptible to us (even susceptible to our susceptibility, a circle that accounts for certain forms of affective and sexual intensity).[15]

Without collapsing Butler's distinction between susceptibility and passionate attachment, the claim being made here is that working on, laboring on, and improving access to awareness of aesthesis as feeling, with what Butler calls the "the relational dimensions of embodiment: passion, desire, touch," can help in negotiating the passionate attachments that form subject life.[16] In these writings Butler makes her turn to the aesthetic aspect of subject relationality rather clear. In considering the vulnerable, inscrutable, bodily not-quite "I" that proceeds the production of an intelligible subject, Butler holds that

> what follows is that form of relationality that we might call "ethical": a certain demand or obligation impinges upon me, and the response relies on my capacity to affirm this having been acted on, formed into one who can respond to this or that call. Aesthetic relationality also follows: something impresses itself upon me, and I develop impressions that cannot be fully separated from what acts on me.[17]

And again without collapsing the distinction between aesthetics and art, the further claim being made here is that art manifests those relational dimensions of embodiment in a superlative fashion with implications for the artful techniques that go into forming the feeling, susceptible, and relational subject. There are, in Butler's words, a series of technological, structural, and institutional supports that condition bodily emergence, and these supports, active and passive, "are already acting on a body with various degrees of success and failure, acting on a localized field of impressionability for which the distinction between passivity and activity is not quite stable and cannot be."[18] The response here is that qualitative improvement beyond mere success and failure (for whom?) might be possible by taking supports of subject life like feeling, vulnerability, and appearance as media for artistic technique. Reclaiming and refashioning these supports might make it possible to build up a bodily edifice more refined and welcoming than a prison formed from darkly artistic surveillance technology.

Stepping back to consider the aims of this particular project, it seems clear that looking at species-level ritual technologies from the perspective of the world observer, as happens with subjectality, represents one way of expanding upon Butler's work. This lends itself to further rhizomatic growth, as Butler's own words point to a connection between affective, felt relevance and the way in which things are given as subject and object—a connection which can be assessed with more of an eye to the species level. To that end, this therefore means bringing phenomenology to bear in order to develop an account of this link in terms of *apprehension* and *appearance* and to consider the possibility of refining appearance as a matter of technique.

With the premise being that emotion in the form of concern serves as the basis for the way in which subjects and objects appear and are apprehended in general, it seems that such concern ought to underlie how apprehension functions as part of subject recognition within a virtual panopticon. If such recognition occurs through interpellation and scenes of address, then the brute appearance of the players on the scene ought to have an emotional quality, one that Butler describes in terms of vulnerability and a desire to persist in being. Appearance in the world and its quality of felt vulnerability is why the self turns back upon itself and submits to the call of authority. This exposure is the emotional basis of subject experience.

Butler is clear that apprehension is prior to recognition.[19] Appearance should be prior as well. Appearance *is* the basic mode of givenness here; it is the manner of relevance for encounters of recognition. Moving away from Butler just for the moment, recall Arendt's insight that appearance and being are but two sides of the same coin.[20] Finding a resource in Arendt's drawing together of reality and appearance, *Sein und Schein*, in the political realm makes sense here given the culmination of surveillance in the constitutive panopticon. For Arendt, appearance is not some superficial layer on top of a substrate of being. Appearance cannot be separated from being in the plural world, and this makes the connotations of quality and aesthetic sensation that come when appearance is actually central to being. Being in the political world involves feeling and quality in appearance in a rather comprehensive way. This all serves to highlight how appearance, apprehension, and the aesthetic domain do more than just dance about on surfaces and instead pervade the very depths of subject life, with it being the inevitability of appearance and exposure on the social-political scene that drives the recognition of subjects within that space.

Now, at this point a word of caution is advised against reading appearance too narrowly in terms of vision. True, there is a tendency toward scopophilia in the Euro-American tradition that lurks even in the notions of more transgressive critical theorists, with Foucault's panopticon serving as a rather obvious example (though Althusser's interpellative hail stands as a similarly obvious counterexample). In any case, it is clear that the aesthetic dimension of appearance and the way in which subjects organize can be dealt with other than visually, as the link in the Chinese lexicon between ritual and musical theater suggests. Appreciating the political space of appearance in terms apart from just the visual sense (even if that is still dominant) adds a needed richness to the account—a need pointed to in Butler's own recent work *Senses of the Subject*, and its exploration, through Maurice Merleau-Ponty, of a synaesthetic intertwining of vision, language, and touch in scenes of inaugurating address and recognition.[21]

With this proviso in mind, the call here is to understand apprehension as twinned with appearance, where the appearance of the vulnerable and the apprehension of vulnerability occur prior to the harmful (mis)recognitions through which subjectivation occurs. Put another way, in an undifferentiated moment before any call can be issued and any misqualified, malqualified, or unqualified type of recognition can take place, one has to appear, appear vulnerable, and be apprehended as vulnerable. Put yet another way, even if there is no gap between the apparently simultaneous moments in the everyday perception of time, one still has to show up before being apprehended, let alone before being apprehended *as* recognizably this or that.

And so, the further suggestion here is that it is possible to appreciate how appearance is a tool just like any other—a tool and technique used to effect the emergence of subjects—meaning that relative mastery of the technique is possible. Here, it is not just the what, but the how; it is not just appearance, but *the mode and quality of appearance* that matters. This quality of appearance is what can be improved, albeit with considerable time and effort being needed to upset established habit and refashion the way in which subjects initially appear on the scene prior to encounters of recognition.

Taking a cue from Confucianism and regarding the idea of ritual *lǐ* as appreciating appearance as not just a technique, but as a technique where qualitative improvement might be possible, and extending this with Bernard Stiegler's analysis of memory, the further claim here in this section is that something profound is forgotten when subject life becomes all about interpellation and being pejoratively hailed into existence.

What is lost is the wider field of possibility for appearance. What is lost is the idea of appearance on the social scene occurring through something other than a hail, something other than being called out. What is lost is the idea of appearance in a world with others occurring not just in the mode of "calling *out*" but in the mode of "calling *to*," which is to say not just in terms of hailing but also in terms of beckoning, or perhaps gathering (*Versammlung*).

What is important here is not the way in which artworks might help in coming to terms with this or that particular loss, since artworks are unlikely to commemorate, in direct fashion, one's dead parent or one's lost and unspeakable desires for this or that person or group (though there certainly are a wide variety of memorial and requiem artworks fitting this description). The key is not the way in which artworks help in dealing with this or that loss, but rather how they help in rethinking the very notions of loss, absence, and permanence that mark the implicit calculus underlying the bargains for survival compelled in the course of subject life.

Artworks can radically alter the dynamics of subjectivation here, because they are able to arrest attention without threatening actual arrest, like the hypothetical interpellating police officer does. Artworks *call to* rather than *call out*. Artworks can touch subjects without pushing them. Artworks can "look" back at a person without necessarily binding them within a purposive gaze.

This stands as a qualitatively different type of relationship between subject and object. With artworks, the constitutive intertwining of appearance and being still occurs, albeit in a different mode. Appreciating artworks and appreciating oneself, one's being, and human being generally in terms of artworks can help in pursuing what Bernard Stiegler terms "the politics of memory" by making conscious what is so often left unconscious in how the human condition appears in the world. Turning to art, artistry, and artfulness can help in realizing how certain possibilities for subject life have been lost and understanding that the common mode of appearance is contingent and could indeed be otherwise. Appreciating art can help in appreciating appearance itself as a tool and technique to be refined. Moving beyond the subjectivating, interpellating small-talk that calls subjects to skin-tight cells within the world of the panopticon, a more salutary type of calling might then be possible, and this might bring a bit of dignity and perhaps nobility to how subjects appear in the world.

It becomes clear that this talk of technique in appearance connotes a turn to phenomenology. Within the macro level of this project and its engagement with human species development, terms like being-toward-death and sedimentation have already become part of the discussion and so there is already something of a natural rhizomatic point of connection to phenomenology, generally speaking. Further growth in this direction calls for an approach that combines being with appearance in a way that addresses the possibility of technique unearthing some of the forgotten sediment that accrues prior to subjects apprehending/being apprehended by others.

The approach here takes Hannah Arendt's view on the inseparability of being and the space of common appearance, which has already been introduced, and Bernard Stiegler's more recent work on technique and memory to address this challenge.[22] Examining, critically analyzing, and reappropriating a combination of these phenomenological insights can show how it might be possible to refine and improve the quality and emotional tenor of the vast manifold of everyday scenes of interpellation and recognition by making the most out of the sedimented material of the panopticon and the relationships that it enables. This language of refining technique in appearance will cash out next chapter in a look at ritual bodily cultivation as described by Richard Shusterman in his platform of somaesthetics and a reconsideration of the Confucian roots of the issue, all of which will point to the possibility of changing the basic stakes of subject life as understood by Butler. First, though, something needs to be said about how Bernard Stiegler also adds to this line of thought with his understanding of such rituals along the lines of the exemplary basic tool and ur-technology of Hellenic and post-Hellenic mythology and philosophy, fire.

Stiegler on Technique and Memory

Fire! Fire! Fire! This is what Prometheus brought, yes? This is what defines humanity; this is what defines technology; this is what defines how the two are intertwined. We humans are human because we, having learned from Prometheus's transgressive gift, make fire—end of story.

If only things were so simple and the story could be boiled down to Prometheus's wrath against the gods and his refusal to submit to Zeus. Indeed, ironies abound with the myth of Prometheus. Of course, the story serves as an influential and enduring cultural archetype of the notion of contesting the powers that be (as is illustrated in the then-contemporary editorial cartoon likening a strident young Marx to a modern-era Prometheus, with his liver being pecked by an eagle for his defiance of the Prussian censors).[23] Indeed, in the youthful estimation of his doctoral dissertation, Marx deems Prometheus to be "the most distinguished saint and martyr in the philosophical calendar" for having raged against the gods and having prefigured the humanist enterprise of philosophy in terms of repudiating those who do not recognize "human self-consciousness . . . as the highest divinity."[24] However, beyond the basic fact of Prometheus's defiance, the story is also important for the point that it makes about how a dual structure of memory and forgetfulness are constitutive of technological human life. The story's origin is based on forgetfulness—on forgetfulness of how humanity is to be defined and how it is to survive—and somehow, amid all of this, Prometheus's *other* gift is itself ironically forgotten, the flame being so transfixing and his sacrifice so great.

This is just part of Bernard Stiegler's view. Working in terms of both phenomenology and the early writings of Marx, Stiegler goes on to describe how the proliferation of "technization" leads humanity to a profound forgetfulness, where access to origins is lost and remembering "originary temporality" occurs through attention not to organic or inorganic matter, but to how we organize matter, that is, to how techniques aesthetically temporalize existence.

As mentioned, contemporary Chinese philosopher Lǐ Zéhòu provides a similar perspective. Following Confucius, he describes early sages elevating shamanic practice in the development of ritual, language, art, and music, and how this occurs in the early proliferation of what Marx calls the humanization of nature and the naturalization of humanity. This is to say that the ritual and discursive arts are themselves material factors in the economy of how human society survives and thrives. Being material, ritual practice grows over time, but in a matter that covers itself over, almost like epochal geological strata, almost like sediment. For Lǐ, forgetfulness sets in as habits then sediment in the most basic use of religious-aesthetic-normative technologies, forming something akin to a Jungian collective unconsciousness, in ways similar to, but crucially different from, Stiegler's view.

And so, Stiegler and Lǐ independently converge in showing how humanity has always had an aesthetic bearing rooted in the ritualized organization of labor and material and why we ceaselessly work to forget this. The contention here is that Stiegler and Lǐ are describing the technology of social ritual in similar ways and that this is connected with a very particular mode of forgetfulness. Simply put, we forget in order *to survive*, and we forget that we have forgotten. And this too is in order *to survive*.

Well then, what has been forgotten? The myth of Prometheus may provide clues, if only indirectly and by way of allegory. In the lay and lazy retelling of the myth, Prometheus, so full of hubris, snatches fire from the gods and brings it back for earthbound humans to enjoy, marking the birth of *Homo sapiens* as such.

However, as Stiegler deftly argues, this profoundly and very ironically misses the point of the Promethean myth. Setting aside the more famous, but perhaps less conceptually rich, telling of the myth in Aeschylus's *Prometheus Bound*, consider the version of the Prometheus myth recounted in Plato's *Protagoras*:

> There once was a time when the gods existed but mortal races did not. When the time came for their appointed genesis, the gods molded them inside the earth, blending together earth and fire and various compounds of earth and fire. When they were ready to bring them to light the gods put Prometheus and Epimetheus in charge of decking them out and assigning to each its appropriate powers and abilities. . . .
>
> To some he assigned strength without quickness; the weaker ones he made quick. Some he armed; others he left unarmed but devised for them some other means for preserving themselves. He compensated for small size by issuing wings for flight or an underground habitat. Size was itself a safeguard for those he made large. And so on down the line, balancing his distribution, making adjustments, and taking precautions against the possible extinction of any of the races.
>
> After supplying them with defenses against mutual destruction, he devised for them protection against the weather. He clothed them with thick pelts and tough hides capable of warding off winter storms, effective against heat, and serving also as built-in, natural bedding when they went to sleep. He also shod them, some with hooves, others with thick pads of bloodless skin. Then he provided them with various forms of nourishment, plants for some, fruit from trees for others, roots for still others. And there were some to whom he gave the consumption of other animals as their sustenance. To some he gave the capacity for few births; to others, ravaged by the former, he gave the capacity for multiple births, and so ensured the survival of their kind.
>
> But Epimetheus was not very wise, and he absentmindedly used up all the powers and abilities on the nonreasoning animals; he was left with the human race, completely unequipped. While he was floundering about at a loss, Prometheus arrived to inspect the distribution and saw that while the other animals were well provided with everything, the human race was naked, unshod, unbedded, and unarmed, and it was already the day on which all

of them, human beings included, were destined to emerge from the earth into the light. It was then that Prometheus, desperate to find some means of survival for the human race, stole from Hephaestus and Athena wisdom in the practical arts together with fire (without which this kind of wisdom is effectively useless) and gave them outright to the human race. The wisdom it acquired was for staying alive; wisdom for living together in society, political wisdom, it did not acquire, because that was in the keeping of Zeus. Prometheus no longer had free access to the high citadel that is the house of Zeus, and besides this, the guards there were terrifying. But he did sneak into the building that Athena and Hephaestus shared to practice their arts, and he stole from Hephaestus the art of fire and from Athena her arts, and he gave them to the human race. And it is from this origin that the resources human beings needed to stay alive came into being. Later, the story goes, Prometheus was charged with theft, all on account of Epimetheus.[25]

As Stiegler explains, Prometheus "makes no sense by itself," since it is the dyad between Prometheus's farseeing prudence and Epimetheus's forgetful, too-late memory that forms the narrative.[26] And so he insists on not approaching the question concerning technology in solely Promethean terms. A certain mode of Epimethean forgetfulness is key.

What does this mean for humanity though? And what does this mean for appearance? Stiegler's reading of the myth contends that "humans are the forgotten ones. Humans only occur through their being forgotten; they only appear in disappearing."[27] Echoing Butler's formulation of a constitutive "double loss" where what is lost in surviving as a subject is itself lost as a loss that might be grievable and speakable, it could be said that for Stiegler, on a species level, humans survive by forgetting and then forgetting that they have forgotten.[28]

Why focus on this particular creation myth, then? Why focus on this notion of forgetting and disappearing? Why and whence Prometheus?

For Stiegler, the key point, independent of any particular Attic Greek allegory, is the vulnerability of humans, which is described in the Promethean myth in terms of a lack of survival traits. This compels technology. This impels technology as prosthesis. This propels technological prosthesis outward, humanizing nature, but also crucially naturalizing humanity, in the sense described by Marx.[29] Despite being originally disposed to survival, *tekhnē*, and with it the temporality of being-toward-death, eventually sediments over time, and, for Stiegler, this constitutes epiphylogenesis, "a rupture with *pure* life" and "*the pursuit of evolution of the living by means other than life.*"[30] This epiphylogenetic emergence is key for humanity and humans, bridging the micro and the macro levels, for it "bestows its identity upon the human individual: the accents of his speech, the style of his approach, the force of his gesture, the unity of his world."[31] From this epiphylogenetic sedimentation, this social *and* biological evolution, tradition grows. *Tekhnē* proliferates in technological traditions, which, being seduced by their own respective narrative histories of progress, lead humans to start to care for a vulgar conception of time, making any sense of originary temporality long forgotten, with the accumulated faults leaving humans in default of origin.[32] This default or fall is "*exteriorization.*"[33] This fall and its abyss take place as the interplay between deficiency vis-à-vis material property for survival (*impropriété*) and supplementary prosthesis creates a scission, an instrumental ur-separation mediating inner and outer, which, in Stiegler's more particular reading of Rousseau, stands as the origin of inequality.[34]

It is important to note here, too, as Stiegler does, that this fall is not just about Promethean fire and that the oft-forgotten practical arts play a crucial role. This is so because, for Stiegler, the two emerge together as a pair, where once again the key is a certain type of forgetfulness springing from excessive care for technology as prosthetic and external—"Fire! Fire! Fire!" indeed.

Taking a broader view, Stiegler defines techniques (*tekhnē*) in terms of savoir-faire or skill, and he points to "politeness, elegance, and cuisine" as examples. For him, only with the latter, cuisine, is technique "*productive*" in the sense of outward manufacture, where *poiēsis* occurs with an artisan (often in command of fire) serving as the efficient cause.[35] As a result, instead of logos, mythos, and cultural rites being thought along the lines of technique and technology, the control and manipulation of fire stands as the dominant model. And so, on yet another level, this narrow focus on technology in the mode of external manipulation leads humanity to a profound forgetfulness, a Promethean-Epimethean forgetfulness. Due to the basic external nature of humanity's technological prostheses, where sediment accrues and leads to traditions, access to origins is lost, and this dynamic generates an illusion of succession and an inauthentic sense of time.

For Stiegler, the only way to access authentic "originary temporality," is through attention neither to humanity's inner organic matter nor to the world's external inorganic matter as such. Calling to mind Derrida's varied words on possible readings of Heidegger as anthropocentric, Stiegler issues his own assessment of shortcomings in how Heidegger conceives of the "dynamic of organization," instead holding that what grants authentic access are techniques that themselves organize, enacting the split between interior and exterior, between the subject and the object, between the technician and the material.[36] With sedimentation occurring along historical, cultural, and economic vectors and concealing the temporality of techniques, a narrative emerges with the interior subject, the technician, and Aristotelian efficient cause at its center, standing over objects in the natural world and mastering increasingly dehumanizing technologies at the cost of authentic technique.[37]

And so Stiegler issues a call for "a politics of memory" that "would be nothing but a thinking of technics (of the unthought, of the immemorial) that would take into consideration the *reflexivity* informing every orthothetic [exact and putatively lossless recording/inscription] form insofar as it does nothing but call for reflection on the originary de-fault of origin."[38]

Here, we have a concise, though dense, statement of Stiegler's view, whereby the same forces that prompt Heidegger's *Being and Time*, the loss of the question of the meaning of being, are also the same forces that lead to the subject-who overshadowing the object-what, with the world set apart in parentheses from other egos who happen to meet inside it.[39] Stiegler's particular reformulation of the question of being lies in considering "the relationship between being and time as *techno-logical*."[40] In Stiegler's view, something is lost when attention turns away from somewhat more subtle techniques like "politeness" and "elegance" and toward more grossly technical activities where the calculable element conceals "the *différance* that *Dasein* is," with it in fact being "*tekhnē* that gives *différance*, that gives time."[41] For Stiegler the rub here is that this technological relation of being and time comes with a founding loss, a primal fall—one well captured by the tragic figure of Epimetheus. This all forms the basis of Stiegler's view that, for humanity, "tools are foresight—*promethes* is the foreseeing one,"[42] where such foresight and relation to human mortality lamentably only happens through an original Epimethean forgetfulness.

Reassessing Stiegler and Ritual Technique in Appearance

Stiegler's analysis is quite useful for this project, especially as it extends the species-level vocabulary for subject life being developed here in conjunction with the views of Hannah Arendt and Lǐ Zéhòu. However, some of his account calls for reexamination, namely, the idea that "inorganic organized beings" stand as a third type of being beyond biological beings like humans and physical entities.

Now, the basic core of his idea concerning these inorganic organized beings has considerable merit; the problem lies in the formulation more than anything. First, there is the somewhat pedantic point that, for early humans, a great deal of the technological innovation in terms of food and shelter pointed to by Stiegler concerned dead plant and dead animal matter, hardly inorganic. Now, this objection can be easily set aside with the qualifier that inorganic means no longer living (as opposed to the technical meaning of being composed of hydrocarbon compounds). However, even here there is a breakdown in the distinctions and qualifiers used by Stiegler in his major formulation that "between the inorganic beings of the physical sciences and the organized beings of biology, there exists a third genre of 'beings,' *inorganic organized beings*, which are technical objects."[43] How does this breakdown occur?

The issue here is that Stiegler's formulation of "inorganic organized beings" (*étants inorganiques organisés*) follows what he might call a "vulgar" temporal narrative a bit too slavishly and gives primacy to the prior organic nature of beings that then become organized, if not subsumed, by the still-living biological (human) being. The primary suggestion here, somewhat taking a cue from Whitehead and his emphasis on process, is that the third genre of being should be designated "beings, organizing," which is to say that, rather than the result (what is organized), emphasis should be given to the process of interplay (organizing) at the threshold of the prior two moments of physical and biological beings.

The further suggestion takes a more direct cue from Arendt and her emphasis on the coextensiveness of being in the political world and appearance. This is to draw a likeness between how the exemplary technique of fire-making organizes and negotiates the after-the-fact boundaries between the fire-making subject and a variety of material objects, on the one hand, and how panoptical interpellation also works as an exemplary technique for organizing a given subject as an object amid a community of similarly objectified subjects, on the other. And so the connection to Stiegler is how epiphylogenetic sedimentation motivated by species-level survival and being-toward-death gives the individual human being bearing and orientation, with the human as such being its result, or, as Stiegler writes:

> *Homo æconomicus, faber, laborans, sapiens*: the logical, reasonable, or speaking animal, the social and political animal, the desiring

animal, all which traditional philosophy has utilized to quantify humankind, from Plato and Aristotle to Marx and Freud, all of this is only arriving after this accident where man enters into the baleful condition of death, into melancholy.[44]

Setting aside for the moment the intriguing connections to Butler's reading of Freudian melancholy, Stiegler's major point is that there is a third class of organized inorganic beings apart from the organic beings of biology and the inorganic beings of the physical sciences. The claim being made in response here is that for these beings, these technical beings, what is key is not this or that phase of matter, but rather technique in the *process* of organizing the intertwined macro-level sedimentary technologies of discourse, politics, desire, and so on, through which individual, micro-level subject life takes shape.

And here in turning to micro-level subject life, resonances begin to emerge with Stiegler's account of the Promethean-Epimethean fault of memory on the level of the human species. Consider how for Butler, even with all of the possible power and fury of self-consciousness, no subject can become the object of any coherent narrative that might extend prior to the formation of self-consciousness and the establishment subject/object relations, as a matter of definition.[45] This is to say that a subject who acquires consciousness as a self-turned-on-self cannot be conscious of nor recount anything before the constitutive psychic turn that occurs with exposure to the social world. This is why, in her reading of Hannah Arendt on the exposure of the subject, Adriana Cavarero describes the fault of memory of every human being and the need to resort to hearsay accounts and mythical biography to fill in gaps in the story.[46] Exposure and mythic fabulation (which is to say artistry) together drive the respective dynamics of both subject and species, binding these levels together in a way that almost demands the expansion of Butler's paradigm.

It is at this point that Lǐ Zéhòu comes back into the discussion with his own account of the quasi-mythic origins of humanity and material organization. In contrast to the supernatural cautionary tale of Prometheus and the covering up of finer techniques by fire brought from above, the Confucian tradition tends to point more to *this* world to explain the invention of ritual technology, in particular the mytho-historical leader Yáo.[47] Recall again Lǐ Zéhòu's observation that

> Chinese sages transformed and rationalized the power of the shamans into rites and rituals and interpreted these powers as

manifested in music and poetry to be constructive. Western scholars considered the powers of the muses attractive and powerful, but whimsical, and a threat to humans' most treasured faculty: reason.[48]

And so, the practical arts of material organization broadly, so overlooked in post-Promethean notions of *tekhnē*, according to Stiegler, take center stage within Lǐ Zéhòu's Confucian-influenced framework. Working with the Confucian sage's employment of ritual and bodily self-cultivation, Lǐ Zéhòu casts the sage as an exemplar figure for understanding the proliferation of the dual processes that Marx calls the humanization of nature and the naturalization of humanity, where, in a manner similar to Stiegler's description, collective unconsciousness accrues and develops. However, Lǐ ends up, much like Stiegler, describing the survival orientation of the ritual-technological development of early humans and how it was thus very much oriented toward death, all sedimenting and inhering in collective unconsciousness (described earlier as a background hum). And so, despite Lǐ not speaking about forgetfulness per se, and despite not speaking in an explicitly phenomenological idiom, he nonetheless ends up advancing something similar to, but with crucial divergences from, Stiegler's account of forgetfulness in human technology with regard to being-toward-death.

In particular, Lǐ breaks down the dialectical counterpart of humanizing nature, naturalizing humanity, into three aspects. He points firstly to the environment as a context for life, secondly to nature as "other" as an object for appreciation and recreation, and thirdly to activities integrating human bodies and the rhythms of nature, with bodily practices like *qìgōng* 气功 standing out as particularly laudable models (with *t'ai chi ch'uan* or *tàijíquán* 太极拳 perhaps being the most familiar proximate example to English speakers).[49] Note how, with similar influence from Marx's earlier work, something similar to the basic threefold dynamic between living biological beings, nonliving physical beings, and organizing nonliving beings described by Stiegler is advanced by Lǐ as well.

If, as Lǐ Zéhòu puts forward, such integrative bodily activities provide a connection to humanizing nature and the sedimentation of artistic, musical, quasi-religious rites at the base of collective unconsciousness and the material organization of humanity, then turning attention to ritual in its bodily dimension makes sense. Now, the objection might be raised that this draws an all-too-hasty equivalence between appearance prior to recognition, the organizing of material in human life, and ritual. While it is true that conflating these very complex notions is problematic, the contention here is something else—rather than being equivalent, these elements, while retaining genuine differences, grow into and out of each other coordinately and rhizomatically. How so?

Ritual, by itself, sounds outmoded, arch, and feudal. However, when read in terms of *lǐ* 礼, *tǐ* 体, and *yuè* 乐, in terms of grand and subtle ritual propriety, dynamic bodily organization over space and time, and musical-social choreography, and then further extended with Lǐ Zéhòu's reading of the felt, aesthetic nature of sedimented human tradition, the idea of ritual is distinct, but with clear connections to both the political space of appearance and the organizing of material in human life.

Hence, this vocabulary of appearance from Arendt, particularly as concerns the appearance of the body, and the uniquely Confucian notion of ritual each add to Stiegler's account, and, moreover, to Butler's framework. Putting these sources together points to how the techniques that temporalize human life and lead to forgetfulness can be called into the service of memory, of remembering and recovering a more originary, authentic sense of technology. This is to say that at least in some regard, artful, ritual, and bodily self-cultivation stands as one way of engaging in the politics of memory for which Stiegler calls.

Fire! Fire! Fire! That is supposed to be the representative avatar of technology and of human beings—but no! Rather, the practical arts are *at least* as important. Perhaps more than the fire itself, the key is how humans organize *around* fire. The issue is how humans organize labor and material *over time* with care for the finitude of life; it is about how humanity collectively survives and how subjects recognize each other individually within the broad sweep of human progress. It is the sedimented, ritualized dynamic of organization itself—this is human thriving, and this is what is forgotten with seeming necessity.

The hidden implication here is that dominant definitions of *tekhnē* and technique in terms of *poiēsis* and bringing forth, like those of Heidegger and Stiegler, may need to be qualified when it comes to the rituals of subjectivation.[50] Proceeding from Arendt's political theory and her drawing together of *Sein* and *Schein*, of being and appearance, "bringing forth" may be inadequate when it comes to the technology of organizing beings, which is to say organizing social and political human beings who *are* and who thus inevitably *appear* as subjects. The issue is not appearance in concealment (and being brought into or out of concealment), but rather subjectivation's medium in each moment of the process is the appearance of the vulnerable (and sometimes still-concealed) body on the social scene. Subjectivation is about emergence and here the grim factory connotation behind Foucault's talk of technologies of the self has merit, especially upon consideration of the functional and mechanistic nature of life in a panoptical society. Subjectivation occurs prior to the question of concealment and the establishment of inner public and outer private realms for objects appearing before observing subjects, and therefore prior to any question of bringing forth *out of concealment* and truth as disclosure, per Heidegger. Considering appearance in technological terms helps in appreciating subjectivation and the ever-nascent ritual organization of persons as just that—a technique, and thus something capable of being refined.

Now it is true that as an exemplary technique, fire-making has been refined into all manner of particular technologies like the atomic bomb, much like ritual subjectivation has also been refined throughout the years into the particularly frightening technology of the virtual panopticon. However, just as, per Heidegger, the essence of technology is nothing technological, such that it is neither the campfire nor the atomic bomb nor any other particular technology, so too is the essence of the ritual technology of organization nothing that resides in any one technology of organization per se, even if it is one as dominant as panoptical interpellation in subjectivation.[51] Refining particular technologies is *not* the same as refining technique. Refining particular technologies leads to *quantitative* changes to being—*more* beings, *more* things, *less* distance. Refining technique leads to qualitative changes to being—changes to *how* being is concerned for and cares for being. As an exemplary technique, ritual appearance in the world can be refined, not just with regard to quantification in bigger and more precise virtual panopticon technologies, but in the very quality and affective, emotional tone of how subjects apprehend and organize themselves and other subjects.

And so, even though the Promethean myth is somewhat culturally specific, Stiegler's point is that it is illustrative of a deeper truth about memory and technology, one that he approaches phenomenologically. Reapproaching Stiegler's platform with the considerations advanced here helps to extend those valuable insights about species-level memory and technology in terms of the more particular technology of ritual organization of appearance, with classical Confucian sources and Lǐ Zéhòu supplying the vocabulary for ritual and Arendt furnishing a robust platform for dealing with appearance as a subject on the political scene.

Conclusion

This idea of technique in appearance builds on the previously introduced notions of subjectivation and subjectality, adding the following points to the emerging argument.

12. Subjectivation occurs through relations of concern, somewhat on the level of undifferentiated being, before any social subjects emerge. Before subjectivation, before interpellation, before recognition, there is an appearance on the scene marked by such concern. Appearance with felt vulnerability comes before subjectivation. However, this type of appearance does not occur in the singular, but occurs reciprocally amongst subjects in a political community where appearance is reality, for all of the good *and* ill that this equation causes. Subjectivation often falls on the unhappy side of this formula, but when looked at in this way, something curious emerges—appearance in the manifold and on the macro level stands prior to subjectivation yet is necessary for the ongoing emergence of subjects as subjects in such encounters. This means that appearance is part of the basic technology of subject life.

13. Subjectality's macro-level complement to micro-level subjectivation becomes a bit clearer upon considering the interplay between technology and memory. The basic technologies of inscription and ritual organization act as prostheses for memory, relieving one of the need to remember this or that fact or this or that reason for organizing in a specific way for survival. Thus, in the twinned processes of humanizing nature and naturalizing humanity, a certain forgetfulness emerges that in many ways mirrors what Nietzsche pejoratively calls "forget[ting] oneself as a subject, and indeed an artistically creating subject."[52] On both a species level and an individual level, we forget in order *to survive*.

14. Looking at macro-, species-level human development through the language of Arendt and Stiegler shows how it might be possible to remember what has been lost for the purpose of survival. Putting their accounts together points to how remainders of what has been lost in human development still inhere unconsciously in human tradition.

Moving forward, these dormant traces remain to be awakened in the kind of ritual interaction appreciated by classical Confucianism and further extended by Lǐ in his own contemporary take on species-level human development already explored in this work. It is at this point that the possibility of self-cultivation through those ritual techniques brings up the question of practice. In using the ideas of subjectality and technique in appearance to account for the historical role of artful ritual in species-level development and to provide a counterweight to the account of normative ritual in individual subjectivation, it has become clear that at least one avenue for improving the subject's situation lies in remembering and making conscious the artful roots of ritual sedimented in the unconscious habits and gestures that mark bodily life. What is needed in order to further the discussion underway is a platform that brings together what has been said on the micro level of subjectivation and what has been said on the macro level of subjectality in a way that bridges theory and practice, ideally in a way that speaks in the idioms of Foucault, Butler, and Confucius (for starters). Rather fortunately and speaking to precisely this need, there is the influential work of Richard Shusterman on bodily practice and his paradigm of somaesthetics, which by and large shares the aim of this project—bettering (a) relational, (b) discursive, (c) bodily, and (d) ritual subject life.

Chapter 6

Somaesthetics

> Entire ideologies of domination can thus be covertly materialized and preserved by encoding them in somatic social norms that, as bodily habits, are typically taken for granted and so escape critical consciousness. . . . Any successful challenge of oppression should thus involve somaesthetic diagnosis of the bodily habits and feelings that express the domination as well as the subtle institutional rules and methods of inculcating them, so that they, along with the oppressive social conditions that generate them, can be overcome.[1]
>
> —Richard Shusterman

Preliminary Remarks: Somaesthetics and Subjectivation

Richard Shusterman's work on somaesthetics represents the last major locus from which this particular rhizomatic inquiry grows. Shusterman defines somaesthetics as being

> concerned with the critical study and meliorative cultivation of how we experience and use the living body (or *soma*) as a site of sensory appreciation (*aesthesis*) and creative self-fashioning.[2]

For Shusterman, somaesthetics is interdisciplinary and takes place *analytically* in the theoretical work of thinkers like Foucault, Bourdieu, and Butler, *pragmatically* in doctrinal methods including diet, yoga, martial arts, erotic arts, and *practically* in the actual performance and refinement of bodily activity where "the less said the better."[3]

Though there is something of a continuum between these domains, this inquiry will, at least at first, mostly deal with Shusterman's remarks in the analytic, theoretical domain. Three items here are of particular interest for this project.

First, there are Shusterman's direct words regarding the project of subjectivation, particularly his reading of Judith Butler's work. Specifically, he speaks against her "insist[ing] on transgressive representational performances with the body [being] coupled with an argument against 'the illusion of an interior' of somatic experience that could serve as a legitimate focus for critical study and transformation."[4] And so, since he speaks of artful bodily practice in critique of Butler, there are certainly links to this project.

Secondly, Shusterman claims that somaesthetics has the power to renew everyday life and the body's interconnection with the prevailing environment, natural *and* social. Shusterman's words here regarding turning unconscious bodily habit into consciously bodily conduct and in the quote opening this section addressing the ideological domination of bodily habit call to mind those of Arno Böhler. Böhler glosses resistance to the material status quo in terms of the ritual performativity talked about by Butler where he speaks of dealing with the thoughtless replication in one's own body of compulsively reenacted rituals of embodiment.[5] Taking this line of thinking and considering it in terms of the problems presented by subjectivation and subjectality for the aim of promoting novel modes of self-recognition in terms of the artful body, the connections of interest here become a bit clearer.

Thirdly, and most importantly for this inquiry, at various points Shusterman draws on East Asian thought, particularly the root school of Confucianism and its distinctive notions of ritualized self-cultivation, in order to express ideas where the European-American idiom is insufficient. Beyond Shusterman's own work, though, there is further to go in exploring the Chinese tradition, particularly since the remarks he does make on the topic hint at a possible tension with the sort of creative self-fashioning that he advocates.[6]

Luckily, though, the most influential debate in Confucianism, the one over human nature being "good" or "bad," ends up being a question of whether embodied ritual self-cultivation is internally spontaneous or externally imposed. This provides a sort of parallel conversation on the nature and status of somaesthetic practice.

On one side of this debate, there is the Confucian tradition's canonical second master, Mèng Zǐ (Mencius), who, working in the fourth century BCE, put forward that such practice arises from good human nature. On the other, there is the tradition's more ambivalently regarded figure, Xún Zǐ, who, working later on in the third century BCE, instead held that good practice is imposed onto dissolute nature. The dialogue that emerges between these two figures within the Confucian tradition both parallels and anticipates issues in Shusterman's much more recent philosophy and in this project more broadly.

Even though Shusterman appears more attracted to Xún Zǐ and his praise for ritual self-cultivation, the argument here is that this is worrisome. Despite having clear admiration for Foucault, Merleau-Ponty, James, and Dewey, Shusterman criticizes his biggest influences when they succumb to dualistic thinking in order to rehabilitate their otherwise valuable insights. The suggestion is that something similar should occur with the ultimately pessimistic view on human nature and ritual propriety held by Xún Zǐ. However, before putting these voices together, more must be said about Shusterman's somaesthetics and the corresponding issues in Confucianism on their own respective terms.

Somaesthetics: Rethinking Bodily Cultivation

Somaesthetics is, of course, a neologism, and so some explanation is in order. Such a term is necessary, in part, because of the way that dominant Euro-American philosophical discourses often go above ignoring the body to disparaging it outright. In her own work, Butler casts the accusation that "philosophy founders time and again on the question of the body, it tends to separate what is called thinking from what is called sensing, from desire, passion, sexuality, and relations of dependency."[7] For Shusterman, the philosopher responsible for coining the term "somaesthetics," conventional approaches often fail to fulfill central aims of philosophy like self-knowledge and right action, because bodily knowledge is left neglected and powers of volition are left undeveloped.[8] This is similar to Arno Böhler's diagnosis of philosophy's primary focus on the mental, which leaves the body a sleep-walking mass in need of a new breed of philosophers of art who do not seek to free thinking from bodily sense, but who instead see thought as the "form of the intensification and bodily ennobling of our desire."[9] A difficulty emerges with this new brand of philosophy, since responding to the state of affairs variously identified by Butler, Shusterman, Böhler, and others, seems to require a way of talking about the body that is not already laden with the kind of unfortunate presuppositions that place it secondary to mind.

As a philosopher of this ilk with a corresponding need to speak in new terms, Shusterman does not confine himself to one particular philosophical school, instead exploiting conceptual overlap in order to address the theoretical dimensions of his somaesthetic project on more amenable terms. That said, the tradition of American pragmatism plays a particularly prominent role in his work, perhaps with John Dewey's influence being the strongest. This line of pragmatist thinking leads Shusterman to reject most classical dualisms in favor of what might be called a type of meliorism strongly based in process thought. This shows through in his unease with the word "body" and his vision "of an essentially situated, relational and symbiotic self rather than the traditional concept of an autonomous self that would be grounded in an individual, monadic, indestructible, and unchanging soul."[10]

Shusterman's paradigm resists the term "body" and the mind/body dualism connected with it for four main reasons. Firstly, there is the problematic reduction of knowledge to the cognitive, to something residing in a wholly mental realm. Secondly, there is the issue of casting the body as some wholly external implement. Thirdly, there is the worry that this diminution of the body is at the base of other distinctions, that is, interrelated notions of high art/low art, art/craft, white collar/blue collar labor, and so on.[11] Fourthly, there is the problem of the body being rendered silent, even in what should be body-friendly movements within philosophy. This occurs in the field of embodied cognition, where third-person observational data of the body as external is emphasized at the expense of first-person accounts of body consciousness. Something similar also happens with a good deal of phenomenology of the body in the wake of Maurice Merleau-Ponty, an enterprise, which in Shusterman's view, is insufficiently culturally pluralistic, too engaged in description at the expense of being prescriptive, and overly influenced by the paradoxical tendency of this "patron saint of the body" to regard the silent, tacit cogito of the body as an impediment to spontaneity in conduct (a criticism that could easily extend to Butler insofar as her approach to inscrutable Aristotelian prime matter resonates with Merleau-Ponty's belief that the tacit cogito is prior to philosophy and only comes to know itself when it is under threat of death or the gaze of another implicitly).[12] Thus, in order to differentiate himself and his project from prevailing notions of the body, both long-standing and recent, Shusterman opts instead to reach back to ancient Greek for the term "soma" to refer to what he calls "a living, feeling, sentient body rather than a mere physical body that could be devoid of life and sensation."[13]

This antidualistic spirit can be further seen in Shusterman's particular use of the term aesthetics, which simultaneously emphasizes soma as both perceiving and self-fashioning, as observer and artist, as it were. "I thus both am body and have a body," as Shusterman says.[14] Here subject and object merge, albeit imperfectly, since the body, not being "a clear object of knowledge," makes somaesthetic knowledge always partial.

Shusterman concedes that somaesthetic awareness may fail to be clear and distinct in a Cartesian sense, and that, per Wittgenstein, it is typically not required for basic orientation in everyday life, falling short of providing solid conceptual knowledge. Shusterman makes his stand here, arguing that failing to be conceptual does not exclude refining the somaesthetic and enriching experience in nonconceptual ways.[15] That there may be theoretical limits to somaesthetic awareness owing to weakness in the human faculties, defects in particular sense organs, or habit-induced blindness in no way hinders cultivating awareness of the soma within those limits.

And so, with parts criticism and parts praise Shusterman looks at a number of doctrines and practices for increasing somatic acuity. These include "various diets, forms of grooming and decoration (including body painting, piercing, and scarification as well as more familiar modes of cosmetics, jewelry, and clothing fashions), dance, yoga, massage, aerobics, bodybuilding, calisthenics, martial and erotic arts, and modern psychosomatic disciplines like Alexander Technique and Feldenkrais Method."[16] These all can provoke somatic awareness, albeit in different ways, but for Shusterman a similar effect obtains.

Putting these approaches together in a way that unites Li's idea of sedimented collective habit and Shusterman's idea of self-cultivation aims to make conduct a matter of deliberate technique. Such an approach can also respond to Dewey's clear definition of the problem facing the modern enterprise of somaesthetics, namely, that mind/body, theory/practice, ideal/actuality dichotomies, and the like underlie the split between thought and habit, presenting a challenge to somaesthetics where, per Dewey,

> the current dualism of mind and body, thought and action, is so rooted that we are taught (and science is said to support the teaching) that the art, the habit, of the artist is acquired by previous mechanical exercises of repetition in which skill apart from thought is the aim, until suddenly, magically, this soulless mechanism is taken possession of by sentiment and imagination

and it becomes a flexible instrument of mind. The fact, the scientific fact, is that even in his exercises, his practice for skill, an artist uses an art he already has. He acquires greater skill because practice of skill is more important to him than practice for skill. Otherwise natural endowment would count for nothing, and sufficient mechanical exercise would make any one an expert in any field. A flexible, sensitive habit grows more varied, more adaptable by practice and use.[17]

With his Dewey-influenced description of the soma as in-process, transactional with the environment, and capable of bringing skill to habit, Shusterman maintains that heightened somatic awareness promotes a new sense of self in everyday relations. This is to say that, as one becomes more attuned to the soma, habit becomes practice. A famous example of this is the focus that many disciplines place on breathing and awareness of breathing. This is supposed to spill over to everyday life, allowing for conscious reflection on typically unconscious changes in breathing, say in states of agitation, arousal, and so on.[18]

And so, one becomes more aware of unconscious, *visceral* reactions, all the way up to the "knee-jerk" revulsion that many lamentably exhibit toward homosexuality, other races, and so on.[19] This highlights the malleability of material, normative habit, which is in fact more like glass, being amorphous and subtly shifting, despite apparent "solidity." When this somaesthetic awareness comes into its own, one's ritual/habitual life thus becomes an object that one can counter and reflect upon—an artful "I" that serves as different type of less pernicious "Other"—stepping outside of oneself in a moments of genuine ecstasy. This idea is performatively enacted in Shusterman's provocative *Adventures of the Man in Gold: Paths between Art and Life*, where Shusterman, the philosopher, "prefers to lend his own silent body as the somatic medium for the Man in Gold's gestural communication, which is far more dramatic and potently expressive than any words that Richard Shusterman can muster as his philosophical spokesman," thus pointing to the possibility of engaging in a liberating "discourse" with ecstatic oneself.[20]

Furthermore, Shusterman holds that somaesthetic attention can work to focus more vaunted experiences, including encounters with art. Here he invokes Wittgenstein's remarks on movement from *Culture and Value* to describe how recalling a melody is often accompanied by somatic changes, for Wittgenstein, teeth grinding, but this could just as well be toe-tapping, changing walking cadence, or something similar.[21]

Shusterman, responding primarily to the William James–inspired thread in Wittgenstein's later work and to remarks of his collected posthumously in the *Vermischte Bemerkungen*, argues that "if somatic feelings are neither the object nor the explanation of our judgments and experience of art, this does not entail, however, that such feelings are not aesthetically important."[22] Just as somaesthetic awareness of the body helps in keying in on unconscious reactions to social situations, it can also clarify the role of physical/emotional reactions to art, helping to avoid the outcome where "art appreciation degenerate[s] into a gushy, vague romanticism."[23] Shusterman's thoughtful account of the often underappreciated role of the body in Wittgenstein's thinking leads him to the critical conclusion that somaesthetic attention hones subjectivity in a variety of contexts. Although Wittgenstein might not himself have cared for the notions of subjectivation, subjectality, and the like, explored in this work, Shusterman's Wittgenstein-critical point regarding somaesthetic awareness nonetheless stands and offers insight into the rituals of subject life.

This does not mean that Shusterman gives an unthinking blanket endorsement to all somaesthetic attention. There remains the genuine corner that the arts and aestheticism have been painted into and indeed into which they have painted themselves, pun intended. As mentioned earlier, there is the very real estrangement of the skeptical, quizzical artworld from the serious, stoic business of the real world, fallout that comes with art setting itself apart as extraordinary. Shusterman is aware of this danger, of the needle that somaesthetics needs to thread in order to avoid the dangers of hedonism, superficiality, and the like, writing:

> But why, to continue this line of argument, should one work so hard, if the aesthetic transformation is merely perfunctory and superficial: a line of mascara, the shallow shimmer-shine of tinted hair? Modernity's sad irony is that art has inherited religion's spiritual authority, while being compartmentalized from the serious business of life. Aestheticism must seem amoral and superficial when art is falsely relegated from ethical praxis and instead confined to the realm of mere *Schein* (i.e., appearance, illusion). Challenging this false dichotomy between art and ethics, pragmatism seeks to synthesize the beautiful and the good. While recognizing (with Montaigne) that our greatest artworks are ourselves (inextricably bound up with and shaped by others), it also brings ethical considerations into the project of aesthetic self-fashioning and the judgment of such art.[24]

As another example of what conventional thinking deems amoral aestheticism, there is of course sexuality. While he does generally support Foucault's goal of increasing somatic awareness through exploring sexuality, Shusterman believes that a narrow nihilistic/hedonistic preoccupation with this aspect (taking Foucault and Sadomasochism as an example) is ultimately counterproductive to somatic cultivation. Accordingly, Shusterman's more recent work in *Thinking through the Body* sees the erotic arts of ancient China and India as "form[ing] the core of this study" as it goes beyond his particular theoretical engagement with Foucault.[25] This belief also takes influence, at least in some regard, from feminist critiques, particularly those of de Beauvoir, which focus on how pernicious modes of body consciousness can and do harm women.[26] For example, increasing gender parity in athletic participation may be putatively good, but even noble care for the body is readily co-opted as another tool of domination, where now the archetype of the "athletic body" all too easily becomes just one more thing to be wielded very decidedly *against* women.

And this highlights another concern, namely, that somaesthetic practices seem always to be in peril of being taken over by market and social forces in ways that would undermine the genuine care for the self of interest to Shusterman. Physical exercise becomes about getting a beach-ready body for summer; Hatha yoga becomes fitness-studio yoga; zen turns into pop-psych, feel-good pabulum; meditation gets enmeshed in speculation about crystals and quantum theory under the misbegotten heading of "metaphysics"; and so forth. Indeed, these perils ironically become real with the misconstrual of Shusterman as "uncritically recommending the concrete performance of all the different body practices falling within the field's general purview, even practices (and their attendant ideologies) that [he] critique[s] rather than endorse[s]" and criticism that his early forays in somaesthetics received for "reflecting today's commercialized obsession with mindless physical delights and superficial stereotypes of good looks, while exacerbating this problematic trend by giving it theoretical backing as well."[27]

Somaesthetic Practice: A Resource for Expanding Subject Life or Another Means of Control?

All of this leads to the question of whether somaesthetic practices genuinely offer novel possibilities for negotiating the relationship between self and the broader environment or whether they ultimately just end up being deceptive and rarified forms of control. After all, as William James cuttingly observes, habit ensnares all in such a way that people are "mere walking bundles of habits," making it so that "habit is . . . the enormous fly-wheel of society, its most precious conservative agent. It alone is what keeps us all within the bounds of ordinance, and saves the children of fortune from the envious uprisings of the poor."[28] Shusterman is aware of the quandary presented by habit, namely, that it both springs from the body's organic plasticity and that it serves to arrest the body in a way that forestalls social change.[29] Therefore, simple habituation without qualification will not do. This curiously finds Shusterman in the position of having to deny a blanket endorsement of habit with regard to its productive/restrictive bind, a corollary of Foucault's challenge not to issue a blanket condemnation of power in recognition of *its* productive/restrictive bind. Though Shusterman quite obviously has faith in certain somaesthetic practices (with Japanese *Zazen* 坐禅 seated meditation, the Alexander Technique, and the Feldenkrais Method being particularly attractive to him), the question persists as to what kind of habituation and cultivation might prove helpful.[30]

When it comes to this project and its goal of escaping the confines of the self as a *pejoratively subject* self, the key is explaining how the effects of such training and cultivation might derive from factors over and above any cultural or discursive determinism. For Shusterman's project, this issue comes to a head where he appears to agree with Michel Foucault and Judith Butler on "how the body is both shaped by power and employed as an instrument to maintain it, how bodily norms of health, skill, and beauty, and even our categories of sex and gender, are constructed to reflect and sustain social forces."[31] Butler in particular puts special weight on how the social construction of the body forecloses the conscious deployment of an intelligent, discursive bodily remainder as a source of novelty over and against the programmatic structure.[32] It should be pointed out that Shusterman does in fact argue against Butler's rigid insistence, mentioned earlier, on there being no inner bodily life that is not a performed effect of discursive power, with Shusterman rather smartly pointing out in response that "being an effect, however, does not mean being an illusion."[33]

To add to this and to follow Shusterman's basic argument against Wittgenstein's devaluation of merely partial knowledge of the body, the response might also be given that, despite Butler being correct in asserting that "to be a body is, in some sense, to be deprived of having a full recollection of one's life. There is a history to my body of which I can have no recollection"; this *does not mean* that attempts at partial recollection and remembering of unconscious habit are either foolish or vain.[34] An arguably misguided insistence on perfection should not stand in the way of ameliorative solutions. Denying the possibility of fully redeeming loss should not forestall the possibility or minimize the merits of what may turn out to be only partial and minor recovery from loss. This being so, it is worth recalling Butler's observation that "conscious experience is only one dimension of psychic life, and that we cannot achieve by consciousness or language a full mastery over those primary relations of dependency and impressionability that form and constitute us in persistent and obscure ways" in the service of remembering that somatic practice may in fact be a major resource for dealing with dimensions of psychic life beyond what is consciously explicit.[35]

And so the claim being made here is that, even if Butler is right where she says that body "cannot be said to be a mere effect of discourse" and that it cannot be easily addressed in the simple grammar of A-leads-to-B narratives, such that it "escapes the terms of the question by which it is approached," there still are less clear and distinct modes of approaching the body outside of interrogation and questioning that may nevertheless provide valuable means of access to these scattered and sedimented origins.[36] Even if it is granted, per Butler's Malebranche-inspired reading of Descartes, that "whereas one can have 'clear and distinct' ideas of a priori truths, such as mathematical ones, it is not possible to have such clarity and distinctness with respect to one's own self, considered as a *sentiment intérieur*," the lack of perfect clarity and distinction concerning the body and its innermost sentiments does not mean that the body is always and forever prevented from any efforts whatsoever, even work outside of the sphere of narrative discourse, to clarify and distinguish the grounds of its feelings.[37]

Fortunately, though, there are resources for dealing with these issues outside of Euro-American traditions. Shusterman himself is quite keen on this, as can be seen in his pluralistic approach, which draws on a number of somaesthetic philosophies and disciplines with origins in East Asia. Shusterman is particularly attracted to the Confucian sage Xún Zǐ, whose extended remarks on the role of ritualized aesthetic self-cultivation seem to anticipate a great deal of somaesthetic theory. However, such an appropriation of Xún Zǐ leads to problems if taken too far. In another stroke of luck, the Confucian tradition's own resources can help here by contributing a response to the question of how somaesthetic practices may or may not coincide with the kind of prior internal source of bodily resistance so roundly rejected by Butler in her own account.

Confucian Perspectives on the Development of Ritual Propriety: Inside or Outside of Human Nature?

Shusterman is familiar with Chinese thought, and this proves useful to him where he advances and clarifies his own thinking amid shortcomings in English-language terminology. He describes his own usage of "soma" in terms of the contemporary Chinese word for body, "*shēntǐ* 身体," writing:

> [The] Chinese term *shenti* 身体, which also denotes the living soma and is formed from the two characters *shen* and *ti*. The character shen 身 was used in classical Chinese to denote the whole person (including the moral and spiritual self that should be cultivated, rather than the mere material animal body), and the character is derived from an image of a standing pregnant woman, a charged symbol of the living, creative, dynamic body that is directionally asymmetrical and also top-heavy.[38]

Elsewhere, Shusterman goes on to explain:

> If the *ti* body in classical thought is closely associated with generative powers of physical life and growth and the multiplicity of parts (such as the [body's] four limbs), the *shen* body is closely identified with the person's ethical, perceptive, purposive body that one cultivates and so it even serves as a term for self. The concept of *shenti* thus suggests the soma's double status as living thing and perceiving subjectivity.[39]

Of particular interest here is the second character *tǐ* 体 (traditionally written 體), where the left side of the traditional character refers to the character's bodily sense with a bone or skeletal framework, *gǔ* 骨. Meanwhile, the right side of the traditional character, *lǐ* 豊 refers to ritual sacrifice. This extends to *lǐ* 礼 (traditionally written with a shared root ideogram 禮), which, to recap, refers to the aesthetically oriented ritual propriety at work in moments of both grandeur and subtlety that, as previously mentioned, forms what leading translators Roger T. Ames and Henry Rosemont, Jr., call a "social grammar"[40] for recognizing one's self in relation to others, or as Confucius playfully puts it, "knowing where to stand *lì* (立)."[41] This fits with using one of the major terms for the body, *tǐ*, to "refer to groups of people organized for special purposes, and even to concrete things in the world . . . [and] to anything that has a definite form and style of organization, such as types of writing styles," to reiterate Cheng Chung-ying's words on the subject.⁴²

Speaking more on the present-day usage of *shēntǐ* for body is Susan Brownell, who ties the first component, *shēn*, to the German notion of *Leib*, referencing the "living, experiential, subject-body," and the second component, *tǐ*, to *Körper*, referencing the "dead, instrumental object-body." She is careful to note that the correspondences are inexact, especially as respects the German language and its tendency toward a much stronger subject/object dualism than is typical of the Chinese language.⁴³ Following Brownell in noting a general avoidance of oppositional subject/object and mind/body dualisms, Yanhua Zhang 张燕化 draws attention to how component parts like *shēn* and *tǐ* work within the paronomastic and rhizomatic framework of the Chinese language, where wordplay and interconnection serve to center words rather than explicitly defining them, noting:

> Even the modern concept of "*tiyu*" 体育 (physical education) need not be reduced to training a physical body object. *Tiyu* is still very much an intense process to embody social values and ideology through a highly formalized body. In this sense, *shenti* (both *shen* and *ti*) is centrally important in Chinese social life.
>
> Besides *shen* and *ti*, other single characters may also have the connotations of "body," for example, *xing* 形 (form, shape), *qu* 躯 (body trunk), and *shi* 尸 (corpse). In modern Chinese, they are often combined with either *shen* or *ti* to create multiple senses that indicate different states of embodiment, for example, *xingti* 形体 (body shape) and *shenqu* 身躯 (body build).⁴⁴

Adding to this is Deborah Sommer and her exhaustive account of the body within the Chinese language. Given the rhizomatic approach taken here as a point of formal methodology, it is interesting to note Sommer's description of the body in classical Chinese thought in terms of a tuber, where she writes that

> *ti* bodies often act more like plants than like humans. When living human bodies are divided, they die: halving, quartering, or fragmenting human or animal bodies inevitably results in dismemberment or death. . . . If one quarters a tuberous root into four segments, each of which flourishes on its own, does

the plant matter from those four segments then belong to the original "mother" plant (to use modern horticultural terminology) or the four new "daughter" plants? Mother and daughter plants are at once autonomous and yet consubstantial.⁴⁵

With her language of mother and daughter being consubstantial, Sommer intentionally echoes Roger T. Ames and his description of the Confucian self as correlational.⁴⁶ What is important here is the particular distinction that she makes between the component parts of the contemporary word for body in Chinese, *shēn* and *tǐ*, where, unlike the *tǐ* sense of body referring to abstract corporeal organization with overlapping loci and levels occurring on the grand scales of life, death, heaven and earth, the *shēn* sense of body refers to something that does not overlap significantly with other *shēn*-bodies—namely, one's *own* person.⁴⁷ This leads Sommer to conclude:

> *Shen* bodies, even though they are living physical frames, are less circumscribed by the flesh than are *ti* bodies; *shen* bodies may routinely be developed through thought and reflection, but *ti* bodies rarely are. One might reflect on one's *shen* body and thus transform it, but one could not do so with one's *ti* body.⁴⁸

Though he shies away from particular Sommer's likening of the *tǐ* body to plants *over* humans, Roger Ames and his connected polyvalent understanding of *tǐ* are helpful here and serve to round out the discussion.⁴⁹ He examines "[the] three alternative classifiers that constitute the variant forms of this character *ti*—*gu* 骨, *shen* 身, and *rou* 肉—as a heuristic for parsing *tǐ*'s range of meaning" to give a fuller description of the concept, whereby

> we must allow that *ti* with the "bones" (*gu* 骨) classifier references the "discursive body" as a process of "structuring," "configuring," "embodying," and thus "knowing" the world not only cognitively and affectively, but also viscerally. Each of us collaborates with the world to discriminate, conceptualize, and theorize the human experience, embodying and giving form to our culture, our language, our habitat.⁵⁰

When this notion of *tǐ* is understood as being part of a complementary rather than oppositional dualism with *shēn* in the modern word for body, *shēntǐ*, things become clearer. *Shēn*, *tǐ*, and *lǐ*—personal body, extended body, and ritual—thus speak to the idea of the self in physical organization, not just statically, but extended over time spanning both one's personal life experience and one's sedimented cultural tradition, *shēn* and *tǐ* respectively. This is the background that becomes the basis for more extended treatments of the relational, ritualized, bodily self in later epochs of Chinese history, like that offered by Lǐ Zéhòu.

With this background information in mind it is possible to turn to the issue of organizing the body in motion. On this point, Confucius identifies a continuum existing between social rites, be they large or small, and choreographed musical performance.[51] Here, rites are encounters of recognition that set relations of power and deference; and the many rites that a person goes through give a sense of where to stand.[52] Musical performance brings heightened attention to choreographed gesture, which in turn hones understanding of everyday rites through the artistic provocation of emotion, as recognized by Confucius in his play on the identical characters for music and joy 乐 (traditionally written 樂).[53] And so, music, standing for the arts generally, affects bodily sensation in a way that helps the self to know, in the bones, where to stand, bringing the connection between the related characters *lǐ* and *tǐ* full circle.

Shusterman finds value for his own work within this conceptual constellation, where he follows Confucius in finding an essential link between personal bodily demeanor and virtue, where the confluence of ritual and music leads to "exemplary virtue [being] somatically formed" in such a way that "social norms and ethical values can sustain their power without any need to make them explicit and enforced by laws [since] they are implicitly observed and enforced through our bodily habits."[54] What draws Shusterman to this conceptual constellation is "the key Confucian doctrine that one's character and somatic comportment are essentially indivisible," which thereby "sees ritual and the fine arts (especially music, poetry, dance, and calligraphy) as the two main pillars of ethics," with a "unity of the mental and somatic," making it so "a teacher can teach without words, [and do so] instead by his embodied example of behavior."[55]

And so, in Confucianism and in Shusterman's own reading of the tradition, people, that is, bodily selves, learn where to stand and thus acquire status as particular persons through social conventions, which is to say because of somaesthetic practice and training, because of *lǐ*. This begets a fork in the conceptual road. If the types of habituation addressed by somaesthetics are external social impositions, then inborn human nature is insufficient in some way. However, if such habituation is not imposed, but is instead internal to humanity, then something in human nature is already good or at least potentially good enough for somaesthetic flourishing to take place. This, in short, forms the basis of the most important debate in classical Confucianism, the disagreement between Mencius and Xún Zǐ, who, working in terms of ritual *lǐ* and the human potential for developing somatic practices, respectively argue in opposing terms about human nature being either "good" or "evil," or perhaps more precisely, either "adept" or "despicable."

Mencius on Human Nature and Ritual

After Confucius, Mencius stands as the second major figure of Confucianism, elaborating and extending the former's aphoristic sayings with more substantial anecdotal reasoning as well as his own conceptual contributions roughly two hundred years after Confucius's initial activity, circa 500 BCE. One of the major contributions that Mencius brings is his dictum "*xìng shàn* 性善" or "human nature is good."[56] The first part of this phrase, *xìng*, refers to the native, living (*shēng* 生) heart-mind (*xīn* 心), indicated by the two parts of the character for *xìng* 性. It is important to note that, according to Mencius, *xìng* is not a static matter of what is given at birth, and that it has more to do with qualitative cultural tendencies differentiating humans from animals.[57]

Shàn is a bit more complex, going beyond the more common contemporary word for good, *hǎo* 好 (e.g., the Chinese greeting "*nǐ hǎo* 你好"). Ames holds that *shàn* is relational in a way that does not really fit well with the essentializing quality of the common translation "good," and that it is more like being "adept at" in a way connoting "aesthetic achievement."[58]

In what does human adeptness consist, then? There is, for Mencius, a type of spontaneity akin to water flowing downhill that marks human moral sense, impelling action in the hypothetical scenario of seeing a child drowning.[59] Likewise, Mencius stresses the spontaneity of family relations, which in turn builds up normative civic communities and the development of culture. And so, Mencius sees *yì* 义, *zhī* 知, *rén* 仁, and *lǐ* 礼—appropriateness, humane conduct, enactive knowledge, and somatic ritual propriety—each as good and natural outgrowths of the human heart-mind, growing like limbs.[60] Furthermore, there is the naturalistic explanation offered by Mencius where the rituals concerning mourning, and thus in a certain sense concerning ritual *lǐ* more generally, grew out of basic emotional reactions that occur upon seeing what happens to corpses when left unattended, particularly when they are of one's own kin (over and above those of any random people, as the somewhat deontological rival Mohist school would have it).[61] These remarks have the effect of casting somatic practice, covered by *lǐ*, by ritual propriety, as a natural good and not an imposed one, indicating an aversion common in classical Chinese thought generally, and Confucianism specifically, to deprecating the human domain in favor of some other realm above and beyond, from which goodness might enter into human life.

Shusterman makes his own reference to Mencius's distinct emphasis on bodily cultivation in his description of the basic logic of somaesthetics, and he elsewhere takes up the provocative imagery of Mencius concerning "cultivating the 'flood-like *qi* [*ch'i*]' that 'fills the body' by giving it the controlling attention of the will and mind." Additionally, the respective lines of thought presented by Shusterman and Mencius further indicate strains of optimism, humanism, and antidualism.[62] All of this would seem to make Mencius an ideal resource for somaesthetics, given its pragmatist bearing.

Mencius also makes a clear connection between *yì* 义 (traditionally written 義) and ritual *lǐ*. On the face of it, the dictionary definition of *yì* as "justice" and its connection to ritual *lǐ* might imply ritual to have an ethical content in opposition to any aesthetic value, as per the standard Euro-American delineation between ethics and aesthetics. However, *yì* really has more to do with appropriateness, as Henry Rosemont, Jr., and Roger T. Ames suggest in their reading of the major text of Mencius's predecessor, *The Analects of Confucius*.[63] Within the tradition as a whole, and certainly within the work of its most prominent mainstream disciple, Mencius, *yì* refers to the "sense of appropriateness that enables one to act in a proper and fitting manner, given the specific situation. . . . By extension, it is also the meaning invested by a cumulative tradition in the forms of ritual propriety [*lǐ*] that define it—import that can be appropriated by a person in the performance of these roles and rituals."[64]

And with this in mind, it is possible to see how Mencius aligns with somaesthetics on the value of ritual *lǐ* in terms of everyday appropriateness, with all of its aesthetic connotations. Indeed, ritual is meant not only to hone action in the everyday, but to be actually constitutive of one's person as such, and, in this sense, the pair of ritual and appropriateness, of *lǐ* and *yì*, address not necessarily the ethical worth of this or that ritually honed action, but the conditions of normativity and subject life as such. This is what leads Mencius to speak of doing violence to oneself, of throwing oneself away when one turns away from ritual propriety and appropriateness, from lǐ and yì, because like the other two virtues, zhī and rén, which together form the four basic limb-like outgrowths of humanity, these are constitutive of the self as Mencius understands it.[65]

Certainly, the notion of ritual lǐ plays a major role in Mencius's view of humanity, with him claiming that lǐ is more important than eating or sex—a view on the crucial role played by lǐ in the growth of humanity that is echoed by Confucian-influenced thinkers today like Lǐ Zéhòu, who see lǐ not in terms of moral worth per se, but in terms of something still normative, which is to say in terms of the kind of social stability, cohesion, and flourishing brought by ritually developed appropriateness.[66] While it should be noted that the way in which Mencius puts it in this passage is somewhat problematic for the purposes of somaesthetics in that it presumes a separation between ritual on the one hand and eating and sex on the other, a separation that somaesthetics seeks to ameliorate, if not eliminate, it is possible to view this as a bit of rhetorical flourish, especially since there are a number of remarks made by both him and Confucius connecting ritual lǐ with sex, eating, and the more quotidian aspects of human life.

However, even with this said, it must be admitted that Mencius's remarks on ritual vis-à-vis somatic life are somewhat limited in depth and breadth, especially when compared to Xún Zǐ. True, in Mencius's corpus there is some continuation of a generally Confucian emphasis on the body and a distinct esteem for wordless action, as Shusterman himself notes.[67] However, Mencius enjoys a much more prominent role within the Confucian tradition in general, and this makes sense upon consideration of how his optimistic view of human nature might prove more attractive when compared to Xún Zǐ, especially as the latter's view has been condemned as pessimistic and has been connected, rightly or wrongly, to some of the authoritarian ills of China's history. It is thus worth asking, then, why is it that Mencius's philosophical antagonist, Xún Zǐ, arguably figures more prominently into Shusterman's work (or at least why he stands more prominently in this body of work than he does in the postclassical Confucian tradition itself). Is there a position within this debate best suited to somaesthetic theory?

Xún Zǐ on Human Nature

Xún Zǐ stands on the other side of this debate, and it is he to whom Shusterman appears to give a great deal of his attention (especially in his notes), likely because of the lofty status granted to ritual self-cultivation in the former's lengthy remarks on the topic.[68] Working in the third century

BCE, some sixty years after Mencius, Xún Zǐ takes up the former's language of *xìng* and gives laudable emphasis to ritual self-cultivation.

However, this emphasis comes at the expense of a questionable idea of human nature, one which he champions explicitly against Mencius in holding that "human nature is detestable" (*xìng è* 性恶) and repeatedly stressing that it is like rough wood in need of a pressboard form.[69] However, unlike Mencius employing the term for the purpose of species differentiation (and not referring to what is the case for this and that human being), Xún Zǐ uses *xìng* to refer to what is common to *each and all*, from the most lowly and dissolute to the most noble and sagacious.[70] This distinction proves decisive.

Xún Zǐ defines what for him are the two major factors of human life, *xìng* 性 and *wěi* 伪, respectively describing the former term for human nature as "beginning root material" and the latter term for artifice as "flourishing discourse," the former being detestable and the latter being admirable and good.[71] *Xìng* thus stands in contradistinction to *wěi*. *Xìng* is inner, including what is there at birth; *wěi* and its goodness is outer, encompassing external morality, codes of conduct, social standards and practices, and self-cultivation.[72] So as *xìng* is to *wěi*, matter is to form, roughly speaking.

On this basis, Xún Zǐ rather boldly declares that human nature (*xìng*) is detestable and that good comes only through willful exertion, through artifice (*wěi*).[73] When culture flourishes with the figure of the sage, all parts of *wěi*, that is, ritual, music, and the correct use of language, all affect and transform inborn natural desires, and it is such an environment that creates deference and Xún Zǐ's model of social harmony.[74]

What makes *xìng* detestable for Xún Zǐ is not that it is evil in the sense of a Christian rejection of the flesh as sinful.[75] Rather, for Xún Zǐ, *xìng* is detestable because, like Aristotelian prime matter, it is undefined and degenerate, a kind of dumb avarice groping for survival in a Hobbes-like state of nature that lacks governance and its imposition of outer form.[76] And so, what for Mencius are four shoots growing spontaneously out of the human heart-mind are for Xún Zǐ goods that must be imposed from without if people are to stand a chance of actually becoming properly human.

Xún Zǐ's Restricted Usefulness for Somaesthetics and the Potential Value of New Approaches to Mencius

And this creeping oppositional dualism begins to show the main problem with taking on Xún Zǐ in support of a pragmatist somaesthetic philosophy.

For Mencius, human nature is in process. For Xún Zǐ, it is a bit more of a static, native quantity. For Mencius, human nature is the acorn, the mighty oak, and all intervening stages. For Xún Zǐ, it is simply the acorn. For Mencius, human nature is part of a holism where the natural meets the socially artificial. For Xún Zǐ, arts and artifice are external, and not part of *xìng*. Put another way, Qing-era scholar Dài Zhèn 戴震 identifies the main issue in the debate as a difference in the scope of *xìng*, with Xún Zǐ talking about what is held in common in the sense of the lowest common denominator and Mencius talking about what differentiates the human species, where Mencius sees artifice, especially in the development of somatic paradigms for ritual propriety, as marking humanity and separating us from animals generally, even if civilization's artifice does not mark each individual human as such (though the detailed contours of Dài's rather nuanced alignment with Mencius in favor of Xún Zǐ should be noted, as he disdains the former's neglect of emotion, even if the latter's dualism is ultimately rejected).[77]

In any case, the particular way in which Xún Zǐ understands *xìng* or human nature ends up being connected to how he arguably abandons one of the most important precepts in the Chinese worldview, a major premise that anticipates the bearing of Shusterman's Dewey-inspired pragmatism—*tiān rén hé yī* 天人合一, the idea that the heavens and humanity are one. Calling this bedrock principle into question, Xún Zǐ argues that cultivating *dào* 道, which would include self-cultivation through ritual, means realizing *the difference* between humanity and the heavens.[78] For him, the establishment of ritual propriety comes from mytho-historical sages like Yáo, who, despite being granted no special favor by the heavens in their nature, in their *xìng*, set forth the rites and established society.[79] For Xún Zǐ, this grand work, attributable to forces external to the lowest common denominator's *xìng*, unites inborn nature with artifice and thereby also unites heaven and earth, further implying a prior separation.[80]

Unfortunately, though, this results in a dichotomy not unlike the well-worn Hellenic view that muses speak from beyond earth, from some transcendental realm, *to* the artist. For Xún Zǐ, such sages receive the arts, here the ritual/musical performance continuum, from without, and use that to impose form on humanity's otherwise despicable bodily urges. These binary oppositions might not present exactly the same problems as those born of the dualisms at the base of Platonic philosophy, Abrahamic religions, and lay Euro-American morality, but the effect is similar—the bodily dimension of human nature is devalued, degraded, despised, detested, or otherwise diminished. Christianity might hold that human nature is evil and sinful, while Xún Zǐ maintains that it is merely unhewn and unlovely. In any case, such oppositional, hierarchical dualisms ill suit pragmatism and somaesthetics.

Though it is just a passing remark, in light of the foregoing, possible problems can nonetheless be seen where Shusterman speaks of "Xunzi argu[ing] that the exemplary person should master 'the method of controlling the vital breath' and be 'absorbed in the examination of his inner self' and 'scorn mere external things.' "[81] The inside/outside dichotomy, here already quite stark, hints at a tendency toward the kind of rigid opposition that Shusterman often avoids as a matter of (cultivated) instinct.

And it is not just on the level of comparative philosophy that Xún Zǐ proves problematic. Indeed, the most famous figure of the Song Dynasty's neo-Confucian renaissance, Zhū Xī 朱熹, famously included Mencius's work when he established what would go on in later eras to become the canonical Four Books of Confucianism, rejecting Xún Zǐ and his dour view that leaders need to *press* human nature into a proper shape for setting a lamentably recurring trend in Chinese history toward heavy-handed, book-burning social control through the influence of his student Lǐ Sī 李斯, a prime minister in the Qin Dynasty.[82] With Zhū Xī's views going on to form the bedrock of Chinese orthodoxy in the centuries to follow, this particular criticism of Xún Zǐ gained traction with generations of intellectuals. Accordingly, Xún Zǐ has been seen (perhaps unjustly) as having "derailed the original Confucian mission and plunged China into a cycle of authoritarianism and corruption that lasted for more than two thousand years" and subsequently definitively excluded from anything that might be called the Confucian mainstream, although his reputation has experienced a bit of a revival in recent years, following rising appreciation for his talent for extended and systematic argument, a state of affairs that Paul R. Goldin aptly summarizes.[83]

And so, to put it simply, because of conceptual reasons owing to pragmatism's tendency to disdain oppositional mind/body dualisms and because of historical reasons stemming from the Chinese intellectual tradition, attempts to appropriate Xún Zǐ and his otherwise worthwhile insights for somaesthetics ought to be critical and circumspect. This is the case with Shusterman's engagement with Foucault, Merleau-Ponty, and James, among others, and a similar standard should apply to Xún Zǐ.

This is not to say that Xún Zǐ simply ought to be excluded from somaesthetics—far from it. Xún Zǐ has much to offer, provided that his use as a resource comes within limits appropriate to the somaesthetic project. So what is it that should be salvaged from Xún Zǐ here? Shusterman's interest in Xún Zǐ is certainly understandable, since, of all classical Confucian thinkers, he has the most to say on matters touching on somaesthetics. As Shusterman indicates, Xún Zǐ's dictum that "learning must never be concluded" has value for the somaesthetic project in terms of its advocacy of a specifically bodily mode of lifelong self-cultivation.[84] The question then becomes what doctrines connected to his view of human nature can be reworked or rethought in support of this distinctively Confucian approach to learning in order to enrich Shusterman's project without smuggling in any unwanted conceptual baggage.

When dealing with Confucianism and somaesthetics, *lǐ* has to be central, and thus the strategy called for here is one that in some way might cleave Xún Zǐ's approach to ritual *lǐ* from the one he takes to human nature. This is no easy task, given the importance of ritual *lǐ* to any Confucian theory of human nature. What then can be said of Xún Zǐ's particular insight into *lǐ*?

Playing with the ambiguity in English, one the one hand, it could be (and has been) said that, for Xún Zǐ, *lǐ* work to distinguish. *Lǐ* "take common belongings for use, take the eminent and humble as prime for refinement, take disparity for distinction, take the lofty and the weak as necessary."[85] As mentioned, Xún Zǐ goes on to describe how ritual *lǐ* involve the aesthetics of distinction vis-à-vis refinement, maintaining that "*lǐ* trim what is long and extend what is short, do away with excess, add to the deficient, reaching to the refinement of love and respect, so that the beauty of conduct flourishes."[86]

Again to recap, taking the ambiguity in another direction, it can be said that *lǐ* distinguish between things, between phenomena in the social field in a rather general and basic sense. For Xún Zǐ, this is so because *lǐ* are about becoming "fond of distinctions," such that "the eminent and the humble have rank, young and old are treated differently, the poor and rich each have different degrees of importance," all of which is meant to keep "distinctions between the noble who serve the noble and the vulgar who serve the base, the grandeur of the great, and the pettiness of the small."[87]

Reiterating their view, David L. Hall and Roger T. Ames point to a general trend in Confucian thought in anticipating a great deal of what Derrida expresses with his term "*différance*."[88] Here applying this thought to Xún Zǐ in particular, it is possible to make a tentative connection between the notion of distinction in Xún Zǐ's account of *lǐ* and Derrida's much later work on how deferring to the authority of sign chains and differing one thing from another—deferring and differing together—serve to generate meaning, broadly speaking. Without drawing any sort of direct equation, further connection can also be made to Pierre Bourdieu's notion of everyday taste as accompanying the kind of distinctions that place the subject within the social field:

> Taste classifies, and it classifies the one who classifies: Social subjects distinguish themselves through the distinctions they affect, between the beautiful and the ugly, the distinguished and the vulgar, and where they express or they reveal their position in objective classifications.[89]

While Derrida and Bourdieu are at times critical in their respective approaches to distinction in the social field, Xún Zǐ is far more upbeat in his assessment; and it is here that some of that authoritarian character for which he is so roundly condemned can be seen. True, Confucianism faces a similar accusation, generally speaking, but the harshness advocated by Xún Zǐ where he identifies the need for human nature to be pressed into shape can come across as a bit hard-hearted when it comes to so-called petty or small people, none of which is helped when Xún Zǐ is tied to the prevalent and negative historical narrative. Nonetheless, there is something of real value to these thoughts, to the insights of Xún Zǐ into ritual propriety and cultivating a fondness of distinction. These can aid the project of somaesthetics, particularly when connected to crucial remarks made by Xún Zǐ regarding the aesthetic side of ritual *lǐ* in his discourse on music.

Xún Zǐ, of all thinkers in the early Confucian canon, does the most to describe a link between ritual and aesthetics, which for him plays out in terms of the conceptual pair of *lǐ* and *yuè* 乐 (traditionally written 樂). *Yuè* is often translated simply as music, but in reality the term is much richer than that, with classical Confucianism taking music to mean not just the phenomenon of rhythm, tone, and timbre, but rather seeing musical theater as involving other domains like dress, dance, gymnastics, and so on, such that in the early Confucian works *yuè* comes to stand for the arts more generally through synecdoche.

So what is the connection? As has been said earlier, the thinking here is that what *lǐ* orients in the everyday, performance of *yuè* on stage amplifies. Giving heightened attention on stage to the ritual gestures of the everyday and using those refined gestures along with song and dance is supposed to entertain and edify the audience. In turn, this is all supposed to educate the community as a whole, making people fond of distinctions through aesthetic pleasure, in such a way that *lǐ* and *yuè* mutually reinforce each other, as can be well seen in Xún Zǐ's statement that "music has harmonies which cannot be changed; ritual has principles which cannot be changed. Music unites; ritual differentiates. The unity of ritual and music conducts the human heart-mind. Music's emotionality deals with change at its most basic level."[90]

Moreover, Xún Zǐ's doctrinal extension of Confucius's aphorism draws upon the connection between the shared characters for joy (lè 乐) and music (yuè 乐), and with them music's conceptual pairing with ritual lǐ in his idea that joy accompanies ritual and music.[91] As regards ritual/musical self-cultivation, Xún Zǐ really fleshes out the core Confucian idea of joy being deeply connected to music in his observation that

> performing music clarifies the will; cultivating ritual perfects conduct. The ear and eye become acute, blood and bodily energy harmonize and balance, movements and customs transform and change, everything under heaven becomes tranquil, and everyone together enjoys what is beautiful and good. Thus it said: music is joy.[92]

And it is here, in the discussion of aesthetic pleasure with respect to the body in connection to human emotion, that Xún Zǐ makes a distinctive contribution to early Confucianism and offers resources for somaesthetics with how he builds on Confucius's aphorism with his own stronger claim—"music is joy, being inevitable in human feeling."[93] In order to understand the value of Xún Zǐ's insight, it is necessary to first have some context though.

And here the crucial point regarding Xún Zǐ comes into view. The main antagonist opposed by Xún Zǐ in his remarks on music is *not* Mencius, his philosophical opponent concerning the status of human nature within Confucianism, but rather the school of Mohism. This is so because of Mohism's hostility toward ritualizing life and not because of anything having to do with the intra-Confucian human nature debate per se. Mohism's leader, Mò Zǐ 墨子, adopts the position that music is extraneous to governance and that it takes away valuable resources from society, distracting people from their proper occupations (farmers in fields, etc.), no matter the pleasure it might yield.[94] All of this leads Mohists to the conclusion that music, especially Confucian notions of ritual and music, are to be condemned.

Xún Zǐ takes aim at the Mohists, since, despite the latter party's contention that ritual and music are grand diversions, they overlook the invaluable regulation and stability that ritual and music bring to other more supposedly necessary human endeavors. This is because, for Confucians, music and rituals are very much about performance, the performance of social roles. The argument against the Mohists is that those endeavors, very much including toil in the fields and the feeding of people, take place through the social coordination of roles that music and ritual bring. To reiterate the point from earlier, music and ritual may seem like wastes of financial resources, but the point is the wider economy, which, following Confucius himself, only works when "the sovereign reigns, ministers minister, fathers father, and sons 'son.' "[95] This is the idea that Xún Zǐ extends in his more particular observation that it is precisely courtly music that brings subordinates and inferiors together while also setting up relationships where sons defer to fathers, younger brothers to elder brothers, and so on.[96] Thus, for Xún Zǐ specifically and Confucianism more generally, music cannot be condemned for being superfluous, as the Mohists would have it.

Xún Zǐ's remarks on ritual and music, particularly where he expresses his ire against Mohists and not his fellow Confucians like Mencius, represent a potential conceptual juncture. It might be possible here to separate the more useful aspects of Xún Zǐ's work, like his remarks on aesthetic pleasure, the arts, and ritual, from the pessimistic position he takes on human nature. True, ultimately Xún Zǐ connects what he says concerning the educative effect of aesthetic pleasure to the pessimistic view that habilitating dissolute human nature is possible *with and only with* certain highly regulated forms of aesthetic pleasure, but this connection between aesthetic education and Xún Zǐ's particular view of human nature is far from necessary.

Indeed, much of what Xún Zǐ has to say against the antiaesthetic/anaesthetic Mohists still holds even if one takes an approach to human nature more similar to that of Mencius, whose account of ritual as spontaneously "self-so-ing," like one of the four limbs, could certainly accommodate the idea that music, ritual, and joy are likewise similarly spontaneous and inevitable in human feeling, as Xún Zǐ maintains against the Mohists. Likewise, the fondness for distinctions that is central to Xún Zǐ's account of self-development and that is cast as one of the major functions of music and ritual, contra the austere Mohists, can be made to work inside of a framework more like that of Mencius, as there is no reason why fondness for distinction and the idea of *lǐ* working to generate meaning in the social field needs to be connected to the specific type of misanthropic hierarchy advocated by Xún Zǐ.

Therefore, there is clear warrant to claim that both Xún Zǐ's work to connect education through aesthetic pleasure to the Confucian idiom of *lǐ* and his efforts to describe *lǐ* in terms of differentiation, distinction, and the proliferation of meaning in discourse are both matters worthy of consideration by Shusterman and advocates of the somaesthetic approach. This is to say nothing of acknowledging the more general service provided to enterprises like somaesthetics by Xún Zǐ's energetic defenses of the value of Confucianism's body-conscious aesthetic against attacks from Mohists opposed to such aesthetic considerations. The suggestion here is that Xún Zǐ's work in areas like these should be evaluated separately from his attack on Mencius's doctrine of good human nature wherever possible, particularly where Xún Zǐ clearly has another target in mind outside of Confucianism, as is the case with ritual/music and the Mohists; and this would continue the trend of critical and partial appropriation one sees in Shusterman's engagement with thinkers from the European-American sphere.

On the other side, Mencius's view that both the origination of standards of ritual propriety and their changing adaptation to circumstance occur as natural outgrowths of the human constitution stands more in line with Shusterman's premises and goals, if only because it avoids the oppositional dualisms that ultimately call for the restricted use of Xún Zǐ as a resource for somaesthetics. Moreover, the way in which Mencius places the creative force behind ritual cultivation not in the self, but in the species and its broader social environment, shows other possibilities for somaesthetics, possibilities taken up in more recent years and briefly explored in what follows. Considering such lines of thought can complement Shusterman's focus on emancipatory *self*-cultivation with one on *social*-cultivation and the emergence of somatic practices from the social manifold, all of which could be helpful in postindustrial, liberal, democratic contexts and in liberationist social movements aligned with pragmatism.

There is, however, the quite reasonable objection that critical approaches from a contemporary enterprise like somaesthetics would likely find much to quibble about within a Mencius-inspired social/political philosophy, given the glaring anachronisms. This is not fatal to the enterprise, though, as the reappraisals in recent literature on both Mencius's protodemocratic people-as-roots (or *mínběn* 民本) theory and his female, maternal sensibility attest.[97] Perhaps one of the better examples of this contemporary revival of Mencius, and one that speaks to somaesthetics more directly, is the previously mentioned recent work on "subjectality" by Lǐ Zéhòu.

All of this points to a real convergence between what Lǐ Zéhòu talks about with laboring on sedimented collective unconscious as an aesthetically structured source of freedom and what Richard Shusterman gets at when he speaks about ameliorating unconscious habits with conscious somaesthetic practice. Indeed, this connects to what Shusterman addresses in his assessment of Butler and her denial that interior bodily resources are available within subjectivation, where he instead argues the point that "intelligent spontaneity is not mere uneducated reflex but rather the acquired product of somatically sedimented habit, which often goes by the name of muscle memory."[98] The use of the term sedimentation here is no coincidence; Shusterman is pointing to something like subjectality as understood by Lǐ Zéhòu. Lǐ is dealing with the ur-historical conditioning and control of the *soma* politic and what conscious somaesthetic practice ought to address and ameliorate.[99] Moreover, where these approaches diverge, with Lǐ Zéhòu's contemporary approach to Mencius giving attention to the development of humanity and rites in the collective unconscious on a macro level and with Richard Shusterman focusing on cultivation on the micro level of the somatic self against a background of unconscious habit, the two can complement each other.

However, despite Mencius providing much less content when it comes to somaesthetics than his philosophical combatant Xún Zǐ, there is a very real sense in which Lǐ Zéhòu's own work hinges on the prevalence of a specific reading preferring Mencius to Xún Zǐ regarding the status of somaesthetic practices vis-à-vis human nature, and this may anticipate a conceptual fork in the road lying ahead for Shusterman as he continues his engagement with East Asian, Chinese, and Confucian sources. All of this is to say that, when it comes to Shusterman's own distinct though proximate project, a similar need might arise at some point where, perhaps more because of Xún Zǐ's negative conceptual baggage than because of Mencius's own positive utility for contemporary somaesthetics, sides need to be chosen. This remains true even if some of Xún Zǐ's insights into ritual, self-cultivation, and the like can be rehabilitated (and they very likely can, to some extent). In any case, the ultimate decision ought to go in favor of Mencius and the mainstream Confucian tenet that human nature is, in some perhaps limited way, good.

Assessing Somaesthetics with Regard to Mencius and Xún Zǐ

Shusterman's somaesthetics addresses a crucially important topic, and it does so in a way that takes intercultural philosophy to heart. Chinese philosophy, and Confucianism in particular, are influential here, and this investigation shows that this influence calls for critical assessment through classical Confucianism's debate on ritual propriety being external or internal with respect to human nature.

Regarding this debate, Shusterman himself observes, "If Confucianism still survives as a flourishing influential philosophy, it is partly because it knew how to embrace the conflicting doctrines of Mencius and Xunzi within the fold of classical Confucianism."[100] However, the foregoing shows that there is good reason not to embrace these conflicting doctrines with the same affection, at least when it comes to somaesthetics.

While Xún Zǐ may be a valuable exponent of rites, practices, and theories that anticipate what we now call somaesthetics, his remarks are entangled in a larger view and connected to quasi-dualistic precepts and an externalism of rites that ultimately devalue the body in a manner contrary to the aims of somaesthetics as Shusterman describes it. While it is undeniable that the way in which Xún Zǐ approaches the particularly aesthetic dimension of ritual and the manner of his detailed account linking ritual and musical theater have real value both for extending Confucius's compelling yet scant remarks on the subject, for refuting anti-Confucian positions, and for the project of somaesthetics, there is clear reason nonetheless to make only qualified use of Xún Zǐ as a resource. The view that Xún Zǐ attacks, the view of Mencius, proves not only to be more in the Confucian mainstream *and* more amenable to somaesthetic approaches, but indeed it *also* offers new avenues for considering the emergence and historical course of sedimented ritual somatic practices in the material ordering of the human environment, as demonstrated by the recent work of Lǐ Zéhòu.

Perhaps on its own, Mencius's doctrine of human nature being good does not have as much useful content for somaesthetics as the counterargument of Xún Zǐ, and perhaps it is only by putting Mencius into conversation with the broader Confucian tradition and with more recent thinkers that this line of thought might then contribute to the project of somaesthetics. Even if this is so, it is in any case true that moving more in the direction of Mencius and those following him can benefit and refine somaesthetics by critically reassessing some of the more troublesome precepts lurking underneath Shusterman's explicit influences and his inherited vocabulary. Moreover, engaging Mencius and more contemporary Mencius-influenced thinkers like Lǐ Zéhòu has the added advantage of enriching somaesthetics by deepening the interdisciplinary and intercultural theoretical engagement already taking place as well as the benefit of resituating ritual somatic practice and the efforts of somaesthetic philosophy within the broader historical sweep of the productive and restrictive factors in human development.

Conclusion

With the argument moving forward, the following points now come into view.

15. Somaesthetics deals with the creative fashioning and refinement of bodily subject life. It thus deals with the physical effects of subjectivation and has the goal of making the varied and several ways in which the body often unconsciously turns on itself it into a matter of conscious awareness.

16. Somaesthetics also has a distinctly Confucian influence, since many of the theoretical and practical notions at play in this approach to bodily cultivation have deep roots in East Asia. Somaesthetics cuts across one of the major quarrels within Confucianism, namely, the debate over the status of ritual propriety being either a natural internal quality or an external imposition onto human nature. While there is some restricted value in the latter and more pessimistic perspective, seeing somaesthetic practice as something growing *out of* and not imposed *onto* human nature is more consistent with taking a long and more hopeful view of humanity in world observation as well as the doctrine of subjectality in general.

And so, as regards the discussion here, bringing in somaesthetics begins a distinctly practical turn, adding to the theoretical take on human development of macro-level subjectality positioned within this project to complement work done on micro-level subjectivation. Now the issue becomes putting all of these theoretical and conceptual sources together into some kind of coordinate unity for the purpose of rhizomatic growth. In this particular context, growth means expanding the limits of how the subject is talked about beyond the confines of melancholy in subjectivation while still responding to Foucault's basic challenge to heed both the productive and restrictive aspects of this process. And so, the task for the remaining portion of the project presented here is clear—showing how a practical turn toward the fashioning of the artful body can change the stakes of subject life.

Final Thoughts

[A] body habituated to timid, subservient, inhibited expression will find it almost impossible to express itself suddenly in the kind of bold and defiantly assertive action needed to challenge social structures that pervasively inculcate inferiority through somatic habit formation that shapes mental attitudes and not merely body postures.[1]

—Richard Shusterman

Changing the Stakes

In Shusterman's remark about facing "the kind of bold and defiantly assertive action needed to challenge social structures that pervasively inculcate inferiority through somatic habit formation" there is something already presupposed about the nature of such a challenge. Boldness, defiance, and assertiveness are all well and good, but such qualities neither exhaust the possibilities for challenging such social structures, nor are they entirely free of conceptual difficulties.

Nonetheless, when the question of resistance likewise arises within Butler's account of subjectivation, it is in such terms that challenges to social structure are posed, with her distinctive addition being that of the language of rage. For her, the issue concerns what happens when life is itself threatened by the compromises and turns-on-self that subjects make in order to get along. If all of the ritual normativity implicitly and explicitly asked of the subject in order to survive is not itself survivable, then recourse needs to be made to some other means of self-preservation, namely, rage. This leads to Butler's finding that

> survival, not precisely the opposite of melancholia, but what melancholia puts in suspension—requires redirecting rage against the lost other, defiling the sanctity of the dead for the purposes of life, raging against the dead in order not to join them.[2]

There is a certain logic to redirecting rage against what has been lost in constitutive bargains for recognition and survival in situations where these compromises yield diminishing returns for the melancholic subject. These considerations lead Butler to see the dynamic underlying subjectivation as ultimately combining a Hegelian notion of recognition with Baruch Spinoza's particular reading of the Latin term *conatus* in reference to how, over and above more particular manifestations of a desire to live or a self-preservation imperative, "each thing, to the extent that it is in itself, strives [*conatur*] to persevere in its being."[3] She notes that,

> for Hegel, it is important to remember, the desire to be, the desire to persist in one's own being—a doctrine first articulated by Spinoza in his *Ethics*—is fulfilled only through the desire *to be recognized*. Spinoza marks for us the desire to live, to persist, upon which any theory of recognition is built. And because the terms by which recognition operates may seek to fix and capture us, they run the risk of arresting desire, and of putting an end to life.[4]

This comment builds upon Butler's previous description of Spinoza's conatus figure in reference to the basic bind of subjectivation wherein the social realm becomes inextricable from psychic life, where she writes:

> If one accepts Spinoza's notion that desire is always the desire to persist in one's own being, and recasts the *metaphysical* substance that forms the ideal for desire as a more pliable notion of social being, one might then be prepared to redescribe the desire to persist in one's own being as something that can be brokered only within the risky terms of social life. The risk of death is thus coextensive with the insurmountability of the social.[5]

Elsewhere, Butler calls back to one of her other major sources of inspiration, Nietzsche, in order to expand upon what she later cashes out as a prefiguration of pre-Freudian death drive somewhat poorly and hesitantly articulated by Spinoza:

> In a Nietzschean vein, such a slave morality may be predicated upon the sober calculation that it is better to "be" enslaved in such a way than not to "be" at all. But the terms that constrain

the option to being versus not being "call for" another kind of response.⁶

However, as previously described, this calculus can be upset if life as an enslaved subject is itself under threat, and this certainly means when normative pressures translate to increased aggression in the turn-on-self and the possibility of self-harm. Open revolt and death become worth the risk if the price of recognition and survival under a regime of subject slavery is too onerous; it is simply a matter of costs outweighing what at one point *might* have passed for benefits.

Now, it is true that Butler has called into question some of her past rhetoric concerning the conatus, particularly where she writes that "it would seem that whatever else a being may be doing, it is persevering in its own being, and at first, this seemed to mean that even various acts of apparent self-destruction have something persistent and at least potentially life-affirming in them."⁷ Her main reason for tempering her views concerning the explanatory power of the conatus figure is the question of what precisely one's "own being" means here, when a subject with its own putative being emerges after the fact, and when, following the basic template of Kant's notion of respect, "it is not possible to refer to one's own singularity without understanding the way in which that singularity becomes implicated in the singularities of others."⁸

Nevertheless, this desire for life, neither wholly located in some singular core of interiority, nor in some external recognizing other, but instead indeterminately in what Butler might call the "*ek-stasis*" of the interplay of the two, can face truly threatening circumstances.⁹ When a desire to live, however disperse in its location, is exploited and twisted into something that threatens life in the singular or a way of life in the plural, it becomes perfectly reasonable to rage against the basic bargain of subjectivation, rejecting what has become lost in becoming subject and defiling that which is dead and departed as far as the subject is concerned, all for the purpose of continuing the life that was *supposed* to be secured by becoming subject.

With there being no inner space from which to launch a revolt, a person's rage must make use of what is at hand in the external social world. Being impoverished when it comes to resources with which to wage this campaign, the raging subject must engage in a kind of guerilla warfare, capturing unsecure enemy weapon caches and redeploying these words in discourse that calls hostile regimes into questions. Put less figuratively, this amounts to taking the basic terms of interpellating discourse, the terms through which subjects are hailed into being and through which they learn to recognize themselves, and exploiting the ability of specifically preexisting terms to be resignified. Put even more simply, this means taking words like "n-----" and "q----" back (but it also means taking back a variety of gestures and behaviors, be they subtle, grand, or in between). In what, precisely, does such ability to resignify consist though?

As previously mentioned, such rage exploits what Butler points to as a weakness inherent in "sign chains," namely, that the actual use of the signs, tokens, and terms of discourse is riddled with temporal gaps, which in Butler's view, open up "the possibility of a reversal of signification, [and also] the way for an inauguration of signifying possibilities that exceed those to which the term has been previously bound."[10]

However, this approach has limits. Butler's way of dealing with this only leaves the subject with a minor ability to struggle and writhe inside of slightly less constricting chains, or inside a more saggy and less skin-tight prison, as it were; but the prison remains well intact. Reflective of this somewhat beleaguered posture, Butler notes that "although such rage may be required to break the melancholic bind, there is no final reprieve from the ambivalence and no final separation of mourning from melancholia"[11] and follows this up by stating that "no rage can sever the attachment to alterity, except perhaps a suicidal rage."[12] With subject melancholia being seemingly intractable and with rage-filled resignification presenting what are only partial and unsatisfying solutions, there still exists the problem of having to survive with the "Other" and with other real people, a problem intensified in the many less than optimal social and political climates that are inimically hostile to the continued survival of suspect classes.

Responding with rage in this manner to the problems that occur in subjectivation is valid and, moreover, it is necessary. Amid threats by social forces to the subject's survival, it is certainly warranted to have a doctrine of overt resistance against power and, moreover, it makes sense to have a lean, if not spartan, view of what is possible in such a combination guerilla war/prison insurrection, if only to avoid fighting with a mistaken and possibly dangerous view of what might be strategically and tactically achievable. Whatever the merits of this approach to rage and resignfication in subjectivation may be, though, this need not be the only way of dealing with the issues raised here.

Consider what has been said about bold and defiant resistance, especially as concerns Butler's specific notion of rage and the inability to sever links to alterity completely. In this case, it makes perfect sense to develop alternate

Final Thoughts

ways of resisting power structures. Addressing the scene in contemporary China and the power of practices like *qigōng*, which certainly falls under the general heading of somaesthetics, to span the political and nonpolitical realms and slip by unnoticed at times and act as part of "subtler" and "ambiguous, ironic and metonymic framing strategies," even within authoritative power structures, Patricia Thornton points to how

> protest movements can and do succeed even in highly repressive political contexts, and in fact often do so by deploying a mix of strategies and repertoires to advance their cause, many of which would appear to be suboptimal, counterproductive or simply ineffective in stable democratic systems.[13]

Adding to this insightful view regarding somaesthetic practice in covert resistance, the suggestion here is that the benefits of plural and at times covert strategies of resistance has its place as a response to subjectivation generally speaking and without regard to the specific level of threat that the subject experiences in less than ideal situations.

The reasoning here is that overt, bold, defiant, and assertive resistance may not always be the best option when it comes to responding to subjectivation, given how disperse, manifold, and anonymous the process of subject-making is. A great number of subjects, even those in severely disempowered groups or classes, do not suffer an absolute and immediate threat to the desire to persist in being at all times. Even for those who do face the extreme archetypal circumstances mentioned here, only rarely does an intimidating voice actually bellow "Hey, you there!" with noncompliance bringing a clear threat of mortal danger.

Rather, death by a thousand cuts is the more common specter haunting the kind of subject that is formed through a variety of recognition encounters in a number of different, often disjointed, contexts. Not being under the threat of death but still being without clear targets for resistance, strategy would dictate marshaling resources for the right time and place, instead of engaging in open warfare (at least not as a first option). Proper settings for resistance may not always be available, but resistance in this mode does not exhaust what comes with being a subject, nor does it deplete the possibilities that a subject might have for dealing with power.

A well-rounded theory of the subject would benefit from having plural strategic responses to power. Out and out resistance is but one way of doing things. How then could somatic feeling be *another* resource for subject life and how could it in any way be *like* the inner resource or space denied by Butler as a possible ground for resistance, given how any such internal wellspring of resistance would be thwarted in advance by pre-existing power structures?

The view advanced here is that feeling, the capacity for aesthesis, is the specific mode of how one appears on the scene prior to any particular instances of interpellation and subjectivation, and that this is at least part of the rhizomatic core of the manifold process of subject life. It can even be claimed that this notion of appearance is something like the kind of prior interior source for resistance so vigorously rejected by Butler. How so?

One suggestion has already been given here by borrowing from Arendt's understanding of appearance and being-in-the-world as occurring (1) prior to particular instances of interpellation/subjectivation and (2) in a way capable of refinement in the form of art surpassing conventional purposiveness. A second suggestion, very much connected to the first, is that appearance and being-in-the-world should, at least within this analysis, include feeling in the multivalent sense of aesthesis proper, because it is not just vulnerability, but rather *felt* vulnerability upon appearing in the world, that is needed for subjectivation to occur.

Butler's work—with its language of threats to survival, with its appropriation of Spinoza's idea of the conatus that would make existence as a prisoner better than no existence at all, and particularly with its talk of violence to the subject—already leans in the direction of the idea of feelings of pain not only greatly affecting the basic topology of consciousness, but pain or its threat enacting and initiating the dynamic. The more general point here is that basic modes of consciousness/self-consciousness are profoundly shaped by pain. Within Butler's telling, consciousness turns on itself and becomes self-consciousness, affecting a dubious but necessary quantum leap because of real or threatened pain, violence, or death.

Now, of course it has to be recognized that pain, violence, and death are not exclusively about feeling or aesthesis, and indeed Butler often employs the more ontic language of the conatus and the desire to persist in being in her description of the turn-on-self in interpellative subjectivation (though her recent work has seen even the conatus reevaluated in terms of the aesthetic language of feeling toward others).[14] In any case, the role of pain, violence, and death in the making of the subject body must be reckoned with to some degree in terms of real feeling and felt threat; these concerns are at least part of the story. And so, the contention here is that *The Psychic Life of Power*, whether in Butler's account of recognition and desire or in the actual lived experience of the subject apart from any book, ought to be reconsidered and in turn supplemented by an appreciation of its felt, aesthetic dimension.

This is so because, upon being drawn into a grim structure of discursive determinism and purposiveness, consciousness becomes self-consciousness precisely because of *feelings* provoked in the course of encounters of recognition with other people. What then prevents self-consciousness from becoming something else or perhaps *something more* through modes of feeling other than those connected to vulnerability, pain, violence, and death? Why not explore sources of aesthetic pleasure and cultivation capable of affecting real change for the subject without the threat of pain or death? Why not take the basic fact of appearance and the brute capacity for feeling, which are prior to and then often subsequently exploited in subjectivation, as things that can be improved upon so as to improve subject life? Why not improve appearance and feeling at the outset? Why should art and felt aesthetic pleasure derived from art not aid the ills of subject self-consciousness, given the alternative framework of appearance, recognition, purposiveness, and endurance at play with artworks?

Stepping back from artworks for a moment to aesthetics more broadly, it is worth pausing to look at how the basic capability to feel, more than any one actual feeling, seems like a very good candidate for the type prior internal source of resistance over and above the processes of subjectivation that Butler rejects. Of course, her point, well explored in her earlier work *Gender Trouble*, and sadly lived out by persons of queer, unacceptable, or foreclosed forms of sexuality, is that the pervasive instantiation of normative self-monitoring behavior ushered by subjectivation changes the very topography of pain and pleasure and the borders between internal and external. With gender performance being so pervasive, there is no prior *and coherent* core of being "born this way" left over that might provide an internal basis for pleasure, satisfaction, and self-fulfillment over and above external norms. This is why, despite the affirmations of well-meaning slogans, closeted queer life is so deeply vexing.[15]

This reading makes pain and pleasure subordinate to desire, such that the desire to persist in being, the conatus figure, overrides all, allowing for pain and pleasure, with their respective bases in bodily matter, to be warped by social normative forms, as is seen in the ugly logic underlying survival in the closet. This is the point of Butler's critical reading of Mladen Dolar's notion of love being possibly beyond interpellation.[16] Taking subjectivation seriously means seeing it as *total* in its effect of initiating reflexive psychic life and making particular subject bodies initially matter within coherent social norms such that no prior internal remainders are left over to offer meaningful resistance.

And the operative word here is internal. There may, in fact, not be any such internal remainder for meaningful, coherent resistance. It may be that the capacity for pleasure and pain, even if drawn back away from particular experience and dealt with in some kind of phenomenology of the conatus, are simply inchoate and inarticulable, following Butler's analysis of the body as a kind of incomprehensible Aristotelian prime matter *made to matter* through the formal and formative imposition of normalizing social recognition. However, the point here is different, but it is still made with an eye toward respecting the basic principle of subjectivation being thorough.

There may, in fact, not be prior *internal* remainders left over for resistance, but there are prior *external* remainders capable of speaking to resistance projects in ways far surpassing silent prime matter. What would such external remainders of subjectivation be, if subjectivation represents such a thorough and complete process of forming and maintaining social reality? The answer presented here, borrowing significantly from Confucian sources old and new, is that it lies in the already fashioned matter of past subject lives that accrue, sediment, and inhere unconsciously in the form of tradition.

Why does a prior remainder of external sediment help here? How might this in any way substitute for a prior internal source of creative, spontaneous resistance against the harms of subjectivation denied by Butler if the internal and the external are two different things?

The answer lies in this—subjectivation and subjectality, respectively referring to the interrelated micro- and macroscopic views of human development, are *processes* and not static things. Strictly speaking, subjectivation does not deal with the subject as a human being, nor does subjectality deal with the survival of human beings. Rather, both of these approaches are ultimately less about being and more about becoming, about human becoming. Subjectivation is about the never-ending *process* of humans becoming subject; subjectality is about the ongoing *process* of plural subject lives collectively becoming the media and material of tradition. What is "internal" to the subject and experienced as psychic becomes internal as such through subjectivation; what is "external" to the subject and experienced as social becomes external as such through subjectality. Internal subject life is really the constitutive internalization of exterior social sediment; and exterior social sediment is really the ongoing externalization of a manifold of "internal" subject lives in the form of cultural tradition. This is precisely what Marx means by the naturalization of humanity and the humanization of nature applied to the micro level of the single human subject.

Butler insists, though, that no internal remainder for resistance exists. However, her comments elsewhere on Pierre Bourdieu show how the nature of the process at play implies a breakdown of the rigid separation of "the 'internal' dimension of performative language over and against what is 'external' language,"[17] leading her to ask the question, "Once the body is established as a site for the working through of performative force, i.e., as the site where performative commands are received, inscribed, carried out, or resisted, can the social and linguistic dimensions that Bourdieu insists on keeping theoretically separate, be separated at all in practice?"[18]

And so, taking subjectivation and expanding upon it with an idea of subjectality, the point is that internal and external, self and society, are not pregiven quantities. Instead, what matters is that the internal, the external, and the subjects negotiating the fluctuating border between internal and external are always in the making. Apart from any more narrowly applied reading of Bourdieu, this is Butler's basic point about the psyche amid ongoing interpellation. However, whereas Butler uses this kind of logic to claim that there is no prior internal remainder for resisting subjectivation on what would be one's own terms, given how obscured any boundary between internal and external might be, the claim here in this work is somewhat different.

The contention here is that what matters for waging effective resistance against the power structures that produce subjects is *not* that such resistance be pure and private but rather that it be prior and with its own proprietary purposiveness. Prior resources for dealing with the dilemmas of the subject, including those putatively belonging to the external social realm, can, through process, *become* internal while still retaining a "prior" socially coherent meaning in connection to the seemingly external temporality of macro-level human tradition. Over time and with practice, some part of these common resources comes to *belong* to the practitioner, but not in a way that would be about exercising pure and private ownership before the fact of any subject life. If "I" take up a musical instrument, a yogic practice, a kind of meditation, a martial art, or a type of dance with the guidance of an instructor, eventually—and it may take years—imitating ceases and improvisation begins. This move to improvisation occurs when a common framework like those mentioned becomes "mine" not as a possessed object, but rather becomes "mine" as *familiar* and as a site of intimate passionate attachment. A practice becoming familiarly "mine" like this allows for novel modes of recognition where the prison walls of everyday self-consciousness cease rigid separation of the "inner" subject realm and the "outer" objective world, thereby exposing the ultimate contingency of the purportedly necessary purpose- and power-driven structures of recognition that make up subject life.

When bodily life involves alternative modes of purposiveness, as is the case in artistic practices marked by a proprietary sense of purposiveness without connection to the prevailing purposiveness of everyday life, then something occurs that surpasses outright determination by social forces in advance of subject, but that still satisfies the requirement of being prior to the subject and thus coherent within subject-forming social discourse. The body can become artful in this regard by developing technique on a personal level through practices aiming at the internalization, the appropriation, and the eventual value-adding appreciation of the unconscious sediment of human tradition. This approach works to expand the scope of subject life by recasting the meaning of purpose and of time beyond the scope of the individual human.

And so, joining subjectivation and subjectality together in somaesthetic practice as described here helps in appreciating the porousness of the bodily boundary between the internal and the external. And this helps in accounting for the origins of self, when, in Butler's words,

> persist[ing] in one's being means to be given over from the start to social terms that are never fully one's own. The desire to persist in one's own being requires submitting to a world of others that is fundamentally not one's own (a submission that does not take place at a later date, but which frames and makes possible the desire to be).[19]

Making the subject body artful with attention, care, and craft and doing so within a framework that *critically* internalizes external latent cultural sediment cannot take care of everything ailing the subject, not by a long shot. However, it can at least help in the project of *Giving an Account of Oneself* when, per Butler, "this self is already implicated in a social temporality that exceeds its own capacities for narration."[20]

The question, then, boils down to how one goes beyond *passively* experiencing this dual process of personal internalization of the psychic and the social externalization of cultural tradition to *also* refining and improving these processes for oneself *actively* through the dormant, unconscious resources developed in the course of cultural history. Since the task lies in appreciating the porous boundary between what is internal and what is external for the subject, then it makes sense to go to the very threshold itself—namely, the body. And since, working at the bodily threshold, the goal is affecting a change in subject self-consciousness, then it also makes sense to bring into play the kind of aesthetic feeling that alters the basic dimensions of recognition and the everyday purposiveness of normative social discourse—namely, art. Bringing these intermediate premises together, the approach here is to combine art and body in order to bring novel purposiveness and less harmful forms of *self*-recognition to subject life.

Within her aesthetic turn to the language of feeling, Butler may be right where she argues with a good deal of emphasis that "if there is no 'I' outside of feeling, and if the 'I' makes this case through giving a report on its feeling, then *the narrative 'I' becomes the transfer point through which the animated 'I' launches an autobiographical construction.*"[21] However, there is, strictly speaking, no reason why the format of the narrative "I" *must* be the only way of telling the subject's story. Literature and literary tropes are not the only means of telling a story. Somaesthetic practices, may *also* work to tell the story of how the subject body emerges in a variety of ways beyond the grammar and strictures of A-leads-to-B narrative. Art, even as performed and honed with one's own body, can tell, in fragments and feelings, stories of archetypes, norms, and unconscious patterns of behavior. Understanding this, there is no reason not to take this aesthetic turn further into the realm of art and technique in consideration of both the formation *and* the refinement of the subject body.

Butler may likewise be correct where she asserts that "only by persisting in alterity does one persist in one's 'own' being."[22] The claim here is that by making the body an artwork and thus a different type of other, persistence in alterity and subject temporality take on novel dimensions that positively change the stakes for what persisting in one's "own" being as conatus might mean. This approach positions artful bodily practice as at least one response to the genuine problems that necessarily occur in the course of subjectivation.

This project therefore responds to some of the friendly concerns raised by long-time coconspirator and constructive critic of Butler, Slavoj Žižek. Summing up the basic state of affairs, he writes:

The paradox at work here is that the very fact that there is no pre-existing positive Body in which one could ontologically ground our resistance to disciplinary power mechanism makes effective resistance possible. That is to say: the standard Habermasian argument against Foucault and "post-structuralists" in general is that since they deny any normative standard exempt from the contingent historical context, they are unable to ground resistance to the existing power edifice. The Foucauldian counter-argument is that the "repressive" disciplinary mechanisms themselves open up the space for resistance, in so far as they generate a surplus in their object.[23]

The response offered here in this book sidesteps the debate and declines to go down either of these two paths. The claim being made here is that it is not necessary for there to be a preexisting body that would resist repressive discipline, but rather that desire, in the form of the conatus, might be driven to find lasting existence or an alternative sense of temporality and purpose through artful bodily life, such that the artful body would essentially do its own thing, "resisting" the mainstream only coincidentally and not in terms of direct opposition.

This line of argument effectively rehabilitates some of Nietzsche's beliefs regarding artistry and subject life, and in a way that preserves the desire to persist in being as prior and primary, in line with Butler's views. Here, artistic creativity is not treated as the original state of psychic life, which is then constrained, as Nietzsche might have it. Instead, the conatus brings with it what Butler's reading of Spinoza casts as the simultaneous desires to live and to live well, with living well pointing to the domains of art and aesthetics not being aftereffects of, but instead being coemergent with, human survival.[24] This lines up to some degree with what Lǐ Zéhòu identifies as the natural human tendency to make it so that "eating is not merely due to hunger but becomes dining; the relationship between the two sexes is not merely one of copulation but becomes love" in a way that elevates survival and the relationship between humanity and nature above simple necessity through the accrual and sedimentation of a common object of aesthetic labor.[25]

Now, Žižek's basic criticism of Butler vis-à-vis resistance has to be acknowledged. He notes Butler's seeming conflation of "two radically opposed uses of the term 'resistance': one is the *socio-critical* use (resistance to power, etc.) the other the *clinical* use operative in psychoanalysis (the patient's resistance to acknowledging the unconscious truth of his symptoms, the meaning of dreams, etc.)."[26]

This may be true and certainly a similar conflation runs throughout this work, although it might be pointed out that elsewhere Žižek explicitly endorses Butler's move to link and even draw outright equivalences between different modes of reflexivity in ways that clearly correspond to how she blurs the lines between modes of resistance, a failing Žižek somehow finds unacceptable solely in the latter case.[27] It might also be that Butler's argument is not that these two modes of resistance *are* in fact the same as a matter of description (for subjectivation initiates the border and the breach between the social and the psychic), but that, as a matter of prescription, social resistance to power and clinical resistance to disclosing psychic life *should* converge or reconverge if an attempt is going to be made to heal that rupture.

In any case, what is outlined here as a possible response to the perils of subject life is *not* about resistance per se, but neither is it meant to counter that idea altogether. This notion of artful bodily practice can at least coincide with and possibly contribute to projects of resistance. But resistance and its entanglements are not primary points of focus here, as they might be with Butler. Instead, the emphasis here is on nonpurposive practice reconfiguring the stakes of subject life.

As for Žižek and his criticism of Butler, though, the conflation of social and clinical/psychic resistance has to be avoided, since

> one should maintain the crucial distinction between a mere "performative reconfiguration," a subversive displacement which remains *within* the hegemonic field and, as it were, conducts an internal guerrilla war of turning the terms the hegemonic field against itself, *and* the much more radical *act* of a thorough reconfiguration of the entire field which redefines the very conditions of socially sustained performativity.[28]

And so it is that Žižek admonishes Butler for being constrained by a framework restricting her version of the subject to only "marginal 'reconfigurations'" while "not allow[ing] for the radical gesture of the thorough restructuring of the hegemonic symbolic order in its totality."[29]

Conclusion

This project takes the aim of thoroughly restructuring this hegemonic symbolic order seriously, but it does so in a way that might be thought of as more subtle than radical. The following points do not build on the previous chapter-ending points, but instead summarize the book as a whole.

A. Subjectivation is the process of selves becoming (a) relational, (b) discursive, (c) bodily, and (d) ritually impelled subjects as prompted by a fundamental need to obtain social recognition for the purpose continued existence. As such, subjectivation is an intractable feature of being subject, one that is often met with rage and rebellious resignification, given the difficulty of finding possible resources for the subject not tainted and thwarted in advance by society's thorough formation of the subject's psychic life.

B. Art can be a resource for subject life, because it points to appearance prior to any subjectivation and to the possibility of a different temporal sense autonomous from the survival of this or that mortal subject or the sense of conventional purposiveness haunting the subject in the course of living according to ritual scripts for what often turns out to be the dubious purpose of bare survival. Refining the body and turning it into something artistic, then, has the potential to upset the dynamic at the root of subjectivation in the everyday.

C. Confucianism and its notion of ritual propriety can help here because it uses language similar to that of the (a) relational, (b) discursive, (c) bodily, and (d) ritually impelled subject while also exceeding more recent Euro-American work on subjectivation, with Confucianism presenting a view of art, artistry, and aesthetic experience as being constitutive of subject life and the basis for its refinement.

D. Subjectality takes the language of ritual and artistry in Confucianism alongside Kantian and Marxian precepts to describe the development of collective unconsciousness on the level of human society in a way that complements the exploration of the development of self-consciousness on individual level that subjectivation theory offers. Subjectality indicates how resources might be present in the unconscious sediment of human tradition and the development of technique and technology.

E. A reconsideration of appearance, technique, and memory shows how the intertwined techniques of interpellation, recognition, and subjectivation all point to resources for subject life. Appearance on the scene and the accompanying feeling of concerned vulnerability occur prior to being called out by any authority or other subject and thus prior to the emergence of the subject as such. This prior appearance/exposure stands as something technical; it deals with how beings organize and emerge in the social scene. Being a matter of technique, appearance does not need to be considered solely in terms of more elaborate technologies for surveillance and for calling out subjects into this and/or that confining role. Technique in appearance points to the possibility of qualitative refinement and possibilities for relating to others beyond the manner typical of most subjects, perhaps even calling to them and demanding thoughtful attention in a manner more like an artwork. However, refinement, so understood, has little do with pursuing technological advances in subjectivation and the confinement of subject life. Rather, such refinement must relate to technique through the resources at hand—the unconscious sedimented rituals that mark how subjects appear and are recognized moment to moment in everyday subject life.

F. Somaesthetics shows how this unconscious sediment of human tradition forms habitual bodily life and how such bodily habit can turn into conscious conduct. Somaesthetics shows how refining the body and its most basic physical presence in social space can bring novel senses of time, purpose, and self-recognition to subject life in ways that rework the exploitative dynamic at the root of subjectivation and that go beyond mere rage or rebellious resignification of the terms of power.

Point F, in particular, shows how, within this project, an undermining, or upheaval, or *Aufhebung*, may not be the goal, where instead the possibility of altering the dynamics of subjectivation is somewhat peripheral—a kind of side effect. This particular, nonexhaustive approach to artful bodily practice aims at habituating a different temporal structure for the body's persistence; it changes the stakes of desire, of the conatus, of the ur-passion, to persist in being. The changes may or may not be radical, for resistance is not itself the point.

Kant's descriptions of nonpurposive purposiveness, of negative freedom, of acts that are spontaneous with respect to cause and effect yet indeterminate with respect to ends, are of interest here, particularly insofar as these remarks prefigure Kant's later notion of the free play of ideas in aesthetic experiences of beauty. Following Arendt's subtle suggestion, perhaps other aesthetic ideals like ugliness, despite Kant's myopic focus on beauty, could also similarly do the job here of supplying an imagined concept without a real-world object and promoting some type of limited, negative freedom.[30] The key point according to this understanding is that aesthetic ideals (like beauty *or* ugliness) and the artworks approximating those ideals do not set forth ends in their demands on subjects, but rather allow for a more open-ended dynamic of recognition informed by a novel sense of how the appearance of an artful body can endure in a way that far surpasses the conventional subject's passionate attachments and desire to persist in being.

Whatever the target aesthetic ideals, be they beauty or some other less appreciated ideals, somaesthetic self-cultivation can work to unsettle prevailing power structures, even if that is not an intended aim. Though it is hardly exhaustive of the field, when pursued in concert with the theoretical framework described here, this particular type of somaesthetic self-cultivation has the potential to generate a new mode in the bodily desire to persist; and just by itself this change in character of the original passionate attachment threatens power mechanisms, even if overt resistance is not involved. This works precisely because this type of somaesthetic practice is not necessarily counterpurposive with regard to those power structures. This is something like what Arendt has in mind where she speaks of quasi-artisanal, individuating types of labor forming "an unpolitical way of life, but . . . certainly . . . not an antipolitical one," with the further claim being that, forming any way of life, however supposedly unconcerned with politics and public life it may be, will inevitably and stealthily verge on the explicitly political realm of active life delineated by Arendt, simply by appearing on the scene.[31]

By setting bodily desire to work, to labor on itself artistically, the body can take on a sense of purposiveness without purpose as determined by the wider social field. This kind of work helps, in piecemeal fashion, to reset the reigning expectation that the subject body indisputably "should" act in certain ways so as to cause certain social effects, for example, continued survival. This type of artful bodily practice does not set forth an end or a hard "should," like bold resistance projects, but this approach nevertheless accomplishes similar goals, thereby adding to the particular theories of subjectivation and subjectality in a way that contributes to subject life more generally. The artful body, at least when considered along these lines, may not take up arms in wars of resistance per se; but its beauty (or ugliness) can still be disarming, even if with its art, nothing particularly martial is the intent.

Notes

Introduction

1. Michel Foucault, *Surveiller et punir: Naissance de la prison* (Paris: Gallimard, 1975), 196. All non-English-language quotations have been translated by the author from the primary sources listed unless otherwise indicated, namely, with Greek-language sources. Likewise, all quoted text preserves original points of emphasis (italics) unless otherwise indicated.

2. Judith Butler, *The Psychic Life of Power: Theories in Subjection* (Stanford, CA: Stanford University Press, 1997), 3; Georg Wilhelm Friedrich Hegel, *Werke*, ed. Eva Moldenhauer and Karl Markus Michel, vol. 3, *Phänomenologie des Geistes* (Frankfurt am Main: Suhrkamp, 1970), 163.

3. Butler, *Psychic Life of Power*, 3, 75; Friedrich Nietzsche, *Zur Genealogie der Moral*, in *Sämtliche Werke: Kritische Studienausgabe in 15 Einzelbänden*, ed. Giorgio Colli and Mazzino Montinari (Berlin: Walter de Gruyter, 1988), 5:305–7 [2.8].

4. Butler, *Psychic Life of Power*, 171.

5. Ibid., 66.

6. Ibid.

7. Judith Butler, *Senses of the Subject* (New York: Fordham University Press, 2015), 8. Emphasis preserved from the original text.

8. Ibid., 115, 123, 147.

9. Louis Althusser, "Idéologie et appareils idéologiques d'État (Notes pour une recherche)," *La Pensée*, no. 151 (1970): 31.

10. Judith Butler, *Bodies that Matter: On the Discursive Limits of "Sex"* (New York: Routledge, 1993), 31–34; Butler, *Psychic Life of Power*, 91.

11. Ibid., 67.

12. Ibid., 67. Emphasis preserved from the original text. Nietzsche, *Zur Genealogie der Moral*, 322 [2.16].

13. Butler, *Bodies that Matter*, 67.

14. Ibid., 75; Nietzsche, *Zur Genealogie der Moral*, 325 [2.17].

15. Butler, *Psychic Life of Power*, 75–76.

16. Friedrich Nietzsche, *Sämtliche Werke: Kritische Studienausgabe in 15 Einzelbänden*, ed. Giorgio Colli and Mazzino Montinari, vol. 4, *Also sprach Zarathustra: Ein Buch für Alle und Keinen* (Berlin: Walter de Gruyter, 1988), 30.

17. Ibid., 29–31.

18. Butler, *Psychic Life of Power*, 67, 75–76; Nietzsche, *Zur Genealogie der Moral*, 322 [2.16].

19. Karl Jaspers, *Vom Ursprung und Ziel der Geschichte* (Zurich: Artemis, 1949), 19–21.

20. Roger T. Ames and Henry Rosemont, Jr., introduction to *The Analects of Confucius* (New York: Ballantine, 1998), 51.

21. Ibid.

22. 孔子, 论语译注, ed. 金良年 (Shanghai: 上海古籍出版社, 2004), §§8.8, 16.13, 20.3.

23. 荀子, *Xunzi*, 2 vols., ed. John Knoblock and Zhang Jue (Changsha: Hunan People's Publishing House, 1999), §§20.2, 20.3, 20.12.

24. 孔子, 论语译注, §§16.5, 17.11; Roger T. Ames, *Confucian Role Ethics: A Vocabulary* (Honolulu: University of Hawai'i Press, 2011), 74; James Garrison, "The Social Value of Ritual and Music in Classical Chinese Thought," *Teorema: Revista internacional de filosofía* 31, no. 3 (2012): 212.

25. 孟子, 孟子今註今譯, 3rd ed., ed. 王雲五 (Taipei: 臺灣商務印書館 中華民國六十七年, 1978), 410 [四一０ 盡心篇第七：七十九 堯舜章, §7.79].

26. David L. Hall and Roger T. Ames, *Thinking Through Confucius* (Albany: State University of New York Press, 1987), 292–93; cf. Jacques Derrida, "La différance," *Marges de la Philosophie* (Paris: Les Éditions de Minuit, 1972), 8–9, 12–13.

27. 孔子, 论语译注, §13.3.

28. Ames, *Confucian Role Ethics*, 109.

29. 荀子, *Xunzi*, §§13.5, 19.3, 19.9; cf. 孔子, 论语译注, §12.11; James Garrison, "Confucianism's Role-Based Political Ethic: Free Speech, Remonstrative Speech, and Political Change in East Asia." *Non-Western Encounters with Democratization: Imagining Democracy after the Arab Spring*, ed. Christopher K. Lamont, Jan van der Harst, and Frank Gaenssmantel (Surrey, UK: Ashgate, 2015), 31–47.

30. 李泽厚, 华夏美学 (Guilin: Guangxi Normal University Press, 2001), 67–71; cf. Karl Marx and Friedrich Engels, *Ökonomisch-philosophische Manuskripte aus dem Jahre 1844*, in *Werke* (Berlin: Dietz, 1956), 40:537–46.

31. 李泽厚, 华夏美学, 67–69.

32. Ibid., 67; 孔子, 论语译注, §8.8.

33. 李泽厚, 华夏美学, 69; 李泽厚, 美学四讲 (Beijing: 三联书店, 1989), 109; Li Zehou, "Subjectivity and 'Subjectality': A Response," *Philosophy East and West* 49, no. 2 (1999): 174–75; cf. Carl Gustav Jung, *Gesammelte Werke*, vol. 9/1, *Die Archetypen und das kollektive Unbewusstse*, ed. Lilly Jung-Merker and Elisabeth Rüf (Zürich: Rascher, 1976), 13–17.

34. 李泽厚, 美学四讲, 75.

35. Ibid., 109.
36. 孔子, 论语译注, §2.4.
37. Foucault, *Surveiller et punir*, 196.
38. Friedrich Nietzsche, "Über Wahrheit und Lüge im außermoralischen Sinne," *Sämtliche Werke: Kritische Studienausgabe in 15 Einzelbänden*, ed. Giorgio Colli and Mazzino Montinari (Berlin: Walter de Gruyter, 1988), 1:883–84.
39. Nietzsche, *Also sprach Zarathustra*, 31.
40. Bernard Stiegler, *La technique et le temps*, vol. 1, *La faute d'Epiméthée* (Paris: Galilée/Cité des sciences et de l'industrie, 1994), 31.
41. Ibid., 151–52.
42. Ibid., 150–53.
43. Ibid., 105–6. Emphasis preserved from original text.
44. Ibid., 151, 248–49. Emphasis preserved from original text.
45. Ibid., 248–49. Emphasis preserved from original text.
46. Hannah Arendt, *The Human Condition*, 2nd ed. (Chicago: University of Chicago Press, 1998), 198–99; Judith Butler, "On This Occasion . . . ," in *Butler on Whitehead: On the Occasion*, ed. Roland Faber, Michael Halewood, and Deena Lin (Lanham, MD: Lexington Books, 2012), 15.
47. Butler, *Psychic Life of Power*, 23; Sigmund Freud, "Trauer und Melancholie," *Gesammelte Werke, chronologisch geordnet*, ed. Anna Freud (London: Imago, 1940), 10:431, 437.
48. Vikki Bell and Judith Butler, "On Speech, Race and Melancholia," *Theory, Culture and Society* 16, no. 2 (1999): 163–74; Judith Butler, "Is Kinship Always Already Heterosexual?," *differences: A Journal of Feminist Cultural Studies* 13, no. 1 (2002): 14–44.
49. Nietzsche "Über Wahrheit und Lüge im außermoralischen Sinne," 883–84.
50. Richard Shusterman, *Body Consciousness: A Philosophy of Mindfulness and Somaesthetics* (Cambridge: Cambridge University Press, 2008), 1.
51. Richard Shusterman, "Somaesthetics and the Utopian Body," *International Yearbook of Aesthetics* 14 (2010): 85.
52. Shusterman, *Body Consciousness*, 3.
53. Ibid., 24.
54. Butler, *Psychic Life of Power*, 72.
55. Butler, *Bodies That Matter*, 223.
56. Judith Butler, "Performativity's Social Magic," in *Bourdieu: A Critical Reader*, ed. Richard Shusterman (Oxford: Blackwell, 1999), 125.
57. Ibid., 146.
58. Frank L. Baum, *The Wonderful Wizard of Oz* (Lawrence: University Press of Kansas, 1999), 128; Victor Fleming, dir., *The Wizard of Oz* (1939; Beverly Hills, CA: Metro-Goldwyn-Mayer, 1997), DVD.
59. Eliza Kania, "Exercising Freedom: Interview with Judith Butler," *R/evolutions: Global Trends and Regional Issues* 1, no. 1 (2013), 39.

60. Slavoj Žižek, *The Ticklish Subject: The Absent Centre of Political Ontology* (London: Verso, 1999), 264.

Intercultural and Interdisciplinary Work

1. Ames, *Confucian Role Ethics*, 21–22.
2. Foucault, *Surveiller et punir*, 196.
3. Gilles Deleuze and Félix Guattari, *Mille plateaux* (Paris: Les Édition de Minuit, 1980), 13.
4. Ibid., 14.
5. Ibid., 13. Emphasis added.
6. Ibid., 14.
7. Ibid.
8. Plato, *Republic*, in *Complete Works*, ed. John Cooper (Indianapolis: Hackett, 1997), 434a–444a; cf. Plato (Πλάτων), *Respublica*, in *Platonis Opera*, ed. John Burnet (Oxford: Oxford University Press, 1903), 434a–444a.
9. John Rawls, *A Theory of Justice*, rev. ed. (Cambridge, MA: Belknap Press of Harvard University Press, 1999), 118n11.
10. Ibid., 118.
11. Butler, *Psychic Life of Power*, 66.
12. Ralph Waldo Emerson, "Experience," in *The Works of Ralph Waldo Emerson* (Boston: Fireside, 1883), 3:72.
13. Friedrich Nietzsche, *Der Antichrist*, in *Sämtliche Werke: Kritische Studienausgabe in 15 Einzelbänden*, ed. Giorgio Colli and Mazzino Montinari (Berlin: Walter de Gruyter, 1988), 6:211 [§39].
14. Alfred North Whitehead, *Science and the Modern World* (New York: Macmillan, 1964), 75, 85–86.
15. Ibid., 85.
16. William James, *The Meaning of Truth* (Cambridge, MA: Harvard University Press, 1975), 135–36.
17. Antony Flew, *Thinking about Thinking: Do I Sincerely Want to Be Right?* (London: Collins Fontana, 1975), 47.
18. Immanuel Kant, "Von der Verschiedenheit der Racen überhaupt," In *Gesammlte Schriften* (Berlin: Preußische Akademie der Wissenschaften, 1900), 2:427–43; Georg Wilhelm Friedrich Hegel, *Enzyklopädie der philosophischen Wissenschaften im Grundrisse* (1830), in *Werke*, ed. Eva Moldenhauer and Karl Markus Michel (Frankfurt am Main: Suhrkamp, 1970), 10:57–63; Georg Wilhelm Friedrich Hegel, *Vorlesungen über die Philosophie der Weltgeschichte* (Hamburg: Felix Meiner Verlag, 1988), 2:418.
19. W. E. B. Du Bois, *The Souls of Black Folk*, ed. Henry Louis Gates, Jr. (Oxford: Oxford University Press, 2007), 3.

20. Brown v. Board of Education of Topeka, 347 U.S. 483 (1954).
21. Deleuze and Guattari, *Mille plateaux*, 14.
22. Gilles Deleuze and Félix Guattari, *Qu'est-ce que la philosophie?* (Paris: Les Éditions de Minuit, 1991), 89.
23. Ibid., 86, 89.
24. Ibid., 89.
25. Ibid., 104–5.
26. Ibid.
27. Ibid., 105.
28. Ibid., 89.
29. Deleuze and Guattari, *Mille plateaux*, 15.
30. Franz Martin Wimmer, *Interkulturelle Philosophie* (Vienna: WUV, 2004), 67.
31. Franz Martin Wimmer, "Thesen, Bedingungen und Aufgaben interkulturell orientierter Philosophie," *polylog* 1 (1998): 10.
32. Wimmer, *Interkulturelle Philosophie*, 67. Emphasis preserved from the original text.
33. Ibid., 72.
34. Wimmer, "Thesen, Bedingungen und Aufgaben interkulturell orientierter Philosophie," 9.
35. Wimmer, *Interkulturelle Philosophie*, 68–69.
36. Ibid., 70.
37. Ibid., 73.
38. Ibid., 66.
39. Ames, *Confucian Role Ethics*, 21; Hilary Putnam, *Realism with a Human Face* (Cambridge, MA: Harvard University Press, 1990), 28.
40. Ames, *Confucian Role Ethics*, 23.
41. Ibid., 37.
42. Ibid., 22.
43. Ibid., 35.
44. Deleuze and Guattari, *Mille plateaux*, 15.
45. Judith Butler, *Giving an Account of Oneself* (New York: Fordham University Press, 2005), 21.
46. Deleuze and Guattari, *Mille plateaux*, 16.
47. Edward S. Herman and Noam Chomsky, *Manufacturing Consent: The Political Economy of the Mass Media* (New York: Pantheon, 2002).

Chapter 1

1. Jean-Paul Sartre, *Les écrits de Sartre: Chronologie, bibliographie commentée*, ed. Michel Contat and Michel Rybalka (Paris: Gallimard, 1970), 101; Jean-Paul Sartre, *Huis clos*, Deutsche Grammophon, 1965, LP.

2. Genesis 1:27 (Authorized King James Version).
3. Exodus 3:14.
4. Jean-Paul Sartre, "Préface à l'édition de 1961," in *Les damnés de la terre*, by Frantz Fanon (Paris: Éditions La Découverte & Syros, 2002), 33.
5. Butler, *Senses of the Subject*, 10.
6. Ibid., 159.
7. Eliza Kania, "Exercising Freedom—Interview with Judith Butler," *R/evolutions* 1, no. 1 (2013): 40.
8. Butler, *Bodies that Matter*, 31.
9. Butler, *Psychic Life of Power*, 3.
10. Hegel, *Phänomenologie des Geistes*, 163.
11. Ibid., 145–46; Butler, *Giving an Account of Oneself*, 43. Emphasis added.
12. Hegel, *Phänomenologie des Geistes*, 147.
13. Butler, *Giving an Account of Oneself*, 27.
14. Ibid.
15. Ibid., 27–28.
16. Hegel, *Phänomenologie des Geistes*, 164.
17. Ibid., 163, 168.
18. Butler, *Psychic Life of Power*, 46.
19. Ibid., 50.
20. Ibid., 171.
21. Ibid., 66.
22. Ibid.
23. Ibid., 67.
24. Adriana Cavarero, *Tu che mi guardi, tu che mi racconti: Filosofia della narrazione* (Milan: Feltrinelli, 1997), 48.
25. Butler, *Giving an Account of Oneself*, 32; cf. Cavarero, *Tu che mi guardi, tu che mi racconti*, 48–49.
26. Butler, *Giving an Account of Oneself*, 33; cf. Cavarero, *Tu che mi guardi, tu che mi racconti*, 51.
27. Butler, *Senses of the Subject*, 16.
28. Butler, *Giving an Account of Oneself*, 7–8.
29. Nietzsche, *Also sprach Zarathustra*, 284.
30. Ibid., 284.
31. Foucault, *Surveiller et punir*, 138.
32. Ibid., 139.
33. Ibid., 140.
34. Ibid., 179.
35. Ibid.
36. Michel Foucault, "Le jeu de Michel Foucault (entretien sur l'Histoire de la sexualité)," in *Dits et écrits: 1954–1988* (Paris: Gallimard, 1994), 3:302. Emphasis preserved from the original text.

37. Foucault, *Surveiller et punir*, p. 179.
38. Ephesians 5:21.
39. Jeremy Bentham, "Panopticon; or, The Inspection-House," in *The Works of Jeremy Bentham* (Bristol: Thoemmes Press, 1995), addendum.
40. Foucault, *Surveiller et punir*, 202–3.
41. Ibid., 194.
42. Ibid., 195.
43. Ibid.
44. Ibid., 196.
45. Ibid.
46. Butler, *Psychic Life of Power*, pp. 86, 94.
47. Ibid., 91.
48. Butler, *Giving an Account of Oneself*, 15–16, 114.
49. Butler, *Senses of the Subject*, 20–21. Emphasis preserved from the original text.
50. Butler, *Giving an Account of Oneself*, 18.
51. Ibid., 17.
52. Butler, *Senses of the Subject*, 9.
53. Butler, *Psychic Life of Power*, 91.
54. Ibid., 92.
55. Ibid., 95; cf. Althusser, "Idéologie et appareils idéologiques d'État," 31.
56. Butler, *Psychic Life of Power*, 111.
57. Ibid., 126, 130.
58. Butler, "Performativity's Social Magic," 120.
59. Butler, *Psychic Life of Power*, 167, 172–73, 177, 182–83, 185, 188; Butler, *Senses of the Subject*, 73–75; Sigmund Freud, *Das Ich und das Es*, in *Studienausgabe* (Frankfurt: Fischer Taschenbuch Verlag, 1982), 3:320; Freud, "Trauer und Melancholie," 431, 437.
60. Butler, "Performativity's Social Magic," 122, 125.
61. Pierre Bourdieu, *La distinction: Critique sociale du jugement* (Paris: Les Éditions de Minuit, 1979), 552–53.
62. Butler, *Giving an Account of Oneself*, 35–39.
63. Ibid., 36; Michel Foucault, "Politics and the Study of Discourse," *The Foucault Effect: Studies in Governmentality*, ed. Graham Burchell, Colin Gordon, and Peter Miller (Chicago: University of Chicago Press, 1991), 72.
64. Butler, *Giving an Account of Oneself*, 11.
65. Butler, *Psychic Life of Power*, 106; cf. Butler, *Giving an Account of Oneself*, 23.
66. Butler, *Psychic Life of Power*, 126.
67. Ibid., 10–11; Butler, *Giving an Account of Oneself*, 20.
68. Butler, *Psychic Life of Power*, 11.
69. Ibid., 195.
70. Ibid., 95.

71. Ibid., 94.
72. Ibid.
73. Butler, *Giving an Account of Oneself*, 26.
74. Butler, *Psychic Life of Power*, 94, 146.
75. Butler, *Senses of the Subject*, 13.
76. Malcolm X and Alex Haley, *The Autobiography of Malcolm X* (New York: Grove Press, 1965), 284.
77. Butler, *Psychic Life of Power*, 185, 192.
78. Ibid., 195.
79. David Kyuman Kim, *Melancholic Freedom: Agency and the Spirit of Politics* (Oxford: Oxford University Press, 2007), 6–7, 12.
80. Ibid., 7.
81. Ibid., 136–37.
82. Ibid., 137.
83. Ibid., 140.
84. Ibid., 8, 128, 136–37, 142.
85. Ibid., 142, 145.
86. Ibid., 140; cf. Stanley Cavell, "Aversive Thinking: Emersonian Representations in Heidegger and Nietzsche," *New Literary History* 22, no. 1 (1991): 153–54.
87. James Garrison, "Revolution in Kant's Relation of Aesthetics to Morality: Regarding Negatively Free Beauty and Respecting Positively Free Will," in *Kant und die Philosophie in weltbürgerlicher Absicht: Akten des XI. Kant-Kongresses 2010*, ed. Stefano Bacin, Alfredo Ferrarin, Claudio La Rocca, and Margit Ruffing (Berlin: Walter de Gruyter, 2013), 4:47–57.
88. Immanuel Kant, *Die Grundlegung zur Metaphysik der Sitten*, in *Gesammlte Schriften* (Berlin: Preußische Akademie der Wissenschaften, 1900), 4:428.
89. Immanuel Kant, *Die Kritik der praktischen Vernunft*, in *Gesammlte Schriften* (Berlin: Preußische Akademie der Wissenschaften, 1900), 5:81; Kant, *Grundlegung zur Metaphysik der Sitten*, 393.
90. Immanuel Kant, *Die Kritik der Urtheilskraft*, in *Gesammlte Schriften* (Berlin: Preußische Akademie der Wissenschaften, 1900), 5:354, 356.
91. Ibid., 314.
92. Immanuel Kant, *Die Kritik der reinen Vernunft*, in *Gesammlte Schriften* (Berlin: Preußische Akademie der Wissenschaften, 1900), 3:254.
93. Kant *Kritik der Urtheilskraft*, 238.
94. Ibid., 316.
95. Ibid., 340.
96. Ibid., 314–15.
97. Ibid., 315.
98. Ibid.
99. Ibid., 314.
100. Kant, *Kritik der reinen Vernunft*, 363.

101. Ibid.
102. Ibid., 364.
103. Kant, *Kritik der praktischen Vernunft*, 33.
104. Ibid.
105. Kant, *Kritik der Urtheilskraft*, 313.
106. Ibid., 315.
107. Ibid., 314–15.
108. Ibid., 306.
109. Georg Wilhelm Friedrich Hegel, "Systemfragment von 1800," in *Werke*, ed. Eva Moldenhauer and Karl Markus Michel (Frankfurt am Main: Suhrkamp, 1971), 1:425.
110. Butler, *Senses of the Subject*, 108.
111. Ibid., 109.
112. Ibid.
113. Ibid., 109–10.
114. Hegel, *Phänomenologie des Geistes*, 510.
115. Ibid., 511.
116. Ibid., 153.
117. Ibid., 517.
118. Ibid., 518.
119. Nietzsche, *Also sprach Zarathustra*, 175.
120. Nietzsche, "Über Wahrheit und Lüge im außermoralischen Sinne," 877; cf. Thomas Hobbes, *Leviathan*, ed. Richard Tuck (Cambridge: Cambridge University Press, 1996), 86–90.
121. Nietzsche, "Über Wahrheit und Lüge im außermoralischen Sinne," 878.
122. Ibid., 883.
123. Ibid., 883–84.
124. Plato, *Protagoras*, in *Complete Works*, ed. John Cooper (Indianapolis: Hackett, 1997), 343b; cf. Plato (Πλάτων), *Protagoras*, in *Platonis Opera*, ed. John Burnet (Oxford: Oxford University Press, 1903), 343b; Rainer Maria Rilke, "Archaïscher Torso Apollos," *Sämtliche Werke* (Berlin: Insel, 1955), 1:557.

Chapter 2

1. Michel Foucault, "On the Genealogy of Ethics: An Overview of a Work in Progress," in *Ethics: Subjectivity and Truth*, vol. 1 of *The Essential Works of Foucault, 1954–1984*, ed. Paul Rainbow (New York: New Press, 1998), 261. Transcript of an English-language interview.
2. Arthur Danto, "The Artworld," *Journal of Philosophy* 61, no. 19 (1964): 580–84.
3. Foucault, *Surveiller et Punir*, 139.

4. Hegel, *Phänomenologie des Geistes*, 157.
5. Ibid., 158.
6. Ibid., 157.
7. Bourdieu, *La distinction*, VIII.
8. Robert L. Solso, *The Psychology of Art and the Evolution of the Conscious Brain* (Cambridge, MA: MIT Press, 2003), 227, 238–39. Cf. Walter Benjamin, "Das Kunstwerk im Zeitalter seiner technischen Reproduzierbarkeit," vol. 1, sect. 2 of *Gesammelte Schriften*, ed. Rolf Tiedemann and Hermann Schweppenhäuser, 3rd ed. (Frankfurt am Main: Suhrkamp, 1980), 475–76n2.
9. Coop Himmelb(l)au, *Architektur muss brennen* (Graz: Institut für Gebäudelehre und Entwerfen, Technische Universität Graz, 1980), 2.
10. Danto, "The Artworld," 581.
11. Joseph Lyons, "Paleolithic Aesthetics: The Psychology of Cave Art," *Journal of Aesthetics and Art Criticism* 26, no. 1 (1967): 109.
12. Lyons, "Paleolithic Aesthetics," 110.
13. Ibid., 111.
14. Ludwig Wittgenstein, *Philosophical Investigations* [*Philosophische Untersuchungen*], trans. G. E. M. Anscombe, 2nd ed. (Oxford: Blackwell, 1997), 194 [part 2, §xi]; cf. Joseph Jastrow, "The Mind's Eye," *Popular Science Monthly* 54 (1899): 312; cf. Wolfgang Köhler, *Gestalt Psychology* (New York: W. W. Norton, 1992), 114; cf. *Fliegende Blätter*, October 23, 1892, 17.
15. Lyons, "Paleolithic Aesthetics," 111–12.
16. Ibid., 113.
17. Arendt, *Human Condition*, 167.
18. Ibid.
19. Ibid., 167–68.
20. Ibid., 197–99; cf. Butler, *Giving an Account of Oneself*, 30–34, 43; Butler, *Senses of the Subject*, 197; Cavarero, *Tu che mi guardi, tu che mi racconti*, 48–56.
21. Butler, *Psychic Life of Power*, 88–89, 92, 128–29; Mladen Dolar, "Beyond Interpellation," *Qui Parle* 6, no. 2 (1993): 87.
22. Arendt, *Human Condition*, 173.
23. Ibid., 168.
24. Kant, *Kritik der Urtheilskraft*, 306; Stanley Cavell, *Must We Mean What We Say?*, updated [3rd] ed. (Cambridge: Cambridge University Press, 2002), 237.

Chapter 3

1. Ames and Rosemont, introduction to *The Analects of Confucius*, 52.
2. Karl Jaspers, *Die grossen Philosophen*, vol. 1 (Munich: R. Piper, 1957), 19–21.

3. Tu Wei-ming, introduction to *Confucian Traditions in East Asian Modernity: Moral Education and Economic Culture in Japan and the Four Mini-Dragons*, ed. Tu Wei-ming (Cambridge, MA: Harvard University Press, 1996), 1.

4. Jaspers, *Die grossen Philosophen*, 161.

5. Kim, *Melancholic Freedom*, 12.

6. Ames, *Confucian Role Ethics*, 71.

7. Ames and Rosemont, introduction to *The Analects of Confucius*, 24–25.

8. Ibid., 27. Emphasis preserved from the original text.

9. Roger T. Ames, and David L. Hall, *Focusing the Familiar: A Translation and Philosophical Interpretation of the Zhongyong* (Honolulu: University of Hawai'i Press, 2001).

10. Ames, *Confucian Role Ethics*, 104–5. Emphasis preserved from the original text.

11. David L. Hall, and Roger T. Ames, "Culture and the Limits of Catholicism: A Chinese Response to *Centesimus Annus*," *Journal of Business Ethics* 12 (1993): 960.

12. Ibid.; cf. 孔子, 论语译注, §2.3.

13. Ruth Benedict, *The Chrysanthemum and the Sword* (Boston: Houghton Mifflin, 2005), 222.

14. Butler, *Psychic Life of Power*, 91.

15. Anthony E. Clark, *Ban Gu's History of Early China* (Amherst, NY: Cambria Press, 2008), 248n462.

16. 孔子, 论语译注, §13.3.

17. Ibid., §12.11.

18. William Butler Yeats, "The Second Coming," in *The Collected Poems of W. B. Yeats*, ed. Richard J. Finneran (New York: Scribner, 1996), lines 2–3.

19. 荀子, *Xunzi*, §§19.3, 19.9.

20. Ames and Rosemont, introduction to *The Analects of Confucius*, 29.

21. 荀子, *Xunzi*, §2.2.

22. 孔子, 论语译注, §§7.9, 9.10, 10.25, 14.40, 19.14, 19.17, 20.1; Ames and Hall, *Focusing the Familiar*, 98–99 [§19]. Emphasis added.

23. Ames and Hall, *Focusing the Familiar*, 97–98 [§18].

24. 孔子, 论语译注, §§12.11, 13.3.

25. Roger T. Ames, "Observing Ritual 'Propriety (*li* 禮)' as Focusing the 'Familiar' in the Affairs of the Day," *Dao* 1, no. 2 (2002): 146.

26. Ibid.

27. Ibid.

28. 孔子, 论语译注, §16.5.

29. Ames and Rosemont, introduction to *The Analects of Confucius*, 56; cf. 李宗侗, 春秋左傳今註今譯 (Taipei: 臺灣商務印書館, 1971), 1221; Li Chenyang, "The Ideal of Harmony in Ancient Chinese and Greek Philosophy," *Dao* 7 (2008): 82–84.

30. 孔子, 论语译注, §13.23; 徐中舒, 左传选 (Beijing: 中华书局, 2009), 187.

31. 张双棣, 张万彬, 殷国光, and 陈涛, 吕氏春秋译注上 (Changchun: 吉林文史出版社, 1987), 125.

32. 欧阳询, 艺文类聚 (Shanghai: 上海古籍出版社, 1982), 358.

33. Roger T. Ames and Henry Rosemont, Jr., introduction to *The Chinese Classic of Family Reverence: A Philosophical Translation of the Xiaojing* (Honolulu: University of Hawai'i Press, 2009), 84.

34. 鍾泰德, 易經通釋 (Taipei: 正中書局, 1999), 豫 §1.

35. Chan Hung Kan and Ho Che Wah, *Citations from the* Shangshu *to Be Found in Pre-Han and Han Texts* (Hong Kong: 香港中文大学, 2003), 76.

36. Chung-ying Cheng, "On the Metaphysical Significance of *Ti* (Body-Embodiment) in Chinese Philosophy: *Benti* (Origin-Substance) and *Ti-Yong* (Substance and Function)," *Journal of Chinese Philosophy* 29, no. 2 (2002): 145.

37. Wei-ming Tu, "Li as a Process of Humanization," *Philosophy East and West* 22, no. 2 (1972): 190, 194, 197.

38. Ibid., 198.

39. Ames and Rosemont, introduction to *The Analects of Confucius*, 51.

40. 孔子, 论语译注, §§8.8, 16.3, 20.3.

41. Ibid., §1.2.

42. Ibid., §17.11.

43. 荀子, *Xunzi*, §19.16.

44. Ibid., §19.20.

45. Ibid., §§19.3, 19.7.

46. Hall and Ames, *Thinking Through Confucius*, 292–93; Derrida, "La différance," 8–9, 12–13.

47. 孔子, 论语译注, §16.5.

48. 荀子, *Xunzi*, §20.1.

49. 嚴靈峯, 墨子簡編 (Taipei: 臺灣商務印書館, 1995), 非乐上 §§1–3, 5.

50. Ibid., 非乐上 §§4, 6.

51. 孔子, 论语译注, §12.11.

52. 荀子, *Xunzi*, §20.6.

53. Ibid., §20.7.

54. Ibid., §20.2.

55. Ibid., §17.1–2.

56. Ibid., §23.17–18.

57. Ibid., §17.1.

58. Erica Brindley, "Music, Cosmos, and the Development of Psychology in Early China," *T'oung Pao* 92, no. 1–3 (2006): 39.

59. 荀子, *Xunzi*, §20.8.

60. 班固, 漢書 (Shanghai: 漢語大詞典出版社, 2004), 776.

61. Wei-ming Tu, "The Creative Tension between *Jên* and *Li*," *Philosophy East and West* 18 (1968): 37.

62. 李泽厚, 美学四讲, 80.

3. Tu Wei-ming, introduction to *Confucian Traditions in East Asian Modernity: Moral Education and Economic Culture in Japan and the Four Mini-Dragons*, ed. Tu Wei-ming (Cambridge, MA: Harvard University Press, 1996), 1.

4. Jaspers, *Die grossen Philosophen*, 161.

5. Kim, *Melancholic Freedom*, 12.

6. Ames, *Confucian Role Ethics*, 71.

7. Ames and Rosemont, introduction to *The Analects of Confucius*, 24–25.

8. Ibid., 27. Emphasis preserved from the original text.

9. Roger T. Ames, and David L. Hall, *Focusing the Familiar: A Translation and Philosophical Interpretation of the Zhongyong* (Honolulu: University of Hawai'i Press, 2001).

10. Ames, *Confucian Role Ethics*, 104–5. Emphasis preserved from the original text.

11. David L. Hall, and Roger T. Ames, "Culture and the Limits of Catholicism: A Chinese Response to *Centesimus Annus*," *Journal of Business Ethics* 12 (1993): 960.

12. Ibid.; cf. 孔子, 论语译注, §2.3.

13. Ruth Benedict, *The Chrysanthemum and the Sword* (Boston: Houghton Mifflin, 2005), 222.

14. Butler, *Psychic Life of Power*, 91.

15. Anthony E. Clark, *Ban Gu's History of Early China* (Amherst, NY: Cambria Press, 2008), 248n462.

16. 孔子, 论语译注, §13.3.

17. Ibid., §12.11.

18. William Butler Yeats, "The Second Coming," in *The Collected Poems of W. B. Yeats*, ed. Richard J. Finneran (New York: Scribner, 1996), lines 2–3.

19. 荀子, *Xunzi*, §§19.3, 19.9.

20. Ames and Rosemont, introduction to *The Analects of Confucius*, 29.

21. 荀子, *Xunzi*, §2.2.

22. 孔子, 论语译注, §§7.9, 9.10, 10.25, 14.40, 19.14, 19.17, 20.1; Ames and Hall, *Focusing the Familiar*, 98–99 [§19]. Emphasis added.

23. Ames and Hall, *Focusing the Familiar*, 97–98 [§18].

24. 孔子, 论语译注, §§12.11, 13.3.

25. Roger T. Ames, "Observing Ritual 'Propriety (*li* 禮)' as Focusing the 'Familiar' in the Affairs of the Day," *Dao* 1, no. 2 (2002): 146.

26. Ibid.

27. Ibid.

28. 孔子, 论语译注, §16.5.

29. Ames and Rosemont, introduction to *The Analects of Confucius*, 56; cf. 李宗侗, 春秋左傳今註今譯 (Taipei: 臺灣商務印書館, 1971), 1221; Li Chenyang, "The Ideal of Harmony in Ancient Chinese and Greek Philosophy," *Dao* 7 (2008): 82–84.

30. 孔子, 论语译注, §13.23; 徐中舒, 左传选 (Beijing: 中华书局, 2009), 187.

31. 张双棣, 张万彬, 殷国光, and 陈涛, 吕氏春秋译注上 (Changchun: 吉林文史出版社, 1987), 125.

32. 欧阳询, 艺文类聚 (Shanghai: 上海古籍出版社, 1982), 358.

33. Roger T. Ames and Henry Rosemont, Jr., introduction to *The Chinese Classic of Family Reverence: A Philosophical Translation of the Xiaojing* (Honolulu: University of Hawai'i Press, 2009), 84.

34. 鍾泰德, 易經通釋 (Taipei: 正中書局, 1999), 豫 §1.

35. Chan Hung Kan and Ho Che Wah, *Citations from the* Shangshu *to Be Found in Pre-Han and Han Texts* (Hong Kong: 香港中文大學, 2003), 76.

36. Chung-ying Cheng, "On the Metaphysical Significance of *Ti* (Body-Embodiment) in Chinese Philosophy: *Benti* (Origin-Substance) and *Ti-Yong* (Substance and Function)," *Journal of Chinese Philosophy* 29, no. 2 (2002): 145.

37. Wei-ming Tu, "Li as a Process of Humanization," *Philosophy East and West* 22, no. 2 (1972): 190, 194, 197.

38. Ibid., 198.

39. Ames and Rosemont, introduction to *The Analects of Confucius*, 51.

40. 孔子, 论语译注, §§8.8, 16.3, 20.3.

41. Ibid., §1.2.

42. Ibid., §17.11.

43. 荀子, *Xunzi*, §19.16.

44. Ibid., §19.20.

45. Ibid., §§19.3, 19.7.

46. Hall and Ames, *Thinking Through Confucius*, 292–93; Derrida, "La différance," 8–9, 12–13.

47. 孔子, 论语译注, §16.5.

48. 荀子, *Xunzi*, §20.1.

49. 嚴靈峯, 墨子簡編 (Taipei: 臺灣商務印書館, 1995), 非乐上 §§1–3, 5.

50. Ibid., 非乐上 §§4, 6.

51. 孔子, 论语译注, §12.11.

52. 荀子, *Xunzi*, §20.6.

53. Ibid., §20.7.

54. Ibid., §20.2.

55. Ibid., §17.1–2.

56. Ibid., §23.17–18.

57. Ibid., §17.1.

58. Erica Brindley, "Music, Cosmos, and the Development of Psychology in Early China," *T'oung Pao* 92, no. 1–3 (2006): 39.

59. 荀子, *Xunzi*, §20.8.

60. 班固, 漢書 (Shanghai: 漢語大詞典出版社, 2004), 776.

61. Wei-ming Tu, "The Creative Tension between *Jên* and *Li*," *Philosophy East and West* 18 (1968): 37.

62. 李泽厚, 美学四讲, 80.

63. Zehou Li and Jane Cauvel, *Four Essays on Aesthetics* (Lanham, MD: Lexington Books, 2006), 178. This text only appears in the English-language version of 美学四讲.

64. Ibid., 26. This text only appears in the English-language version of 美学四讲.

65. Butler, *Giving an Account of Oneself*, 8, 28.

Chapter 4

1. Li and Cauvel, *Four Essays on Aesthetics*, 177. This text only appears in the English-language version of 美学四讲.

2. Ames and Rosemont, introduction to *The Analects of Confucius*, 51; 荀子, *Xunzi*, §19.3; 孔子, 论语译注, §§16.5, 17.11; Hall and Ames, *Thinking Through Confucius*, 292–93; Ames, *Confucian Role Ethics*, 74, 109.

3. 荀子, *Xunzi*, §23.13.

4. Li and Cauvel, *Four Essays on Aesthetics*, 26. This text only appears in the English-language version of 美学四讲.

5. 李泽厚, 华夏美学, 67–71; cf. Marx and Engels, *Ökonomisch-philosophische Manuskripte aus dem Jahre 1844*, 537–46.

6. 李泽厚, 华夏美学, 67–69.

7. Bourdieu, *La distinction*, 552.

8. 李泽厚, 美学四讲, 113.

9. Ibid., 67; 孔子, 论语译注, §8.8.

10. 李泽厚, 华夏美学, 69; 李泽厚, 美学四讲, 109; Li, "Subjectivity and 'Subjectality,'" 174–75; cf. Jung, *Die Archetypen und das kollektive Unbewusstse*, 13–17.

11. Li Zehou, "Of Human Nature and Aesthetic Metaphysics," *International Yearbook of Aesthetics* 14 (2010): 4.

12. Li, "Subjectivity and 'Subjectality,'" 175.

13. 李泽厚, 美学四讲, 75; 孟子, 孟子今註今譯, 291 [二九一 告子篇第六：二 湍水章 §6.2].

14. 李泽厚, 美学四讲, 109.

15. Ibid., 83.

16. Li and Cauvel, *Four Essays on Aesthetics*, 178. This text only appears in the English-language version of 美学四讲.

17. 李泽厚, 华夏美学, 148.

18. Ibid., 75.

19. Ibid.

20. Ibid., 75–77.

21. Kant, *Kritik der Urtheilskraft*, 293, 304.

22. Immanuel Kant, "Zum Ewigen Frieden: Ein philosophischer Entwurf," in *Gesammlte Schriften* (Berlin: Preußische Akademie der Wissenschaften, 1900), 8:360.

23. Immanuel Kant, *Die Metaphysik der Sitten*, in *Gesammlte Schriften* (Berlin: Preußische Akademie der Wissenschaften, 1900), 6:365–68.

24. Ibid., 338.

25. James Garrison, "Kant's Aesthetic Judgment and His Progressing Treatment of Peace," in *Sovereign Justice: Global Justice in a World of Nations*, ed. Diogo P. Aurélio, Gabriele De Angelis, and Regina Queiroz (Berlin: Walter de Gruyter, 2011), 179–97.

26. Immanuel Kant, *Die Metaphysik der Sitten*, 354–55.

27. Ibid., 350–51.

28. Hannah Arendt, *Lectures on Kant's Political Philosophy* (Chicago: University of Chicago Press, 1982), 16.

29. Kant, *Die Metaphysik der Sitten*, 381–83.

30. Arendt, *Lectures on Kant's Political Philosophy*, 18, 49.

31. Ibid., 76.

32. Ibid., 61.

33. Ibid., 61–62.

34. Ibid., 50–51.

35. Ibid., 51.

36. 李泽厚, 美学四讲, 69–70.

37. Li and Cauvel, *Four Essays on Aesthetics*, 88. This text appears in the English-language version of 美学四讲.

38. Ibid., 177. This text only appears in the English-language version of 美学四讲.

39. Li Zehou, "The Philosophy of Kant and a Theory of Subjectivity," *Analecta Husserliana* 21 (1986): 141–42.

40. Ibid., 137.

41. Jing Wang, *High Culture Fever: Politics, Aesthetics, and Ideology in Deng's China* (Berkeley: University of California Press, 1996), 96; cf. Li, "The Philosophy of Kant and a Theory of Subjectivity," 137.

42. Li, "The Philosophy of Kant and a Theory of Subjectivity," 138.

43. Wang, *High Culture Fever*, 109.

44. Li, "The Philosophy of Kant and a Theory of Subjectivity," 139.

45. Ibid., 143.

46. 李泽厚, 美学四讲, 83.

47. Ibid., 121.

48. Li, "The Philosophy of Kant and a Theory of Subjectivity," 143–44.

49. 李泽厚, 美学四讲, 109; cf. Kant, *Kritik der Urtheilskraft*, 293.

50. 李泽厚, 美学四讲, 69.

51. Li, "The Philosophy of Kant and a Theory of Subjectivity," 146; cf. 李泽厚, 批判哲学的批判: 康德述评 (Beijing: 人民出版社, 2001), 413.

52. 李泽厚, 美学四讲, 116.

53. 李泽厚, 美学四讲, 115, 195; Li and Cauvel, *Four Essays on Aesthetics*, 176. This text only appears in the English-language version of 美学四讲. Kant, "Von der Verschiedenheit der Racen überhaupt," 427–43.
54. 李泽厚, 美学四讲, 86.
55. Arendt, *Human Condition*, 9.
56. Ibid., 8–9, 214.
57. Ibid., 9.
58. Ibid., 246.

Chapter 5

1. Butler, "On This Occasion . . . ," 15.
2. Alfred North Whitehead, *Process and Reality: An Essay in Cosmology*, ed. David Ray Griffin and Donald W. Sherburne (New York: Free Press, 1978), 52.
3. Butler, "On This Occasion . . . ," 16.
4. Ibid., 16.
5. Ibid., 16.
6. Ibid., 4, 16; cf. Alfred North Whitehead, *Adventures of Ideas* (New York: Free Press, 1967), 176.
7. Whitehead, *Adventures of Ideas*, 176.
8. Martin Heidegger, *Sein und Zeit*, vol. 2 of *Gesamtausgabe*, ed. Friedrich-Wilhelm von Hermann (Frankfurt am Main: Vittorio Klostermann, 1977), 242, 257–61; Martin Heidegger, *Sein und Zeit*, 11th ed. (Tübingen: Max Niemeyer Verlag, 1967), 182, 194–96 [subsequent references to Heidegger's *Sein und Zeit* use this latter volume's pagination].
9. Whitehead, *Process and Reality*, 166; Heidegger, *Sein und Zeit*, 3.
10. Butler, *Senses of the Subject*, 14.
11. Heidegger, *Sein und Zeit*, 242, 257.
12. Butler, "On This Occasion . . . ," 16–17.
13. Butler, *Senses of the Subject*, 2.
14. Ibid., 5; cf. Butler, *Bodies that Matter*, 31–34; Butler, *Psychic Life of Power*, 91.
15. Butler, *Senses of the Subject*, 7.
16. Ibid., 10.
17. Ibid., 11.
18. Ibid., 14.
19. Butler, "On This Occasion . . . ," 15.
20. Arendt, *Human Condition*, 199; cf. Sophie Loidolt, *Phenomenology of Plurality: Hannah Arendt on Political Intersubjectivity* (New York: Routledge, 2018).
21. Butler, *Senses of the Subject*, 13–14, 37, 42–44, 155–56.

22. Arendt, *Human Condition*, 198–99.
23. Karl Marx and Friedrich Engels, "Prometheus Bound: Allegory on the prohibition of the Rheinische Zeitung," in *Collected Works* (New York: International Publishers, 1975), 1:375.
24. Karl Marx, "Differenz der demokritischen und epikureischen Naturphilosophie nebst einem Anhange [die Doktordissertation]," in *Werke* (Berlin: Dietz, 1956), 40:262–63; cf. Aeschylus, *Prometheus Bound* [Προμηθεὺς Δεσμώτης], in *Persians*; *Seven against Thebes*; *The Suppliants*; and *Prometheus Bound*, ed. and trans. Alan H. Sommerstein (Cambridge, MA: Harvard University Press, 2008), 548–51 [lines 965–75].
25. Plato, *Protagoras*, 320a–323d. Text cited from translation. cf. Plato (Πλάτων), *Protagoras*, 320a–323d.
26. Stiegler, *La technique et le temps*, 194.
27. Ibid., 196.
28. Butler, *Psychic Life of Power*, 23, 173.
29. Stiegler, *La technique et le temps*, 151–52, 201; cf. Marx & Engels, *Ökonomisch-philosophische Manuskripte aus dem Jahre 1844*, 537–46.
30. Stiegler, *La technique et le temps*, 146, 151. Respective emphases preserved from the original text.
31. Ibid., 151.
32. Ibid., 263.
33. Ibid., 127. Emphasis preserved from the original text.
34. Ibid., 142–43.
35. Ibid., 105–6. Emphasis preserved from the original text.
36. Ibid., 151, 248–50. Emphasis preserved from the original text. Cf. Jacques Derrida, "Les fins de l'homme," in *Marges de la Philosophie* (Paris: Les Éditions de Minuit, 1972), 139–42; Jacques Derrida, "La Main de Heidegger (Geschlecht II)," in *Psyché: Inventions de l'autre* (Paris: Galilée, 1987), 45.
37. Ibid., 248–49.
38. Ibid., 262, 279. Emphasis preserved from the original text.
39. Ibid., 257.
40. Ibid., 143. Emphasis and orthography preserved from the original text.
41. Ibid., 227, 240.
42. Ibid., 263.
43. Ibid., 30. Emphasis preserved from the original text.
44. Ibid., 141.
45. Butler, *Senses of the Subject*, 35.
46. Cavarero, *Tu che mi guardi, tu che mi racconti*, 57.
47. 荀子, *Xunzi*, §23.13.
48. Li and Cauvel, *Four Discourses on Aesthetics*, 26. This text only appears in the English-language version of 美学四讲.
49. 李泽厚, 美学四讲, 95.

50. Martin Heidegger, "Die Frage nach der Technik," in *Gesamtausgabe*, ed. Friedrich-Wilhelm von Hermann (Frankfurt am Main: Vittorio Klostermann, 2000), 7:13; Stiegler, *La technique et le temps*, 23.
51. Heidegger, "Die Frage nach der Technik," 7, 36.
52. Nietzsche, "Über Wahrheit und Lüge im außermoralischen Sinne," 883–84.

Chapter 6

1. Shusterman, *Body Consciousness*, 22.
2. Ibid., 1.
3. Ibid., 1, 22, 23, 24, 29.
4. Ibid., 97.
5. Arno Böhler, "Philosophie ALS künstlerische Forschung: Philosophy on Stage," *Korporeale Performanz: Zur bedeutungsgenerierenden Dimension des Leibes*, ed. Arno Böhler, Christian Herzog, and Alice Pechriggl (Bielefeld, Germany: Transcript Verlag, 2013), 13.
6. James Garrison, "Reconsidering Richard Shusterman's Somaesthetics: The Confucian Debate between Mèng Zǐ and Xún Zǐ," *Contemporary Pragmatism* 12, no. 1 (2015): 135–55.
7. Butler, *Senses of the Subject*, 15.
8. Shusterman, *Body Consciousness*, ix, 20.
9. Arno Böhler, "Wissen wir, was ein Körper kann?," in *Wissen wir, was ein Körper vermag?: Rhizomatische Körper in Religion, Kunst, Philosophie*, ed. Arno Böhler, Krassimira Kruschkova, and Susanne Valerie (Bielefeld, Germany: Transcript Verlag, 2013), 249.
10. Shusterman, *Body Consciousness*, xii, 8.
11. Ibid., 7.
12. Richard Shusterman, "Affective Cognition: From Pragmatism to Somaesthetics," *Intellectica* 60, no. 2 (2013): 67; Richard Shusterman, *Thinking through the Body* (Cambridge, UK: Cambridge University Press, 2012), 4; Shusterman, *Body Consciousness*, 49–51; Maurice Merleau-Ponty, *Phénoménologie de la perception* (Paris: Gallimard, 1945), 460–63.
13. Shusterman, *Body Consciousness*, 1.
14. Ibid., 3.
15. Ibid., 119–21, 134.
16. Ibid., 24.
17. John Dewey, *Human Nature and Conduct*, vol. 14 of *The Middle Works of John Dewey* (Carbondale: Southern Illinois University Press, 2008), 51.
18. Ibid., 20, 131.
19. Shusterman, *Thinking through the Body*, 106.

20. Richard Shusterman and Yann Toma, *The Adventures of the Man in Gold: Paths between Art and Life* (Paris: Hermann Éditeurs, 2016), 19.

21. Shusterman, *Body Consciousness*, 125; cf. Ludwig Wittgenstein, *Vermischte Bemerkungen*, ed. Georg Henrik von Wright, with Heikki Nyman (Franfurt am Main: Suhrkamp, 1977), 59.

22. Shusterman, *Body Consciousness*, 124.

23. Ibid., 125.

24. Ibid., 47.

25. Ibid., p. 130–31; Shusterman, *Thinking through the Body*, 266, 269–71.

26. Shusterman, *Body Consciousness*, 99.

27. Shusterman, *Thinking through the Body*, 13, 14.

28. William James, *The Principles of Psychology* (Cambridge, MA: Harvard University Press, 1981), 125, 130.

29. Shusterman, *Body Consciousness*, 140–41; James, *Principles of Psychology*, 110.

30. Shusterman, *Thinking through the Body*, 13, 14.

31. Shusterman, *Body Consciousness*, 23.

32. Butler, *Psychic Life of Power*, 88.

33. Shusterman, *Body Consciousness*, 97.

34. Ibid., 124; Butler, *Giving an Account of Oneself*, 124.

35. Butler, *Giving an Account of Oneself*, 58.

36. Butler, *Senses of the Subject*, 34.

37. Ibid., 38.

38. Shusterman, *Thinking through the Body*, 227.

39. Shusterman, "Somaesthetics and the Utopian Body," 85.

40. Ames and Rosemont, introduction to *The Analects of Confucius*, 51.

41. 孔子, 论语译注, §§8.8, 16.3, 20.3.

42. Cheng Chung-ying, "On the Metaphysical Significance of *Ti* (Body-Embodiment) in Chinese Philosophy," 145.

43. Susan Brownell, *Training the Body for China: Sports in the Moral Order of the People's Republic* (Chicago: University of Chicago Press, 1995), 16nn3–4.

44. Yanhua Zhang, *Transforming Emotions with Chinese Medicine: An Ethnographic Account from Contemporary China* (Albany: State University of New York Press, 2007), 36.

45. Deborah Sommer, "Boundaries of the *Ti* Body," *Asia Major* 21, no. 1 (2008): 296.

46. Ibid., 295.

47. Ibid., 303, 306, 309, 324.

48. Ibid., 304.

49. Ames, *Confucian Role Ethics*, 110.

50. Ibid., 106.

51. 孔子, 论语译注, §§1.2, 16.5, 17.11.

52. Ibid., §§8.8, 16.3, 20.3.

53. Ibid., §16.5.
54. Shusterman, *Thinking through the Body*.
55. Ibid., 319–20.
56. 孟子, 孟子今註今譯, 291 [二九一 告子篇第六：二 湍水章 §6.2].
57. Ibid., 292 [二九二 告子篇第六：三 生之章 §6.3], 294 [二九四 告子篇第六：四 食色章 §6.4].
58. Ames and Rosemont, introduction to *The Analects of Confucius*, 57–58.
59. 孟子, 孟子今註今譯, 78 [七八 公孫丑篇第二：六 不忍章 §2A6], 291 [二九一 告子篇第六：二 湍水章 §6A2].
60. Ibid., 78 [七八 公孫丑篇第三：六 不忍章 §2A6], 297–99 [二九七到二九九 告子篇第六：六 公都章 §6A6].
61. Ibid., 138 [一三八 滕文公篇第三：五 墨者夷 §3A5].
62. Shusterman, *Thinking through the Body*, 34, 200; cf. 孟子, 孟子今註今譯, 61 [六一 公孫丑篇第二：二 加齊章 §2A2].
63. Ames and Rosemont, introduction to *The Analects of Confucius*, 53–55.
64. Ibid., 54.
65. 孟子, 孟子今註今譯, 186–87 [一八六到一八七 離婁篇第四：十自暴章 §4A10].
66. Ibid., 318 [三一八 告子篇第六：二十一 任人章 §6B1].
67. Shusterman, *Thinking through the Body*, 141.
68. Shusterman, *Body Consciousness*, 115n4; Richard Shusterman, "Somatic Style," *Journal of Aesthetics and Art Criticism* 69, no. 2 (2011): 159n10; Richard Shusterman, "Pragmatism and East-Asian Thought," *Metaphilosophy* 35, no. 1–2 (2004): 19n30, 20n12, 25, 35n37.
69. 荀子, *Xunzi*, §§23.1, 23.3, 23.7, 23.11, 23.19.
70. Ibid., §23.12.
71. Ibid., §19.15.
72. Ibid., §§23.8, 2.1.
73. Ibid., §23.1.
74. Ibid., §§19–20, 22.
75. Romans 7:14–23, 8:3–9; Galatians 5:13–26; Ephesians 2:3.
76. 荀子, *Xunzi*, §§23.6, 23.9; cf. Hobbes, *Leviathan*, 86–90.
77. 戴震, 孟子字義疏證 (Beijing: 中華書局, 1982), 100; cf. Pamela Kyle Crossley, *A Translucent Mirror: History and Identity in Qing Imperial Ideology* (Berkeley: University of California Press, 1999), 267–68; Justin Tiwald, "Dai Zhen on Human Nature and Moral Cultivation," *Dao Companion to Neo-Confucian Philosophy*, ed. John Makeham (Dordrecht: Springer, 2010), 405; cf. 孟子, 78 [七八 公孫丑篇第三：六 不忍章 §2A6].
78. 荀子, *Xunzi*, §§17.1, §17.2.
79. Ibid., §23.13.
80. Ibid., §§19.7, 19.15, 23.14; cf. 史記今註, ed. 馬持盈, vol. 3, 5th ed. (Taipei: 臺灣商務印書館, 1979), 1168.
81. Shusterman, *Thinking through the Body*, 200; cf. 荀子, *Xunzi*, §§2.4, 2.5.

82. 朱熹, 朱子语类选注, vol. 1 (Guilin: Guangxi Normal University Press, 1998), 29.

83. Paul R.Goldin, "Xunzi and Early Han Philosophy," *Harvard Journal of Asiatic Studies* 67, no. 1 (2007): 136–37.

84. Shusterman, *Thinking through the Body*, 205; cf. 荀子, *Xunzi*, §1.8.

85. 荀子, *Xunzi*, §19.16.

86. Ibid., §19.20.

87. Ibid., §§19.3, §19.7.

88. Hall and Ames, *Thinking Through Confucius*, 292–93; cf. Derrida, "La différance," 8–9.

89. Bourdieu, *La distinction*, VI.

90. 荀子, *Xunzi*, §20.8.

91. 孔子, 论语译注, §16.5.

92. 荀子, *Xunzi*, §20.7.

93. Ibid., §20.1.

94. 嚴靈峯, 墨子簡編, 非乐上 §1–6.

95. 孔子, 论语译注, §12.11.

96. 荀子, *Xunzi*, §20.2.

97. Sor-Hoon Tan, *Confucian Democracy: A Deweyan Reconstruction* (Albany: State University of New York Press, 2004), 132–44; Joanne D. Birdwhistell, *Mencius and Masculinities: Dynamics of Power, Morality, and Maternal Thinking* (Albany: State University of New York Press, 2007).

98. Shusterman, *Thinking through the Body*, 92; cf. Shusterman, *Body Consciousness*, 97.

99. Shusterman, *Thinking through the Body*, 75, 109.

100. Shusterman, "Pragmatism and East Asian Thought," 27.

Final Thoughts

1. Shusterman, *Body Consciousness*, 141.

2. Butler, *Psychic Life of Power*, 193.

3. Benedicti di Spinoza, *Ethices*, in *Opera Quae Supersunt Omnia* (Leipzig: Carolus Hermannus Bruder, 1843), 1:278 [pars. 6, propos. 6]; Butler, *Senses of the Subject*, 63.

4. Butler, *Giving an Account of Oneself*, 43–44. Emphasis preserved from the original text.

5. Butler, *Psychic Life of Power*, 27–28.

6. Ibid., 130; Butler, *Senses of the Subject*, 67–70, 84.

7. Butler, *Senses of the Subject*, 64–65.

8. Ibid., 65.

9. Ibid., 67. Emphasis preserved from the original text.

10. Butler, *Psychic Life of Power*, 94.
11. Ibid., 193.
12. Ibid., 195.
13. Patricia M. Thornton, "Framing Dissent in Contemporary China: Irony, Ambiguity and Metonymy," *China Quarterly*, no. 171 (2002), 680–81.
14. Butler, *Senses of the Subject*, 65–66.
15. Judith Butler, *Gender Trouble: Feminism and the Subversion of Identity* (New York: Routledge, 1990), 136.
16. Butler, *Psychic Life of Power*, 128–29; Dolar, "Beyond Interpellation," 87.
17. Butler, "Performativity's Social Magic," 114.
18. Ibid., 115.
19. Butler, *Psychic Life of Power*, 28.
20. Butler, *Giving an Account of Oneself*, 8.
21. Butler, *Senses of the Subject*, 45. Emphasis preserved from the original text.
22. Butler, *Psychic Life of Power*, 28.
23. Žižek, *The Ticklish Subject*, 254.
24. Butler, *Senses of the Subject*, 68.
25. 李泽厚, 美学四讲, 69–70; Li, "The Philosophy of Kant and a Theory of Subjectivity," 146; cf. 李泽厚, 批判哲学的批判: 康德述评 (Beijing: 人民出版社, 2001), 413.
26. Ibid., 262.
27. Ibid., 290.
28. Ibid., 264.
29. Ibid.
30. Arendt, *Human Condition*, 168, 173.
31. Arendt, *Human Condition*, 212.

Index

abstraction, 30–33, 40–41
aesthetics, 15–16, 77, 138–39, 190, 195–96
Althusser, Louis, 1, 3, 59–62, 65, 92, 135
Ames, Roger T.: and ritual (*lǐ* 禮/礼), 21, 97, 167; and relationality, 58, 99–101, 169; and self-conscious translation, 39–42
appearance, 12–13, 19, 89–91, 133–34, 140–55, 198–99
apprehension, 135, 140
Arendt, Hannah: and appearance, 13, 42, 89–91, 143, 152–54, 190, 199, 199–200; and exposure/vulnerability, 54, 150; and Kant, 125–27; and Lǐ Zéhòu 李泽厚, 130–33, 148; and phenomenology, 23
Aristotle Ἀριστοτέλης, 13, 28, 58, 138, 160, 192
art(s)/artworks: and abstraction, 87; and artistry/artfulness, 4–7; and early humans, 86; and freedom, 65–69; and ritual (*lǐ* 禮/礼), 8–10; and magic, 87–89, 95; and Prometheus, 146; and self-consciousness/self-recognition, 6, 76–78, 191, 195; and somaesthetics 16–17, 163; and technique, 13–15
artworld, 81–85, 94

Aufhebung, 60, 84, 85, 199
autonomy, 5–7, 11, 19, 79
autonomy of artworks, 6, 66–69
axial age, 7

bad conscience, 1, 4
body: and artfulness, 93, 95, 200; and bodily nature of self, 3–4; in Butler's work, 51, 58–59; in Confucianism, 7–10, 102, 151; in Foucault's work, 55, 56, 58–59; in Lǐ Zéhòu's 李泽厚 work, 151; in Nietzsche's work, 55, 59; and ritual, 12, 15; and self as relational, discursive, and ritually impelled, 19, 22, 28, 43, 78–79, 82, 99, 116, 155, 198; and self-cultivation, 18–19; as *shēntǐ* 身體/身体, 8–9, 16, 21, 108, 152, 167–71; as soma/in somaesthetics, 15, 157–84, 185, 199; and vulnerability, 53
Bourdieu, Pierre, 60–61, 157, 178, 193
Buddhism, 44
Böhler, Arno, 158–59
Butler, Judith: and Arendt, 13, 54, 90, 150; and Cavarero, 53–54, 90; and Confucianism, 94, 115–16; foreclosure/loss, 12, 14, 146; and Foucault, 22–23, 26–27, 42, 55–56, 58, 85; and Hegel, 53, 65, 70–71,

Butler, Judith *(continued)*
73, 77, 88; and Nietzsche, 53,
54–55, 65, 73–76, 186, 196; and
somaesthetics, 15, 17, 155, 157–60,
165–66, 182, 185; subjectivation,
1–4, 9, 14, 18, 43, 49–56, 58,
60–62, 64–65, 90–91, 123, 133,
137–41, 150, 152, 185–88,
190, 190–97; and susceptibility/
vulnerability, 138–39; and technique
in appearance 13–14, 133, 135; and
Žižek, 19, 195–97

Cavarero, Adriana, 53–54, 90, 150
Cavell, Stanley, 65
choreography, 8, 70, 97, 119, 150, 152
collective unconsciousness, 12, 130
conatus. *See* Spinoza, Baruch
consciousness. *See* self-consciousness
Confucianism (*rújiā* 儒家): and the
body (*shēntǐ* 身體/身体), 16, 21,
71, 102, 106, 151, 158, 198;
and Foucault, 54, 57–58; and
intercultural philosophy, 28, 37,
39; and ritual (*lǐ* 禮/礼), 1, 7–10,
16, 19, 21, 28, 41–42, 44, 50–51,
95, 97–117, 119, 136, 141, 143,
150–54, 167, 169–73, 177–84,
198; ritual and music within, 8–9,
11, 16, 106–16, 119, 150–52,
170, 178–81; and sedimentation,
192; and somaesthetics, 143, 144,
150–54, 158–59, 165, 167–84; and
subjectivation, 22–23, 26, 49–51,
64, 94–95
Confucius (Kǒng Zǐ 孔子), 8, 10, 11,
98, 155, 170

dance. *See* choreography
de Beauvoir, Simone, 164
Deleuze, Gilles, 23–24, 27, 33–36,
42–46, 71

Derrida, Jacques, 8, 13, 110, 177
Dewey, John, 160–62
différance, 8, 13, 110, 177
discipline, 21, 23–24, 27, 55
discourse: and Confucianism (*rújiā* 儒
家), 7–9, 102; and self as relational,
discursive, and ritually impelled, 19,
22, 28, 43, 78–79, 82, 99, 116,
155, 198; and sign chains, 17, 188;
and subjectivation, 3, 194–95
Dolar, Mladen, 90, 191
drag, 17, 62
Du Bois, W. E. B., 32

Emerson, Ralph Waldo, 26–26, 64–
65
exposure. *See* vulnerability

fallacy of misplaced concreteness, 29
Flew, Anthony, 30
foreclosure, 13–14
forgetfulness. *See* memory
Foucault, Michel: and art 81; and
Confucianism (*rújiā* 儒家), 54,
57–58; and the panopticon, 55–59,
94, 141; and somaesthetics, 155,
157, 164–65; and subjectivation,
1–3, 9, 11–12, 14–16, 22–23,
26–28, 42, 43, 50, 61, 62, 65, 75,
85, 86, 94, 115, 153, 184, 196
freedom: and the artful body 51–52;
and artworks, 50–51, 63, 65–69,
76–78, 84–85, 92–93; in Foucault's
work, 55–56; negative freedom,
65–69, 84, 199 (*see also* Immanuel
Kant); and sign chains, 62–64; and
subjectivation, 2, 4–5, 10, 16–18,
22, 48
Freud, Sigmund, 1–2, 4, 14, 50, 60,
150, 186

gender, 17, 32, 49–50, 165, 191

Index

Guattari, Félix, 23–24, 27, 33–36, 42–46, 71

Hall, David L., 58, 100–101, 177
heap. *See* sorites
Hegel, Georg Wilhelm Friedrich: on the artisan and recognition, 69–73; and double consciousness, 32; and freedom of artworks, 69–73, 82; in Lǐ Zéhòu's 李泽厚 work, 128; and self-recognition in art 76–77, 88; and subjectivation, 1–3, 186; and unhappy consciousness, 50, 51–52, 82–83, 84
Heidegger, Martin, 12–13, 55, 137–38, 148
hope, 18, 123–24, 126, 130–33, 184
human nature (*xìng* 性), 171–76, 184
humanization of nature: in Lǐ Zéhòu's 李泽厚 work, 10, 115, 120–21, 127, 130–31, 144, 151, 154, 196 (*see also* subjectality); in Stiegler's work, 13, 146, 151, 146, 151, 154; and subjectivation, 193. *See also* Marx, Karl

intercultural philosophy, 19, 21, 27–36, 45
interdiscplinarity, 21, 23–24, 27, 45
interpellation, 1–2, 59–62, 90–92, 135, 154, 189

James, William, 19, 29–30, 163, 165
Jaspers, Karl, 7, 98–99
Jung, Carl Gustav, 12, 130

Kant, Immanuel: in Arendt's work, 130–32; and art 65–69, 73, 76–77 (*see also under* freedom, negative); and Butler, 187; in Deleuze and Guattari's work 35; in Lǐ Zéhòu's 李泽厚 work, 9–10, 127–30, 133, 198–99 (*see also* subjectality); and Rawls on moral agency 25–26; and subjectivation, 64–70
Kierkegaard, Søren, 3
Kim, David Kyuman, 64–65, 99
Kǒng Zǐ 孔子. *See* Confucius
Kyoto School, 44

lǐ 禮/礼. *See* ritual as *lǐ* 禮/礼
Lǐ Zéhòu 李泽厚: and Butler, 28; and Confucianism (*rújiā* 儒家), 114–16, 144, 170; and the humanization of nature, 10, 115, 120–21, 127, 130–31, 144, 151, 154, 196; and Kant, 120, 127–33; as Marxian 1, 42, 114–16, 120, 123, 127, 133, 198; and somaesthetics, 170, 181–83, 196; and Stiegler 14, 15, 148, 150, 153–54; and subjectality, 9, 10, 11, 119–24, 181–83, 196
loss, 14, 17, 52–54, 59, 88, 142, 146
Lyons, Joseph, 86–89

martial arts, 10, 16, 71, 157, 161, 193, 200
Marx, Karl, 9–10, 128, 136, 143–44, 146, 193. *See also* humanization of nature
master-slave dialectic, 3, 52, 70–72, 84. *See also* Hegel, Georg Wilhelm Friedrich
melancholy: and gender, 17, 62; and subjectivation, 2, 4, 48, 50, 60, 64, 71, 77, 88, 131, 150
memory: and intercultural philosophy, 33; and Lǐ Zéhòu 李泽厚, 150–54, 198; as relational, 26; and rhizomatic philosophy, 42; and Stiegler, 141–46, 148, 150–54, 198; and subjectality, 12, 14, 122–23, 133–34; and subjectivation 12, 14

Mencius (Mèng Zǐ 孟子), 8, 121, 158, 171–73, 180–83
misrecognition. See recognition
Mò Zǐ 墨子, 111, 179–80
music. See under ritual and music

narrative, 53–54, 194–95
naturalization of humanity. See humanization of nature
Nietzsche, Friedrich, on the artistically creating subject, 50–51, 73–76, 154; and intercultural philosophy, 28–29, 37; and subjectivation, 1, 4–6, 12, 14–15, 17–18, 50, 53–55, 59–60, 154, 186, 196
"no true Scotsman," 30–31

the "Other," 6, 16–17, 76–78, 93, 151, 162, 188

panopticism, 3, 55–59, 137
Plato Πλάτων, 25–26, 75, 145–46
poiēsis, 59, 147, 152
polylog, 36–39, 49
power: and art, 76; and the panopticon, 55–57; and resistance, 1, 2, 166, 185, 188–200; and subjectivation, 2, 11, 14–15, 50, 189, 200
prison: and the panopticon 55–56, 137; and subjectivation, 2–4, 9, 11, 15, 58, 76, 78, 90, 92–93, 103, 139, 188
Prometheus, 12, 143–48, 150, 152
psyche, 2–4, 25–26, 50, 53, 100
psychoanalysis, 2, 50, 94, 196
purposiveness: and art, 69–70, 82, 89–91, 142, 191, 199–200; and the body, 15–16; and subjectivation, 78–79, 191, 194, 199–200

rage, 2, 50, 86, 97, 185–86, 188

Rawls, John, 25, 26
recognition: and art, 76–78, 92–94, 191, 195; in Hegel's work, 52, 73, 76; and misrecognition, 60, 62, 63; and somaesthetics, 158, 167, 199; and subjectivation, 4, 6, 11, 16–19, 154, 189, 191, 195
rectification of names (*zhèngmíng* 正名), 51, 102, 105
redemption, 4, 18–19, 48–49, 55, 75–76
relationality: and Butler, 139; and Confucianism, 100, 101; and self as bodily, discursive, and ritually impelled, 19, 22, 28, 43, 78–79, 82, 99, 116, 155, 198; and subjectivation, 3, 7, 8, 9, 47, 48
rhizome/rhizomatic philosophy, 23–25, 27, 33–36, 42–46, 140, 157, 184
ritual: as *lǐ* 禮/礼, 1, 7–10, 16, 19, 21, 28, 41–42, 44, 50–51, 94–95, 97–117, 119, 136, 141, 143, 150–54, 167, 169–73, 177–84, 198; and Lǐ Zéhòu 李泽厚 151–52, 154–55; and music, 8–9, 11, 16, 106–16, 119, 150–52, 170, 178–81; and self as bodily, discursive, and relational, 19, 22, 28, 43, 78–79, 82, 99, 116, 155, 198; and somaesthetics 160–61, 171–72; and subjectivation, 1–2, 4, 8–10, 13–15, 18, 94–95
role, 9
Rosemont, Henry Jr., 58, 97, 100, 167
rújiā 儒家. See Confucianism

Sartre, Jean-Paul, 47–48, 94
sedimentation, 4, 10, 53, 127–30, 192, 194
self-consciousness: and art 78, 82, 84, 86, 88, 94; and Hegel 66, 70–73 (*see* unhappy consciousness); in interpretation, 40–42; and Nietzsche

75–76; and subjectality, 119–23, 133; and subjectivation, 2, 6, 11–12, 14, 51–53, 59, 190–96, 198
self-cultivation (*xiūshēn* 修身), 8, 11, 157, 161
shēntǐ 身體/身体. *See under* body as *shēntǐ* 身體/身体
Shusterman, Richard. *See* somaesthetics
sign chain, 17–19, 62–63, 188
skeptic, 84–85, 94
slur, 2, 17, 62–63, 188
somaesthetics: and Confucianism, 167–84; and self-cultivation, 157–84, 189, 199–200; and Stiegler 143, 155; and subjectivation, 1, 15, 19, 23, 42, 199
sorites, 29, 41
Spinoza, Baruch, 186–87, 190, 196
Stiegler, Bernard, 12–15, 23, 28, 42, 134, 141–54. *See also* technique
stoicism, 83, 85, 94
subjectality (*zhǔtǐxìng* 主体性): and Confucianism, 115–17, 119–23, 198; and Kant, 127–34, 198; and subjectivation, 9–11, 18–19, 192, 194. *See also* Lǐ Zéhòu 李泽厚
subject. *See* subjectivation
subjection. *See* subjectivation
subjectivation: and Arendt, 89–90; and art, 78–79, 92–95, 142, 195, 198; and Butler and 1, 2–5, 18–19, 22–23, 43, 53, 59–62, 78–79, 85–86, 88, 182, 185, 190–94, 195, 197, 198; and Confucianism, 9, 97–100, 102, 103, 105, 115, 116–17, 198; and Foucault, 22–23, 42, 82; and somaesthetics, 155, 157–58, 182, 184, 194, 199; and

subjectality, 119, 123–24, 131–34, 192, 198, 200; and vulnerability, 137, 141, 152–54
susceptibility. *See* vulnerability

t'ai chi ch'uan (*tàijíquán* 太极拳), 10, 151
technique/technology, 12–13, 19, 133–34, 198–99. *See also* Bernard Stiegler

unhappy consciousness, 1, 51–52, 71–73, 76, 82, 88. *See also* Hegel, Georg Wilhelm Friedrich
unconsciousness. *See* self-consciousness.

vulnerability, 137–39, 146, 154, 190, 198

Whitehead, Alfred North, 29, 135–38, 149
the will, 2–3, 6, 19, 26, 53, 55, 74
Wimmer, Franz Martin, 36, 37, 38, 39, 42, 49
Wittgenstein, Ludwig, 87, 161–63
The Wizard of Oz, 18
world observer, 124–27, 130–32

xìng 性. *See* human nature
xiūshēn 修身. *See* self-cultivation
Xún Zǐ 荀子, 8, 104, 109–13, 159, 166, 173–83

Zarathustra, 5, 11, 12, 17, 19, 54–55
Žižek, Slavoj, 19, 195–97
zhèngmíng 正名. *See* rectification of names
zhǔtǐxìng 主体性. *See* subjectality

www.ingramcontent.com/pod-product-compliance
Lightning Source LLC
Chambersburg PA
CBHW020651230426
43665CB00008B/397